# EXPERIENCE

## THE BOOK OF

# ACTS

**Dennis McCallum**

Cover design by Reed Costello

New Paradigm Publishing

# CONTENTS

# EXPERIENCE

## THE BOOK OF

# ACTS

# INTRODUCTION

## Life without Acts

Imagine reading your New Testament without the book of Acts. At one moment you would be reading about Jesus' teaching, death, and resurrection. The action takes place in the province of Judea and the city of Jerusalem. Jesus and his followers are all Jewish.

You turn the page, and you're reading a letter by some person named Paul to a group in the city of Rome, made up of mostly non-Jewish people! The author would be discussing theology that never appeared in Jesus' teaching or anywhere else in the Bible up to that point.

Without Acts, the rest of the New Testament would also be incomprehensible, full of names and places unknown in the Gospels. It's clear that something has caused followers of Jesus to appear in cities all over the eastern Mediterranean, but there's no explanation for how they got there.

Only one thing makes sense of the story at this point: the book of Acts. It's an indication of how unique and important this book is.

The so-called "Lukan Corpus" of Luke and Acts comprises the largest book in the New Testament (Luke) and the third largest (Acts). Acts is only slightly smaller than Matthew. Taken together, Luke's books make up 30% of the New Testament by word count. That's more than all of Paul's or John's books put together!

Acts is our only biblical source for the history of this period. Paul's letters refer to a few events (for example, in Galatians 1 and 2), but usually without much historical context. As New Testament scholar Richard Longenecker said, "If one or two of the four Gospels had been lost, we would be much the poorer; but we would still have the others. Acts, however, stands alone."[1]

## Who Wrote Acts?

To appreciate the question of authorship of Acts, you have to read the opening verses of the book of Luke:

> Inasmuch as many have undertaken to compile an account of the things accomplished among us, just as they were handed down to us by those who from the beginning were eyewitnesses and servants of the word, it seemed fitting for me as well, having investigated everything carefully from the beginning, to write it out for you in consecutive order, most excellent Theophilus; so that you may know the exact truth about the things you have been taught. (Luke 1:1-4)

You can see the book of Luke is addressed to "most excellent Theophilus." Most authorities think this form of address signals that Theophilus is a patrician, or semi-noble person. He must be of some importance to have two books written for him.

The author doesn't claim to be an eyewitness, but says he got his material from "those who from the beginning were eyewitnesses." In other words, he's done his research. You can see that he's a believer in Jesus and a historian relying on multiple pre-existing sources.

Now read the beginning of Acts:

> The first account I composed, Theophilus, about all that Jesus began to do and teach, until the day when He was taken up

---

1. Richard N. Longenecker, "The Acts of the Apostles," The Expositor's Bible Commentary, (Grand Rapids: Zondervan Academic), 2017, 208.

to heaven, after He had by the Holy Spirit given orders to the apostles whom He had chosen. To these He also presented Himself alive after His suffering, by many convincing proofs, appearing to them over a period of forty days and speaking of the things concerning the kingdom of God. (1:1-3)

Here the author refers to his "first account," and addresses his book again to Theophilus. The Greek writing style also matches. It's clear that we are dealing with the same author in both books.

According to early church tradition, the author is Luke, whom Paul calls "the beloved physician" (Colossians 4:14). And in this case, tradition is correct.

It's not surprising that early Christians would know from the beginning who wrote such an important text. Neither is it surprising that they kept track of that knowledge over time. Not only were the earliest church fathers unanimous on Luke's authorship, but none of them proposed any other author. We have no good reason to doubt the universal testimony of the early church that Luke wrote both Luke and Acts.

Additionally, the very early papyrus p[75] (late second century) lists Luke as the author, as does the Muratorian Canon (AD 170).

# Internal Evidence

In this case, we have more than early tradition to go on. At three different points in the book of Acts, the author joins the action. In these sections, he no longer refers to the apostolic group as "they," but rather as "we." He has become one of them.

Other people show up in these same passages, and clearly none of them could be the author. Otherwise, the author wouldn't have named those people or referred to them as "them" in a "we" passage. These "we" passages are important for other reasons, as we will see later. For now, the important point is that these passages give us a list of people we can rule out as possible authors.[2]

Of special interest is the third and final section of "we" passages, which continues through the end of the book. At that point, Paul spends two

---

2. The list of men excluded from authorship includes Sopater of Berea, the son of Pyrrhus; Aristarchus; Secundus of the Thessalonians; Gaius of Derbe; Timothy; Tychicus; Trophimus of Asia; Aristarchus, a Macedonian of Thessalonica; Julius a Roman; Publius of Malta; and the apostle Paul.

years in a rented house in Rome, and our author is right there with him. During those years Paul also wrote four books, which are called the "prison epistles": Ephesians, Colossians, Philippians, and Philemon. In these epistles, he lets his readers know who is with him in Rome. One of those he names is our author, Luke.

By comparing the list of people with Paul in Rome to the list of those ruled out by the "we" passages, we are left with just two possible names: Luke the physician and Jesus Justus, with Luke being the far more plausible candidate.

Luke is a prominent companion to Paul (Colossians 4:14; Philemon 24; 2 Timothy 4:11). Of Jesus Justus we know nothing but his name, making it all but certain that Luke wrote both Acts and the book that bears his name.

Of course, higher critical, skeptical scholars don't believe Luke wrote Acts. They don't believe Luke was a physician. They don't believe Colossians, Ephesians, or 2 Timothy were written by Paul. And, in a word, they don't believe.

Early higher critics suggested that Acts was written by an unknown editor in the second century, mainly to harmonize the Judaic views of Peter with the novel views of Paul. More recent liberal scholarship has tended to reject that construct, and after the work of Adolf Harnack and Sir William Ramsay, Acts was restored to the first century, where it belongs. Liberal scholars still place it decades later than AD 60 and claim it is full of errors. We will consider some of these claims as we encounter them in the text.

## Apostolic Authority

As the author, Luke was working under the guidance and oversight of the Apostle Paul. The last "we" section spans the whole voyage Paul made to Rome. But it adjoins the previous "we" section going all the way back to Paul's third missionary journey, more than two years earlier. That means the author was with Paul during his entire journey from Troas to Jerusalem, his two-year imprisonment at Caesarea, his nearly year-long voyage to Rome, and two further years in Rome.

## At Caesarea

As Luke spent two years during Paul's imprisonment in Caesarea, this is likely where he wrote the book that bears his name. He could have interviewed people in nearby Jerusalem who were actually there when Jesus lived, as well as witnesses of Pentecost and the early years before Paul showed up. These would be combined with Paul's memories for the rest of Acts.

Acts ends abruptly at the end of the two years in Rome, not even revealing the verdict in Paul's trial. That can only mean the author was writing up to that moment, and no further. It was time to turn the work in to Theophilus. In this scenario, Luke would have had around three years to write the book of Acts.

# 1

# GETTING READY

## ACTS 1

## After the Resurrection

Jesus appeared periodically to his disciples and to his unbelieving brothers during the forty days between his resurrection and his ascension. A number of these appearances are detailed at the end of each Gospel. One of the most interesting events is Jesus' teaching session with his disciples, summarized in Luke:

> Then he said, "When I was with you before, I told you that everything written about me in the Law of Moses and the prophets and in the Psalms must be fulfilled." Then he opened their minds to understand the Scriptures. And he said, "Yes, it was written long ago that the Messiah would suffer and die and rise from the dead on the third day. It was also written that this message would be proclaimed in the authority of his name to all the nations, beginning in Jerusalem: 'There is forgiveness of sins for all who repent.' You are witnesses of all these things." (Luke 24:44-48)

This must have been a completely mind-blowing session for these men. It was the first time they understood how God's plan worked, as implied in the statement, "Then he opened their minds to understand the Scriptures."

All the suffering servant songs in Isaiah, the messianic Psalms, and the other prophetic passages suddenly came into focus. Jesus must have also explained the many connections between Old Testament typology, like the sacrificial system and the festivals. That's implied when he says, "everything written about me in the Law of Moses." Suddenly it all made sense like never before!

This disclosure is summarized in Acts 1:3:

> During the forty days after he suffered and died, he appeared to the apostles from time to time, and he proved to them in many ways that he was actually alive. And he talked to them about the Kingdom of God.

The disciples were so locked into their old paradigm that they at first refused to believe that Jesus was actually back from the dead. They thought he was a ghost. To prove otherwise, he had to eat fish in their presence (Luke 24:43). It was probably his teaching on fulfilled prophecy that finally enabled them to undergo a full paradigm shift from the Old Testament to the New Covenant.

In the book of Acts, Luke makes it sound like the discussion in the following verses happened very soon after that remarkable teaching session:

> Gathering them together, He commanded them not to leave Jerusalem, but to wait for what the Father had promised, "which," He said, "you heard of from me; for John baptized with water, but you will be baptized with the Holy Spirit not many days from now." (vs. 4-5)

It would be pointless for them to go out and try to begin their mission without the indwelling power of the Holy Spirit. He had previously bestowed a temporary presence of the Spirit, no doubt in the Old Testament sense (John 20:22). That was totally different from what was about to happen.

# What about the Kingdom?

In their conversation with Jesus, his disciples asked the most obvious question:

> So when they had come together, they were asking Him, saying, "Lord, is it at this time you are restoring the kingdom to Israel?" (v. 6)

Of course! What else was there to do, now that they understood his death and resurrection?

Under some theologies, Jesus would have to explain at this point, "Well, you see guys, that 'kingdom of Israel' thing isn't going to happen... The Jews broke their covenant, so that now goes to you guys, the church." But that's not what he said. Instead,

> He said to them, "It is not for you to know times or epochs which the Father has fixed by His own authority." (v. 7)

This answer implies that God *will* restore the kingdom to Israel at some future date. It's only times and epochs that are not for them to know. If no kingdom comes to Israel, this reply would be very misleading. So Jesus was not a "replacement theologian." He didn't hold that God's Old Testament promises that Israel would inherit a kingdom now only applied to the church, as some interpreters suggest.

# The Spirit's Coming

Then Jesus made clear what was coming:

> "You will receive power when the Holy Spirit has come upon you; and you shall be my witnesses both in Jerusalem, and in all Judea and Samaria, and even to the remotest part of the earth." (v. 8)

Here we have a summary of what the rest of the book of Acts will unfold. The gospel would begin in Jerusalem with Jews, then spread to Samaria with half-Jewish Samaritans, then to the rest of the world with Gentiles. Each of the transitions mentioned would prove to be major sticking points. Only when God exerted powerful pressure would his people overcome their resistance to including other ethnic groups.

Before any of that, they would need the promised new power.

The Spirit's power wasn't just power for the disciples to do whatever they want. The sequence, "you will receive power... and you shall be my witnesses" makes God's intent clear. This spiritual power will make possible the expansion of the people of God to worldwide proportions.

This prediction—that this little group would spread the gospel to the whole world—is one of Jesus' most remarkable fulfilled prophecies. To think that a handful of people standing out on this hill would impact every people group on earth is incredibly improbable. But it happened! Never bet against biblical prophecy coming true.[1]

## And Then, What?

Then, apparently without any preparation, Jesus' body began to ascend! With bulging eyes and mouths hanging open, the disciples stared as he went higher and higher. Finally, he disappeared into a cloud. They kept staring in astonishment. They're left looking at each other, probably murmuring, "Now what? Can you believe that just happened?"

God sent two angels to break the spell:

> As they strained to see him rising into heaven, two white-robed men suddenly stood among them. "Men of Galilee," they said, "why are you standing here staring into heaven? Jesus has been taken from you into heaven, but someday he will return from heaven in the same way you saw him go!" (vs. 10-11)

Did they discuss things further? Or did the angels suddenly disappear? Someone must have suggested, "Let's head back into town," a walk of two miles.

The ascension of Jesus is a jarring account. What a way to exit! But as you think about it, you realize this was a strong statement from God. Where had Jesus come from? A good clue would be where he left to. Heaven.

How else could he have exited? Just disappear? No good alternative suggests itself.

---

1. Jesus also said this worldwide spread of the gospel would be linked to the last days: "This gospel of the kingdom shall be preached in the whole world as a testimony to all the nations, and then the end will come" (Matthew 24:14). If this statement refers to nation states, it is already fulfilled. Every nation state on earth has believers in it. Missions experts argue, however, that the statement won't be fulfilled until every people group is reached. That still leaves 11,000 unreached cultural and linguistic groups. Most are small. When I was a student (in the early 70s), the number of unreached groups was over twenty thousand, according to the U. S. Center for World Missions.

And we have the promise that he will return in the same way that he left at the end of history as we know it. No baby in a manger this time. Jesus said his return would be like lightning flashing "from the east even to the west" (Matthew 24:27). Everyone will know when Jesus returns.

Jesus' second coming is a critical event, promised here and also by Jesus in the clearest terms (e.g., John 14:3). If Jesus doesn't return, his own words would lose all credibility. If he doesn't keep this promise to return, how many other promises won't be kept? The whole biblical story would end in mid-air, unless Jesus returns to take over the world as King Messiah.

## The Upper Room

The believers had an "upper room" they could use in Jerusalem, probably the same "upper room" Jesus and his disciples used for the Last Supper (Luke 22:9-13). Jesus described that room as "large," and we read that about 120 of Jesus' followers were able to fit in it (v. 15).

Participants in the group included the eleven remaining disciples, some unnamed women, and Jesus' mother, and brothers. These brothers were unbelievers earlier (John 7:3-5). But since those earlier days, a significant event had changed their minds: a personal visit from the resurrected Jesus (1 Corinthians 15:7)!

Of all the shocking confrontations he lined up after the resurrection, this one might have been the most enjoyable for Jesus after a lifetime of scoffing from his brothers. I picture him with a big smile as James looks up from his work and recoils in astonishment. "Yeah, that's right," Jesus probably nodded. They must have filled in the other half-brothers later.

Other people were in the upper room as well, based on the total of "about 120" in verse 15.

What was it like in that room? We can imagine the excitement and awe they must have felt. We read that they were continually devoting themselves to prayer (v. 14). Much of their prayer must have been a questioning type of prayer. Many questions remained unanswered. They must have pored over the Old Testament passages Jesus had just explained to them for the first time. What did the future hold?

We also see in the last verse of Luke that the believers "were continually in the temple praising God" (Luke 24:53). So they must have been moving between the temple and the upper room.

Certainly, they would have been busy writing down everything they could remember Jesus saying. It's unthinkable that they would be satisfied with oral accounts. The only natural response would be to get it down while they still remembered it clearly.

## Papias

Around the end of the first century, the early church father Papias wrote a five-book account on how the gospel books were written. Papias was one of our earliest sources. He had actually sat under the Apostle John's teaching. He also had other very early streams of information about this period, like interviews with people who had known one or more of the original apostles.

He talks about what he calls *The Logia* (The Sayings), which he says was the earliest piece written about Jesus. It was apparently a collection of things Jesus said—exactly what you would expect the apostles to produce during these key days. Papias names Matthew as the first collector of Jesus' sayings, and that makes sense, since Matthew would have already had good literacy and writing skills as a head tax collector. The Logia apparently was a forerunner of the Gospels.[2]

Danger was still afoot during these days of waiting. Jesus had been crucified before their eyes just days earlier, and all the perpetrators of his murder were still present and in power. The believers were probably

---

2. This list of sayings could be the so-called Q source. New Testament scholars have shown that while both Luke and Matthew use Mark's gospel extensively, they also have access to another source not found in Mark. This common material is mostly made up of Jesus' sayings. Scholars dubbed it "Q" for quelle (source). We don't have a copy of this document if it did exist, but it makes sense that the disciples would have immediately scrambled to find paper and pen to write Jesus' sayings down. Wouldn't you? Papias says Matthew used this source and others to write his gospel, originally in "the language of the Hebrews," probably Aramaic. We have no good reason to accept the liberal claim that Q was passed on orally for decades. We no longer have Papias' books, just what early church historian Eusebius quotes from them. Copies of Papias lasted into the Middle Ages, but war and fires eventually destroyed them.

Paul shows evidence of having a written source of Jesus' sayings as well. His attribution to Jesus of the saying, "It is more blessed to give than receive" (Acts 20:35), doesn't appear in our gospels (although the concept certainly does). Also, in 1 Corinthians 7 he is apparently consulting a written source on Jesus' teachings on marriage and divorce when he says, "I give instructions, not I, but the Lord" (v. 10; see also 1 Corinthians 15:3). Luke also confirms he had written sources that "were handed down to us by those who from the beginning were eyewitnesses and servants of the word" (Luke 1:2). So these earlier sources could easily go all the way back to this period shortly after Jesus' ascension.

laying as low as possible. But while they were probably worried, their overarching feeling must have been ecstasy and expectancy as they waited for whatever Jesus had promised was coming in a matter of days.

## Replacing Judas

At some point, Peter began to fulfill Jesus' prediction that he would be their leader:

> During this time, when about 120 believers were together in one place, Peter stood up and addressed them. "Brothers," he said, "the Scriptures had to be fulfilled concerning Judas, who guided those who arrested Jesus. This was predicted long ago by the Holy Spirit, speaking through King David. Judas was one of us and shared in the ministry with us." (vs. 15-17)

Peter referred to an Old Testament prophecy by King David. But Judas' betrayal was also predicted in Zechariah. In chapter 11, Zechariah poses as a shepherd, representing God as Israel's unwanted shepherd. He prophesies against the oppressive shepherds exploiting the sheep of Israel. Then,

> I said to them, "If you like, give me my wages, whatever I am worth; but only if you want to." So they counted out for my wages thirty pieces of silver. And the Lord said to me, "Throw it to the potter"—this magnificent sum at which they valued me! So I took the thirty coins and threw them to the potter in the Temple of the Lord. (vs. 12-13)

Here we see God saying that the thirty pieces of silver is "this magnificent sum at which they valued me." So God was sold for thirty pieces of silver. That's the same price Judas received for betraying Jesus (Matthew 26:15).

Then comes a cryptic but amazing part of Zechariah's prophecy. God tells him to throw the money to "the potter" and Zechariah said he did so "in the temple."

Hundreds of years later, Judas felt remorse for betraying Jesus, and tried to give the money back. "'I have sinned by betraying innocent blood,' he said. But the priests refused to take it. they said, "What is that to us? See to that yourself!" (Matthew 27:4).

Judas was so exasperated that he threw the coins into the temple sanctuary and departed to kill himself. The priests gathered up the money and discussed what they should do with it. Under cleanliness laws, they couldn't put it into the temple treasury because it was blood money. Instead, they used it to buy a field for the burial of vagrants. And the man from whom they bought the field? He was a local potter (Matthew 27:5-7)!

This is an amazing, detailed prediction unknowingly fulfilled by Judas and the priests. The thirty pieces paid for Jesus' life went to a potter, but only after first being thrown into the temple.[3]

## Judas' End

The purchase of this field owned by a potter comes up again in Acts 1:

> (Judas had bought a field with the money he received for his treachery. Falling headfirst there, his body split open, spilling out all his intestines. The news of his death spread to all the people of Jerusalem, and they gave the place the Aramaic name *Akeldama*, which means "Field of Blood.") (vs. 18-19)

We know Judas didn't actually buy the field himself, but his money was used for the purchase. That meant the field was purchased with blood money; hence, the name.

The following story is not a variant from what the Gospels say (i.e. that Judas hanged himself). Rather, it should be obvious that they found Judas' dead body hanging and cut him down. Then they took him to the field and flipped him into a burial site. Having already decomposed to some extent, it's plausible that his abdomen would rupture as described. That would never happen to a living person. Judas must have been dead for days. It's a fitting end to his story. Judas' life ended poorly.

## Matthias

When he alluded to a few psalms, Peter wasn't necessarily saying they

---

3. Matthew alludes to this prophecy in 27:9-10, but he attributes the prophecy to Jeremiah instead of Zechariah. One possible reason has to do with the setup of the Old Testament in Matthew's day. The collection of the Prophets began with the book of Jeremiah. The scrolls were sometimes referred to by the name of the first book, which in the case of the Prophets would be Jeremiah. Another plausible view is that Matthew is conflating two different prophecies, one from Zechariah and one from Jeremiah (Jeremiah 18:2; 19:1-4). Then, in typical practice of the day, he attributes the two prophecies only to the first and more well-known prophet. It could also be a copyist's error, although it would have to be very early, because we don't have manuscript evidence for such an error.

were written to predict what was happening in that moment. Rather, he was saying something like, "We're going to do something like what David said, but in a different context." Psalm 69 in particular is loaded with apparent prophetic references.[4]

Peter went on:

> "Therefore it is necessary that of the men who have accompanied us all the time that the Lord Jesus went in and out among us—beginning with the baptism of John until the day that He was taken up from us—one of these must become a witness with us of His resurrection." So they put forward two men, Joseph called Barsabbas (who was also called Justus), and Matthias. (vs. 21-23)

Some readers wonder whether Peter may have jumped the gun here, adding a twelfth apostle when perhaps Paul was the true twelfth apostle. But the account is given in a positive tone and contains no suggestion of error. Although we don't hear about Matthias again, neither do we hear of most of the Twelve after this chapter.

Why did Peter think it was "necessary" to add another apostle? The answer goes back to Jesus, who had earlier said that the disciples would "sit on twelve thrones, judging the twelve tribes of Israel" (Matthew 19:28).[5]

This passage shows that the remaining apostles expected another apostle to have witnessed Jesus after his resurrection. Paul echoes that expectation for apostles in 1 Corinthians 9:1.

> And they prayed and said, "You, Lord, who know the hearts of all men, show which one of these two you have chosen to occupy this ministry and apostleship from which Judas turned

---

4. Williams explains, "While this psalm arises out of personal crisis, it also is prophetic. Verses throughout the psalm find their fulfillment in Christ. For example, Jesus has 'zeal for [God's] house' as does the psalmist (v. 9; see John 2:17). Also, reproaches directed toward God fell on him (v. 9; see Rom. 15:3). And like the psalmist, Jesus was given vinegar to drink (v. 21; see John 19:28–29). There are other allusions to this psalm in the New Testament; see, for example, verse 4 and John 15:25; verse 25 and Matthew 23:38." Don Williams, The Preacher's Commentary: Vol. 13, Psalm 1-72, (Thomas Nelson, 2004), 468. Yet the overall context of the psalm doesn't refer to Jesus. The author refers to his own sin and foolishness, for instance (v. 5). Perhaps these points of contact are more like a simile than an actual fulfillment. The same goes for Psalm 109, which Peter refers to next. Is this imprecatory psalm really about Judas? Or is it just typical of the anger one feels in the face of betrayal?

5. Later, John would see the "Holy City, Jerusalem, coming down out of heaven from God having... twelve foundations," with "the names of the twelve apostles of the Lamb" written on them (Revelation 21:10, 14). So this number 12 was symbolically linked to the twelve tribes.

aside to go to his own place." And they drew lots for them, and the lot fell to Matthias; and he was added to the eleven apostles. (vs. 24-26)

They drew lots to pick Matthias, which, for some, adds to the impression that this move was unspiritual. But in the Old Testament, casting lots was considered a valid way to discover God's will under certain circumstances—and this passage technically falls within the bounds of the Old Testament, because the New Covenant doesn't begin until the day of Pentecost. After the coming of the Spirit, we never again see this method of decision making.

Should the apostles have waited until the coming of the Spirit as Jesus said? Was making such an important decision this way a mistake? If so, the text doesn't suggest any criticism.[6]

## The Big Picture

During these ten days, the apostles and other believers were getting their bearings after the shock of recent events. We don't know what was going on in heaven or why there was a delay. Perhaps some ceremonies? A victorious procession? Jesus said earlier that the Spirit couldn't come unless he (Jesus) first departed (John 16:7). John also comments that the Spirit was not yet given because Jesus was not yet glorified (John 7:39).

Alternatively, Jesus may have waited just so the coming of the Spirit happened on the day of Pentecost, which fulfilled a series of Old Testament types.

- The day of Passover—Jesus was crucified on Passover, signifying the death of the lamb (John 1:29). "The next day he [John the Baptist] saw Jesus coming to him and said, 'Behold, the Lamb of God who takes away the sin of the world!'"

- The offering of the first fruits three days later—this signifies Jesus' resurrection: "But now Christ has been raised

---

6. Catholics argue that this passage validates the idea of an "apostolic succession," where the authority of the Twelve is passed down all the way to today through the teaching magisterium of the church. The concept of apostolic succession was a gateway into their belief that they had the authority to add to Scripture, and that only their interpretations were correct. In fact, this passage argues against such a succession. Only those who walked with Jesus and saw him after his resurrection were qualified, so there would be no such witnesses after the first generation.

from the dead, the first fruits of those who are asleep"
(1 Corinthians 15:20).

- Pentecost, the full harvest festival—This represents the
  outpouring of the Spirit to all of Jesus' followers (Acts 2:38).

God had carefully laid his plans, giving inspiration to Moses in symbols
and festivals, selecting and training his spokesmen. Now he was ready.

# 2

# PENTECOST

## ACTS 2

## Ten Days After Jesus' Ascension

> When the day of Pentecost had come, they were all together in one place. And suddenly there came from heaven a noise like a violent rushing wind, and it filled the whole house where they were sitting. (Acts 2:1-2)

What did the believers feel as this experience exploded around them? Was it frightening? It couldn't have taken long for them to connect the dots with what Jesus had predicted, and encounters with God's Spirit are usually exhilarating. People in the gathering crowds soon interpreted the apostles' affect as drunkenness.

## The City Responds

The sound from heaven is said to be "like a violent rushing wind," and that might be an understatement. This wind made a noise so loud that people all over the city heard it and came running to see what it was. Did it sound like a jet engine? Like a tornado? It's immediately clear that God wants to make a powerful statement.

And no wonder. The Jews in Jerusalem for the festival of Pentecost came from the one faith based on the unique, authentic word of God, and they knew it. They correctly saw themselves at the head of the river of God's working in human history, extending into the future kingdom of the Messiah. Their training in the things of God began in childhood, and every aspect of their lives was governed by the detailed exposition of the Old Testament by their rabbis. They viewed other religions with contempt.

To deviate from rabbinic Judaism in any way was the most serious sin possible. Any suggestion that God was going to move in a new direction from now on would be unthinkable. Against this backdrop, we can see the need for God to provide an astonishing demonstration of something none of them had seen before.

The roaring wind continued. The text doesn't mention any damage, just noise.

> And there appeared to them tongues as of fire distributing themselves, and they rested on each one of them. (v. 3)

Out of the central whirlwind came lights. It wasn't fire. It was "like" fire. Ancient people had never seen anything that gave off bright light except fire or lightning. These could have been balls of radiance. It's reminiscent of the Shekinah glory in the Old Testament.

The radiance came from a center and split out, settling on each person. It was a graphic picture of the Holy Spirit coming down and going out to indwell each believer. But for effect, the radiant glow continued, suggesting that they now had new power. Were the lights over their heads? Or were their faces lit up like Moses' when he came down from being in God's presence?

As people gathered in a growing crowd, they looked around, dazzled and confused. What's happening here? What's going on? What do we do now? Maybe we should listen to these guys with fire energy coming off their faces!

> And they were all filled with the Holy Spirit and began to speak with other tongues, as the Spirit was giving them utterance. (v. 4)

Here, the gift of tongues first emerges. In the pages to come, it will become a key signal that people have received the Spirit.

This instance of tongues was different from the others, because the believers were speaking to the crowd in known human languages:

> The crowd came together, and were bewildered because each one of them was hearing them speak in his own language. They were amazed and astonished, saying, "Why, are not all these who are speaking Galileans? "And how is it that we each hear them in our own language to which we were born?" (vs. 6-8)

At this point, those in the crowd had seen the blazing lights, heard the howling wind, and then were hearing unlearned men speaking in their own languages. God was making sure they couldn't miss the supernatural nature of this event.

## The Foreigners

The disciples were speaking an impressive number of languages:

> "Parthians and Medes and Elamites, and residents of Mesopotamia, Judea and Cappadocia, Pontus and Asia, Phrygia and Pamphylia, Egypt and the districts of Libya around Cyrene, and visitors from Rome, both Jews and proselytes, Cretans and Arabs—we hear them in our own tongues speaking of the mighty deeds of God." And they all continued in amazement and great perplexity, saying to one another, "What does this mean?" (vs. 9-12)

Because it was the festival of Pentecost, Jews and Gentile converts had streamed into Jerusalem from all over the known world. These visitors included people from Rome and Egypt, both of which saw churches planted very early. The presence of Parthians, Arabs, and people from Mesopotamia meant the gospel would spread to the east, beyond the Roman Empire.

Because of what happened on this day, most of these people went home carrying the teachings of Jesus and the indwelling Holy Spirit. And they would excitedly recount to friends and neighbors what they had seen and heard.

The result was house churches springing up in hundreds of locations all around the Mediterranean and eastward. Satan's determination to destroy the church before it got going just became a whole lot harder; in fact, it became impossible. But as we will see, he didn't stop trying.

## The Skeptical View

Some of those present refused to see what was so obvious: "But others were mocking and saying, 'They are full of sweet wine'" (v. 13). Wherever the gospel goes, then or now, there will be those with an alternative explanation. Believers should not feel discouraged when their best efforts to do good are characterized as evil. It always hurts, but it always happens.

In their charge of drunkenness, you can tell that the apostles' behavior must have been such that drunkenness was a plausible counter-explanation. This strongly suggests that the believers were wildly ecstatic and joyful, laughing like inebriated people would. Pentecost was not a somber, stoic event.

## Peter's Speech

Then Peter stepped forward, with the other apostles at his side.

> But Peter, taking his stand with the eleven, raised his voice and declared to them: "Men of Judea and all you who live in Jerusalem, let this be known to you and give heed to my words. For these men are not drunk, as you suppose, for it is only the third hour of the day." (vs. 14-15)

Perhaps he spoke in Aramaic and the others would translate to the other languages line by line. Anyone who has spoken to foreign audiences through translation knows what this is like.

Peter went on:

> "This is what was spoken by the prophet Joel:
>
> 'In the last days, God says, I will pour out my Spirit on all people. Your sons and daughters will prophesy, your young men will see visions, your old men will dream dreams. Even on my servants, both men and women, I will pour out my Spirit in those days, and they will prophesy. I will show wonders in the heavens above and signs on the earth below, blood and fire and billows of smoke. The sun will be turned to darkness and the

moon to blood before the coming of the great and glorious day of the Lord. And everyone who calls on the name of the Lord will be saved.'" (vs. 16-21)

# Interpreting Joel

This prophecy in Joel partly matches what was happening on the day of Pentecost, but partly does not. The Spirit was poured out. People were prophesying. But there was no billowing smoke. The sun didn't turn dark or the moon to blood.

In the original context, this prophecy in Joel goes on, "*In those days and at that time*, when I restore the fortunes of Judah and Jerusalem, I will gather all nations and bring them down to the Valley of Jehoshaphat. Then I will enter into judgment with them there" (Joel 3:1-2, emphasis added). This part of Joel's prophecy didn't happen on the day of Pentecost, and it still hasn't happened today.

Several suggestions have been offered to explain Peter's use of Joel.

## Rabbinic Interpretation

More liberal interpreters argue that Peter is using Scripture like rabbinic *midrashic* or *pesher* methods of interpretation. Both of these approaches interpret the Old Testament passages without regard for their original context.

*Pesher* tends to see current history as fulfilling prophecies, even when careful reading of the original prophecies doesn't fit the details of the current situation. According to some scholars, this passage from Acts is a *pesher* interpretation. The Dead Sea Essenes often employed *pesher* to show that current events pointed to their community having been predicted in Old Testament prophecy.

*Midrash* brings multiple passages together based on word association or similarity of phrases, again ignoring the original context. The result can often be a novel message never intended by the author. Additionally, the message derived is not legitimate according to the grammatical-historical method (the method used by Protestants for normal Scripture interpretation). According to the grammatical-historical method, context is the number one consideration when interpreting.

It's not clear that *midrashic* interpretation was in use when Acts was written. Our examples of *midrash* come from later rabbinic texts like the *Mishnah* or *Talmud* (AD 200-400).

Because the issue of rabbinic interpretation comes up multiple times in Acts, we will be dealing with it as necessary. We will show that turning to this explanation is unnecessary and misguided.

## Spiritualizing

Other commentators see this passage as an introduction to a new way of reading the Old Testament based on changes that Jesus brought about. Specifically, these readers hold that the original meaning of Old Testament prophecies promising a millennial kingdom to the Jewish people—or prophecies about other end-times themes—have been abrogated. Instead, these predictions are "spiritualized" and applied to the church, and that's what Peter was doing in this instance.

But you can see major problems with this view. What about when Peter quotes Joel saying, "And I will cause wonders in the heavens above and signs on the earth below—blood and fire and clouds of smoke. The sun will become dark, and the moon will turn blood red before that great and glorious day of the Lord arrives" (vs. 19-20). Clearly, none of these things happened on Pentecost. If it were about the church, what message would these words convey?

Or, how are we to spiritualize the next verses in Joel where he mentions the restoration of Israel and the judgment of the nations? "For behold, in those days and at that time, when I restore the fortunes of Judah and Jerusalem, I will gather all the nations and bring them down to the valley of Jehoshaphat. Then I will enter into judgment with them there" (Joel 3:1-2). This judgment of the nations doesn't apply at all on the day of Pentecost or to the church. Yet the day of judgment is going to happen. The passage is still unfulfilled, but it will happen later. It was only partially fulfilled.

## Unforeseen Partial Fulfillment?

The best way to understand Peter's use of Joel's prophecy is as an "unforeseen partial fulfillment." These happen when a prophecy refers to more than one event or person.

For example, Jesus quoted Isaiah 61, saying it was fulfilled in his audience's sight that day. But he stopped reading right after it predicted he would "proclaim the favorable year of the Lord" (Isaiah 61:2a). He didn't read the next phrase, "and the day of vengeance of our God" (Isaiah 61:2b). That part was not fulfilled in Jesus' day, because it refers to the judgment day.

Jesus also left out the following verses, where the prophecy goes on to predict the world peace that accompanies the Messiah's second coming. So the prophecy was only partially fulfilled as far as Jesus read it, and the rest was not. But just because only one part of the prophecy was fulfilled doesn't mean the rest of the prophecy isn't going to be fulfilled as well. The rest will be fulfilled later, when Jesus returns. This gap of over 2000 years is not announced in the text, so it's "unforeseen."

In the same way, the prophecy from Joel that Peter quoted was only partially fulfilled at Pentecost—the part about God pouring out his Spirit. Peter probably kept reciting it further in order to reach verse 21, "And everyone who calls on the name of the Lord will be saved." That part was also fulfilled as Peter spoke. The rest of Joel's prophecy, including the darkening of the sun, pillars of smoke, and the judgment of the nations, was not fulfilled then, but will be later.

The partial fulfillment of Joel was also unforeseen because the only cue in the text signaling the leap from Joel's day to AD 33 is the tiny phrase, "It will come about after this" (Joel 2:28a).

## Overview of Jesus' Ministry

Peter continued:

> "Men of Israel, listen to these words: Jesus the Nazarene, a man attested to you by God with miracles and wonders and signs which God performed through Him in your midst, just as you yourselves know..." (v. 22)

Can you imagine someone claiming to be the Messiah? What would it take to convince you that he really is? Surely the ability to do miracles would be one key requirement. Someone rightly called the Son of God would have to do what only God can do.

Jesus' miracles were widely acclaimed, especially the more public miracles like his healing of the man born blind (John 9). Everyone in the relatively small town of Jerusalem knew who the blind man was. He had been begging for decades near the temple, where everyone passed. And no doubt the full text of Peter's sermon would include some reminders of other miracles they all knew.

Notice that Peter describes Jesus' miracles as "wonders and signs which God performed through him." That squares with what Jesus said: "The words that I say to you I do not speak on my own initiative, but the Father abiding in me does his works" (John 14:10). As Paul puts it, Jesus "emptied himself" when he was incarnated (Philippians 2:7). He temporarily laid aside the use of his divine attributes. That's why he was sometimes hungry, tired, or unsure when he would return.[1]

## Confrontation

Then Peter fearlessly confronted his audience:

> "This Man, delivered over by the predetermined plan and foreknowledge of God, you nailed to a cross by the hands of godless men and put Him to death." (v. 23)

How many of those standing there had cried out, "Crucify! Crucify!" before Pilate? Probably quite a few. We later read that these same people "were cut to the heart" (v. 37).

Peter pressed on:

> "But God raised Him up again, putting an end to the agony of death, since it was impossible for Him to be held in its power." (v. 24)

The crowd knew about Jesus' ministry, teaching, and miracle working. But this was the first time they had heard about the resurrection.

How difficult it must have been for them to believe Jesus was alive from the dead! And just because these guys say so? Of course, these were the

---

1. The clearest discussion of Jesus' emptying is in Philippians 2:5-11. This emptying explains many accounts where Jesus appears to lack divine attributes like omniscience (Matthew 24:36; Luke 2:52; 8: 45), omnipotence (Mark 6:5; John 5:19), omnipresence (John 4:4), righteousness (Hebrews 4:15), justice (John 5:30), and self-existence (Luke 4:2). Failure to grasp Jesus' emptying can easily lead to Christological errors, seeing him as less than divine. Although Jesus had access to his divine attributes while incarnated, he laid aside that prerogative and assumed a humble and subservient posture. He performed miracles through the power of the Holy Spirit, as we see here in Acts 2 and throughout the Gospels.

people with light streaming off their faces and speaking in other languages... that roaring wind. Yes. Maybe it was true after all.

The bodily resurrection of Jesus is always a crucial part of the gospel. Without it, we are left with the tragic martyrdom of an innocent man. With it, we have a victorious rescuer.

# Psalm 16

Peter goes on to argue that Psalm 16 predicts the resurrection. He says that, although the psalm appears to be about David and his relationship with God, part of it is about Jesus. David said, "You will not leave my soul among the dead or allow your Holy One to rot in the grave" (Psalm 16:10). Here, the NLT has capitalized Holy One, signifying that it refers to Jesus. David must have been saying that the Holy One's body would not decay, resulting in his own salvation and escape from *Sheol*, the pit of death. Peter points out that this can't refer to David, whose body did decay:

> "Dear brothers, think about this! You can be sure that the patriarch David wasn't referring to himself, for he died and was buried, and his tomb is still here among us. But he was a prophet, and he knew God had promised with an oath that one of David's own descendants would sit on his throne. David was looking into the future and speaking of the Messiah's resurrection. He was saying that God would not leave him among the dead or allow his body to rot in the grave." (Acts 2:29-31)

So did David know about the resurrection? Or did God cause him to write this without fully understanding it? We know of several psalms where David spoke as a namesake for his famous descendent, Jesus. And we can safely assume that David never expected that his own body wouldn't decompose in the grave. So either answer is possible.

Psalm 16 must have been among the passages Jesus showed Peter and the others when he "opened their minds to understand the Scriptures" (Luke 24:45).

The New Testament's use of the Old Testament is an important area of scholarly study. In this very complex field scholars debate the methods used by New Testament writers and speakers when they handle

Old Testament texts. Such questions have a major effect on how we view the whole task of interpretation. Unless the apostles were using grammatical-historical interpretation, it opens the door for other methods that rob Scripture of authority.

Some scholars argue that the part of Peter's speech dealing with Psalm 16 is rabbinic *pesher* interpretation, described earlier. In *pesher*, the interpreter reads the present day into prophecies that actually apply to something else. But when Peter specifically refers to the issue of decomposition and to the historical fact that David's body did decompose, he is using the grammatical-historical method. He shows that this messianic meaning is subtly implied in the original text. It was not David, but "Your Holy One" whose body would not decay.

## Jesus' Ascension

As Peter drew to his climax, he claimed what must have seemed utterly outlandish to this crowd:

> "Therefore having been exalted to the right hand of God, and having received from the Father the promise of the Holy Spirit, [Jesus] has poured forth this which you both see and hear." (v. 33)

That a man could sit at the right hand of God—Jewish teaching had no category for that. Maybe he was a good teacher, a miracle worker, a man of God...but sitting at the right hand of God? Even to entertain this would require an extreme paradigm shift. Yet Peter ends with the relevant reminder, "this which you both see and hear." The crowd heard the wind; the tongues like fire were apparently still there, because he refers to "what you see." So no matter how far out Peter's claims seemed, it would be hard to argue with the guy who has something like fire coming off his head!

Peter is remembering the last supper, when Jesus said,

> "I tell you the truth, it is to your advantage that I go away; for if I do not go away, the Helper will not come to you; but if I go, I will send Him to you," and, "I will ask the Father, and He will give you another Helper, that He may be with you forever; that is the Spirit of truth" (John 16:7; 14:16-17).

Passages like these make it crystal clear that the Holy Spirit's indwelling lay in the future relative to when Jesus uttered these words.

Peter points out that Scripture also predicted the ascension:

> "For David did not ascend to heaven, and yet he said, 'The Lord said to my Lord: "Sit at my right hand until I make your enemies a footstool for your feet."'" (vs. 34-35)

Psalm 110 was already known to be a messianic psalm, and Jesus had earlier called attention to the inconsistencies of the rabbinic view that the Messiah would be both David's son and his Lord (see Luke 20:41-44). The messianic aspect of the psalm becomes clear in verses 5-6: "The Lord is at your right hand; He will shatter kings in the day of His wrath. He will judge among the nations."

But the rabbis didn't focus on King Messiah becoming a child and growing up like a normal man. They either saw him as coming down from the sky (Daniel 9:13) or just appearing. The idea of a carpenter's son sitting at God's right hand was really a stretch.

The Jews didn't believe that King Messiah would be God. For a human to be deity was unthinkable to Jews then, and still today, even though Isaiah says the Messiah will be a child born and his name will be "mighty God" and "eternal father" (Isaiah 9:6).

## Now What?

Peter concluded:

> "Therefore let all Israel be assured of this: God has made this Jesus, whom you crucified, both Lord and Messiah." (v. 36)[2]

Imagine yourself standing there. This man making the most incredible claims you've ever heard now ends with an awful charge: you just killed the Messiah! Naturally, you would strongly resist this message. But again, there's the wind and the fire... Everyone knew about the miracles Jesus performed. Even his enemies admitted he was a miracle worker. They just said he used power from Satan (Matthew 12:24). As the Holy Spirit

---

2. Peter also apparently already understood the worldwide spread of the gospel. "The promise is for you and your children and for all who are far off," he declared (v. 39). It's likely that the believers in the upper room had spent time discussing what the Great Commission meant. In practice it would take significant pressure to get them to actually take action.

convicted hearts throughout the crowd, minds changed. With throbbing heads, they realized it was true:

> When the people heard this, they were cut to the heart and said to Peter and the other apostles, "Brothers, what shall we do?" (v. 37)

This cry of desperation speaks eloquently of repentant hearts. They don't suggest, "Well, maybe we should do this, or offer that...." They had no idea what to do when they realized they were part of the group that killed God's promised one, the Messiah. They came to God with the empty hands of faith.

# The Call

Peter somehow knew exactly what to say:

> Peter replied, "Repent and be baptized, every one of you, in the name of Jesus Christ for the forgiveness of your sins. And you will receive the gift of the Holy Spirit." (v. 38)

Had they discussed during the days in the upper room how a gospel call should be framed? Or did God inspire Peter to put it this way?

Unfortunately, this verse has become ground zero for two false teachings, both of which attempt to reinsert works into God's terms for salvation.

## Baptismal Regeneration

This false teaching claims that Peter prescribed water baptism is required for and also conveys salvation. People are regenerated (spiritually reborn) only upon receiving water baptism.

You can easily see this argument is incorrect by examining several parallel passages where baptism and regeneration appear. For example, we will see that when Peter preached to Cornelius and his household in Acts 10:44-48 the first thing that happened was that the "Spirit fell upon all those who were listening to the message" (v. 44).

Next, seeing these new believers speaking in tongues and glorifying God, Peter turned to his companions and said, "Surely no one can refuse the water for these to be baptized who have received the Holy Spirit just as we did, can he?" (v. 47). So the order is clear: first came faith, then regeneration and the indwelling Holy Spirit, and then water baptism. Baptism is an outward sign of an inward reality.[3]

## Repentance

Peter calls on the crowd to repent. Again, modern teachers err when they expand the meaning of Peter's word "repent."

Teachers of deep repentance argue that repentance means turning away from sin, thus implying that people have to commit to stopping any sin they might be involved in before they can receive conversion.

This view is connected to so-called "lordship theology" or "lordship salvation." It teaches that strict moral demands are an indispensable part of the gospel call. Under lordship theology, any claim that people can come to faith and only later see growth and victory over sin will result in pseudo-conversions.[4]

The Greek word for repent is *metanoia*. It comes from the word for "mind" (*nous*), and a prefix meaning "to change." So repentance literally means a change of mind. Those rejecting lordship theology argue that repenting is simply changing one's mind from avoiding or refusing God to accepting him and his gospel.

Of course, repentance can refer to turning away from a sin, but when used in the context of conversion, it means to turn from unbelief to faith. The easiest way to verify this is to browse through Luke's use of the word for yourself, and see whether the context sustains the lordship view.[5]

Under the free grace understanding, repentance isn't an additional

---

3. Baptismal regeneration also contradicts many other passages, like Acts 16:30-31. There, a jailor asked Paul and Silas, "Sirs, what must I do to be saved?" Their answer was ""Believe in the Lord Jesus, and you will be saved." If baptismal regeneration is correct, then Paul's answer here is false. The only way to harmonize these and dozens of other passages is to single out the lowest common denominator: salvation by faith.

4. Louis Berkhof is typical, defining repentance as "that change wrought in the conscious life of the sinner, by which he turns away from sin." Louis Berkhof, Systematic Theology, (Woodstock, ON: Devoted Publishing, 2017), 486. Lordship theologian John MacArthur explains what he dislikes about the free grace view: "They set up a concept of faith that eliminates submission, yieldedness, or turning from sin, and they categorize all the practical elements of salvation as human works. They stumble over the twin truths that salvation is a gift, yet, it costs everything. Those ideas are paradoxical, but they are not mutually exclusive." John MacArthur, The Gospel According to Jesus (Grand Rapids: Zondervan, 2008), 31. I think it's a flat contradiction, and therefore necessarily false. It's no different than saying 1 million = 0.

5. These are Luke's uses of *metanoeo* (the verb form of *metanoia*): Luke 10:13; 11:32; 13:3; 13:5; 15:7; 15:10; 16:30; 17:3; 17:4; Acts 2:38; 3:19; 8:22; 17:30; 26:20.

requirement, along with faith. Rather, it is implied or entailed by faith. One repents from unbelief to belief.

That's what Peter called for when he said to repent.

Luke points out that Peter admonished the crowd with many other words, which makes sense. You can read this whole sermon in two minutes. It's a summary of the key points he made. This is true throughout Acts wherever speeches are recorded. But if you've ever explained something you have recently taught, you know it's not difficult to summarize your points.[6]

## Three Thousand New Believers

Then comes the victorious conclusion: "Those who accepted his message were baptized, and about three thousand were added to their number that day" (v. 41). All the apostles and probably other believers must have been working at this mass baptism for hours! Probably no ritual or testimonies, just people lining up and being baptized one after another. They must have used one or more of the pools in ancient Jerusalem (several of which have since been excavated).

They probably also told people to meet up at Solomon's Portico in the days to come for further teaching (5:12). Somehow, they were able to channel this surging crowd into a growing orderly community, as the next passage shows.

## The Big Picture

With this harvest, God had already launched the body of Christ out into dozens of cities scattered over the known world. He had also planted a large, strong body in Jerusalem that would carry his work forward in the coming months. Such a large number of believers would be daunting to anyone who had persecution in mind.

---

6. Falsely, see Cadbury, of whom Longnecker says his dictum "reigns supreme in NT circles: 'Instead of accuracy the purpose of ancient historians tended to make the form the chief point of emphasis' and 'from Thucydides downwards, speeches reported by the historians are confessedly pure imagination." Longnecker, *Acts*, 213. That may be true of Thucydides, but not of Acts, where Luke had direct access to Peter and Paul, who could have easily recounted the essence of what they spoke.

# 3

# WHAT HAPPENED TO THESE PEOPLE?

## ACTS 2

Luke says the believers were "filled with the Holy Spirit" (Acts 2:4). Some readers are confused because some of the same believers are later said to be filled with the Spirit on another occasion. For instance, Acts 4:8 and 4:31 both say Peter and the believers were filled with the Spirit again. What does it mean to be filled with the Holy Spirit? Is it a temporary state?

Just a chapter earlier, Luke recounted Jesus saying, "You will be baptized with the Holy Spirit not many days from now" (1:5). That was ten days before Pentecost. Surely, Pentecost must be the baptism of the Holy Spirit Jesus was referring to. If it is (and most agree that it is), what is the relationship between the baptism of the Holy Spirit and being filled with the Spirit?

## Modern Explanations

Early in the twentieth century a group of Christian leaders arrived at the conclusion that the experience described in Acts 2 is the baptism of the Holy Spirit, and that this baptism is a second work of grace (after spiritual rebirth). They held that this second work is available to all believers, but often missed because people don't ask for it and seek it. They argued that speaking in tongues was and is the sign that one has been baptized with the Spirit.

The followers of this view are known as Pentecostals. Today, numbering in the millions, they have reached vast numbers worldwide with the gospel. Although I don't agree with Pentecostal doctrine, I admire the enormous evangelistic work they have done, especially in the developing world. But as part of teaching the book of Acts, it will be necessary to interact with their views on the Holy Spirit.

## What Is Spiritual Baptism?

John the Baptist predicted that Jesus would bring a baptism in, with, or by[1] the Spirit:

> "As for me, I baptize you with water for repentance, but He who is coming after me is mightier than I, and I am not fit to remove His sandals; He will baptize you with the Holy Spirit and fire. His winnowing fork is in His hand, and He will thoroughly clear His threshing floor; and He will gather His wheat into the barn, but He will burn up the chaff with unquenchable fire." (Matthew 3:11-12)

John explained his prophecy that Jesus would baptize "with the Holy Spirit and fire" in the next verse when he said that Jesus' winnowing fork is in his hand. A winnowing fork is like a wooden pitch fork that farmers used when threshing grain.

The farmer first laid the dried sheaves on a wooden platform called a threshing floor and then either beat the grain with a pole or rolled a stone over it. In either case the point was to break the grains loose from the pods or husks. Then, with the winnowing fork, the farmer threw the pile into the air on a breezy day. The dense grain would fall back to the floor, but the lighter "chaff" (the dried stems and empty husks) would blow away.

After doing this a few times, the farmer had "cleansed" his threshing

---

1. The particle en here can be translated "in," "with," or "by." The LID case means the particle could be locative (having to do with location) therefore "in." If it is instrumental, the word would be "by." And if it is dative, the appropriate word would be "with." Which of the three fits best here is up for debate.

floor. A pile of grain lay on the floor, while the chaff lay nearby on the ground. He gathered the grain and put it in the barn. He gathered the chaff, which was useless, and burned it.

## Applying the Analogy

The word "baptize" is not a translation of the Greek word as much as a transliteration. The word is *baptizo*, and it means to immerse or to put into. While our English word usually refers to the ritual of water baptism, the Greek word was used in common speech and often had nothing to do with water baptism.

In Matthew 3 we encounter baptism with the Holy Spirit and baptism with fire. In context, the baptism in, with, or by the Holy Spirit would correspond to putting the grain into the barn. The baptism with fire would be like burning the chaff. In other words, you have two alternatives: you can either go into the barn or go into the fire. In Matthew 3, baptism with the Spirit is conversion, while baptism with unquenchable fire is damnation.

Clearly, the view held by some commentators[2] that the baptism of fire refers to the tongues of fire on Pentecost is incorrect. An important principle in interpretation is to interpret based on context, not word association. Just because something like fire came into play on the day of Pentecost is no reason to overthrow John's own explanation for his statement.

# 1 Corinthians 12:13

Fortunately, God provides a straightforward definition of spiritual baptism in 1 Corinthians 12:13:

> For by one Spirit we were all baptized into one body, whether Jews or Greeks, whether slaves or free, and we were all made to drink of one Spirit.

Notice the following in this one verse:

---

2. For example, The General Council of the Assemblies of God position paper says, "Fundamental Truth 7: All believers are entitled to and should ardently expect and earnestly seek the promise of the Father, the baptism in the Holy Ghost and fire." "The Baptism in the Holy Spirit: The Initial Experience and Continuing Evidences of the Spirit-Filled Life," (Adopted by General Presbytery The General Council of the Assemblies of God August 11, 2000), 3. You can see the baptism of fire is viewed as a good thing.

1. The baptism by the Spirit applies to "we all." So the idea that some (or even most) Christians haven't been baptized by the Spirit is wrong.

2. This baptism is not into water, but into the body of Christ.

3. The same particle in Matthew 3, with the same options for translation, appears in the opening phrase "by one Spirit."

4. The verse says that "we were all made to drink of one Spirit." That refers to the indwelling of the Spirit, when he comes to live within each believer (1 Corinthians 6:19). So we are put into Christ, and he indwells us through the Spirit. Jesus promised this ahead of time: "In that day you will know that I am in My Father, and you in me, and I in you" (John 14:20).

5. Finally, while Paul says we all were baptized by the Spirit, later in the same chapter, he asks, "All do not speak with tongues, do they?" (1 Corinthians 12:30). This construction requires a negative answer. So since all are baptized by the Spirit but not all speak with tongues, the idea that speaking in tongues is the evidence of being baptized by the Spirit is proven wrong.

This is the only passage we have that defines what the baptism by the Spirit is. Some later passages in Acts are said to support the Pentecostal position, and we will deal with those as they arise in the text. Here in 1 Corinthians 12, we see clearly that to be baptized by the Spirit means to be placed into Jesus and into his body, the church.

## What Is the Filling of the Spirit?

The filling of the Spirit is different from spiritual baptism, although both can happen concurrently. That's what happened on the day of Pentecost. As the Spirit baptized the believers into Christ, they were also filled with the Spirit.

Filling happens when believers come completely under the influence of the Holy Spirit. Many have correctly noted that it's not that *we* get more of the Spirit, but that *he* gets more of us. To be filled with the Holy Spirit means you are completely submitted to the Spirit and sensitive to his leading.

Unlike spiritual baptism, spiritual filling can happen multiple times. The strength of spiritual influence can wax and wane. It's something we can ask for, especially in ministry situations. That's why being filled with the Spirit is given as an imperative in Ephesians 5:18: "Be filled with the Spirit."

# Indwelling

On the last night of his life before the cross, Jesus explained to his disciples that the Spirit "abides with you and will be in you" (John 14:17). In other words, this indwelling is a new ministry of the Holy Spirit not known before Pentecost. In the Old Testament, the Spirit would "come upon" a prophet when he prophesied (e.g., Ezekiel 11:5). But this indwelling was something different.

Jesus predicted that the Spirit would actually enter into the believers' lives. At that point, God's Spirit is fused with our spirit. Paul explains, "The one who joins himself to the Lord is one spirit with Him" (1 Corinthians 6:17). This fusion is so complete that we can rest assured it is permanent.

The Old Testament's temporary anointing could leave David pleading, "Do not cast me away from your presence, and do not take your Holy Spirit from me" (Psalm 51:11). That would be a totally inappropriate prayer for New Covenant believers, about whom Jesus said, "I will ask the Father, and he will give you another Helper, that he may be with you forever" (John 14:16).

This new indwelling of every believer is not only permanent, it is also universal, applying to all Christians. There are no exceptions. Paul insists that, "If anyone does not have the Spirit of Christ, he does not belong to Him" (Romans 8:9).

The indwelling of the Holy Spirit gives us a new outlook on our relationship with God. It also gives us new insight. Our ability to understand Scripture more deeply and to resonate when it speaks to our heart is a direct result of his presence (see 1 Corinthians 2:14-16). We also experience new sensitivity to evil and goodness. The Spirit also causes us to feel drawn to Christian fellowship.

His promptings are usually subtle. He doesn't bowl us over. And if we don't bother to listen, we probably won't hear him.

# Empowering

When Jesus talked to his disciples just before ascending to heaven, he told them to go to Jerusalem and wait for the Holy Spirit. Then he said, "You will receive power when the Holy Spirit has come upon you; and you shall be my witnesses both in Jerusalem, and in all Judea and Samaria, and even to the remotest part of the earth" (Acts 1:8).

Here Jesus promised that in addition to spiritual baptism and indwelling would come power. But it wasn't power for the disciples to use to do whatever they wanted. The power was specifically so that "you will be my witnesses."

Bringing people to a living faith in Jesus is a supernatural task. Believers who experience success in outreach and discipleship also know how essential God's empowering is to those tasks. The Spirit gave the apostles power to perform miracles and to speak with conviction, not to mention a roaring wind and fire-like balls of energy.

All spiritual ministry requires divine power. How do we help people grow or change their lives? We don't know, but it happens all the time. And that's because the Holy Spirit empowers ministry.

Counseling, serving, and helping all require spiritual power as well. Jesus said, "Apart from me you can do nothing" (John 15:5). He didn't mean that we can't do literally anything at all, but rather that we can't do anything spiritually significant. We need to abide in Jesus in order to become attuned to him and to the promptings of the Spirit.

# The New Covenant

What changed in the transition from the Old to the New Covenant? It wasn't salvation by faith apart from works. That's always been the only pathway, as Paul explains in Romans 4. It wasn't the definition of good and evil. God's character hasn't changed either.

The main change involves these new ministries of the Holy Spirit—joining believers to God, dwelling within them, empowering them to serve him, and several others we have not discussed. None of these ministries existed before Pentecost. With these new ministries of the Spirit, believers experience new intimacy with God, resulting in a new hardiness and increased potency in ministry.

The Old Covenant focused on having God's people stay in the land, have nothing to do with neighboring nations, and survive (Deuteronomy 7:1-11). Even with that fairly low bar, true faith barely survived at several points. Now, with a new commission to go out into every nation, God equipped believers with the strength and knowledge they would need in order to invade the world system successfully.

The New Testament raises the spiritual bar for everything. On the negative side, it would be unthinkable that a key leader like Peter or Paul would commit adultery and murder a man to cover his sin, like David did. On the positive side, we see descriptions of dynamic local bodies, like the one described in the next chapter. We know of no such communities in ancient Israel before Jesus.

## Formation of the Body of Christ

"The body of Christ" is another term for the church, as we see in verses like Colossians 1:18: "He [Jesus] is also head of the body, the church." To create the body, the Spirit baptizes believers into Jesus, as we just read. Since spiritual baptism results in the formation of the body of Christ, we can infer that the body, the church, was a new development on the day of Pentecost. Theologians call this putting of believers into Jesus the "mystical union."

Although a people of God existed under the Old Covenant, that was different from the church. The Jewish people included believers and nonbelievers. They were not joined to Jesus and each other by spiritual baptism and indwelling, as members of the New Testament church are.

This distinction is important, because many theologians think the church began with Abraham 2000 years earlier. If that were so, it would suggest that features from the Old Testament like priests, holy days, the temple, and infant circumcision should also be features of the church. If the church began here on the day of Pentecost, however, then we would need to erase the blackboard and start over. Rituals and roles from the Old Covenant should be discarded or reinterpreted to fit the new situation of the people of God.

## The Big Picture

The day of Pentecost changed everything for the people of God. Because of the cross, God was able to fuse his people to Jesus in the mystical union. These new ministries of the Holy Spirit were all novel on that day. This is the "power from on high" Jesus told his disciples to wait for (1:8). We could go further on the ministries of the Holy Spirit, discussing:

- The illumining ministry, where the Spirit opens our eyes to comprehend Scripture (1 Corinthians 2:12; Ephesians 1:17-19).

- The convicting ministry, where the Spirit convicts the world of their sin and their need for Christ (John 16:8-11; 1 Thess. 1:5).

- The sealing ministry, where the Spirit puts a stamp of guarantee on our eternal life (Ephesians 1:13-14; 4:30).

- Regeneration, where the Spirit causes a spiritual rebirth at the moment of salvation (John 3:3; Titus 3:5).

- The guiding ministry, where the Spirit leads the people of God in their lives and ministries (Acts 11:12; 11:27-30; 16:6; 20:22-3; Galatians 2:2).

- The transforming ministry, where the Spirit gives us the power and motivation to grow spiritually and see our characters become more Christ-like (Romans 5:5; 8:4ff; Galatians 5:22-3; 1 Thessalonians 5:23-24; 2 Corinthians 3:18).

With the coming of the Spirit in his New Covenant ministries, believers now live at a spiritual level unknown in earlier ages. As a result, expectations also rise—those from God and our expectations on ourselves and each other. The rest of the book of Acts illustrates how this new supernatural lifestyle plays out.

# 4

# LIFE IN THE EARLIEST CHURCH

## ACTS 2:41-47

The people of God immediately congregated and began their lives together. Luke gives us a short list of seven key characteristics found in the group. The approving language implies that this local body was the ideal followed by later communities.

The list begins with the expression, "They were continually devoting themselves to..." followed by four activities. The phrase "continually devoting themselves" is strong language, indicating intensity, frequency, and duration.

## The Apostles' Teaching

> They were continually devoting themselves to the apostles'
> teaching... (Acts 2:42)

Jesus had earlier established the apostles as the gold standard for truth in teaching. He said, "He who receives you receives me, and he who receives me receives Him who sent Me" (Mathew 10:40; see also Luke 10:16). Later, in the upper room, the night before his death, he said, "The Helper, the Holy Spirit, whom the Father will send in my name, He will teach you all things, and bring to your remembrance all that I said to you" (John 14:26).

And he added, "When the Helper comes, whom I will send to you from the Father, that is the Spirit of truth who proceeds from the Father, he will testify about me, and you will testify also, because you have been with me from the beginning" (John 15:26-27).

Being with Jesus from the beginning clearly distinguished the Apostles (with a capital A) from other New Testament apostles.[1] It also meant the original apostles couldn't pass their doctrinal authority to later generations, as claimed by the Catholic, Orthodox, and Anglican churches. How can later church leaders have been with Jesus from the beginning? The Bible never says the apostles could pass their authority to others. What they did pass on are the books found in the New Testament.

Jesus also told the Twelve, "When he, the Spirit of truth, comes, he will guide you into all the truth; for he will not speak on his own initiative, but whatever he hears, he will speak; and he will disclose to you what is to come" (John 16:13). The apostles' ability to deliver definitive truth therefore also includes new revelation beyond what Jesus had already said.

Much of our teaching in the rest of the New Testament goes beyond anything Jesus taught. For example, the relationship between following Jesus and the temple, rituals, and festivals isn't completely cleared up until the book of Hebrews. Therefore, Jesus' promise that the Spirit would reveal further truth to the apostles is important to our understanding of New Testament doctrine as a whole.

Taken together, these promises from Jesus pre-authenticated the apostles as authoritative arbiters of truth, including being authors of Scripture. Only books with apostolic authority were admitted into the canon of Scripture, but the canon came later. In the days following Pentecost, people were mainly listening to the apostles' preaching and teaching. Of

---

1. Apostles other than the Twelve are evident in the New Testament. For instance, Paul says Jesus appeared to the Twelve after his resurrection (1 Corinthians 15:5), but later he appeared to "all the apostles" (1 Corinthians 15:7). Apostleship also appears in lists of spiritual gifts (1 Corinthians 12:28; Ephesians 4:11), so believers expected that some of their number would have that gift. Barnabas was an example. The word "apostle" means "a sent one," so apostles roughly correspond to missionaries or church planters. However, the original twelve had unique authority to declare doctrine that defines the boundaries of true Christianity. No one else has that authority.

course, they may have had written accounts as well, but not fully completed books.

Today, we have "the apostles' teaching" in writing—that is, the New Testament. If we want to imitate the first Christian church, we will continually devote ourselves to the apostles' teaching. That means expounding the word, learning the word, remembering the word, and sharing the word on a regular basis. Language later in this passage shows that they gathered to hear the word taught most days, if not daily.

Local bodies that devote themselves to the word are rewarded with spiritual health. God can regularly correct or remind believers of the great truths on which we stand. The body of Christ is a community of truth, and delving deeply into God's word brings joy and needed insight to its members.

Arguably, congregations nourished with weekly exposition of Scripture in context—disciplined study of whole books of the Bible, chapter by chapter—will be healthier than those given light topical fare and entertainment.

The early believers called the apostles' body of teaching "tradition" (*paradosis*, that which is handed over) that could be passed on to others (cf. 1 Corinthians 11:2; 1 Thessalonians 2:13; 2 Thessalonians 2:15; 3:6). But they weren't talking about a body of material different from Scripture. New Testament tradition *is* Scripture, properly interpreted. Part of the believers' task was integrating the whole Old Testament with what Jesus taught.

# Fellowship

> They were continually devoting themselves to... fellowship. (v. 42)

The New Testament word for fellowship is *koinonia*. It comes from a word meaning "to have in common" or" to share," and it became a favorite word in the early church when referring to what happened when believers assembled.

Early followers of Jesus believed they could share the life of God through gathering with others who had the Spirit in common. When a group of people indwelt with the Spirit gather, the potential for building community is elevated to a new level.

Quality fellowship requires that people gather in smaller groups, like this group did. Verse 46 says, "Day by day continuing with one mind in the temple, and breaking bread from house to house, they were taking their meals together with gladness and sincerity of heart."

You see that the believers met in their homes. Houses were smaller then than they are today. Most houses wouldn't have held more than a dozen or so. That means there must have been scores of house gatherings, at least.

Why meet in homes? The main reason was to build community. Large gatherings also have a purpose, but they are not suitable for building community. They are too diffuse and too public for honest sharing. Believers need gatherings where everyone participates. Later in the New Testament, we learn about spiritual gifts and the universal call to learn how to serve. The first believers were probably just beginning to learn about these things at this time.

The New International Version translates the expression "day by day" as "every day." That is the sense of the expression. Every day, or at least most days, they found time to get together. This is far from the "Sunday go to church" picture.

In real Christian community, believers build quality love relationships with each other. That takes time and focus. Even small groups are not enough. People really need to get together in even smaller groups (two or three) and open up about what's happening in their lives. They need to pray for each other, asking God how they can invest most effectively in one another's lives. Real community is terrifically exciting and energizing to members. They can't get enough.

All this is why it was necessary that "they were continually devoting themselves." They had jobs and families to take care of, but they found plenty of time for building *koinonia*.

## The Breaking of Bread

> They were continually devoting themselves to... the breaking of bread... (v. 42)

Is breaking bread referring to communion? Or is it another way of describing having meals together? It hardly matters, because the apostolic church celebrated communion as part of a larger meal.

Sharing meals is a natural venue for friendship building. Eating together feels good, and people usually become more talkative during and after dinner. Picnics and cookouts were in play then, as they are today. When you have good friends in the body of Christ, it's natural to want to eat together.

Historical evidence from a later period in the early church suggests that house churches met for dinner and fellowship once a week, calling their dinners "love feasts" (Jude 12). They usually also practiced communion. Spending time using bread and wine to remember what Jesus did at the cross is always a good idea, but Scripture never says how often we should do it. Paul simply says, "as often as you do it" (1 Corinthians 11:26).

In later church history, communion came to be viewed in an almost magical way. The early, simple view expressed when Jesus said, "Do this in remembrance of me" was nowhere in sight (1 Corinthians 11:25). Eventually, only ordained priests could change bread and wine into flesh and blood, and the mass actually conveyed forgiveness of sin. Like most changes introduced later in church history, none of these had any basis in Scripture, and all were changes in the wrong direction.[2]

# Prayer

> They were continually devoting themselves to... prayer. (v. 42)

This was a God-centered group. You can imagine how zealously one would turn to God when realizing what he had so recently done through Jesus. But this passage isn't primarily talking about private prayer. Rather, it's about public (sometimes called corporate) prayer.

---

2. The view that communion was effectual in forgiving sin comes from John 6. There Jesus said he was "the bread of life" and that "if anyone eats of this bread, he will live forever (John 6:48, 51). However, this passage is not referring to communion for several reasons. First, communion had not yet been given or explained, so Jesus' audience would not take that meaning. Second, the context for the symbolism in communion is Passover. The symbolism in John 6 comes from manna (vs. 31-32). Eating bread here in John means something completely different than communion. Third, the context makes clear that "eating Jesus' flesh and drinking his blood" means nothing other than believing in him. He explained in this same talk, "For this is the will of My Father, that everyone who beholds the Son and believes in Him will have eternal life" (v. 40; cf. vs. 29, 35, 47). Fourth, Jesus himself made clear in context that his words should not be taken literally: "It is the Spirit who gives life; the flesh profits nothing; the words that I have spoken to you are spirit and are life" (v. 63).

We know the early church continued to observe the times of prayer at the temple (see, e.g., Acts 3:1). The God-intended role of the temple in the spiritual lives of these believers may have been fuzzy at this point. Indeed, it remained unclear for decades to come, if we accept (as I do) that the book of Hebrews was addressed to the descendants of this same group. Jewish Christians were very reluctant to see that Jesus had made the temple obsolete.

While sin offerings would have been completely out of bounds, going to pray the regular, twice-daily public prayers wouldn't have been a problem. The believers were apparently engaging in both formal and informal prayer, because the Greek here uses the definite pronoun and the plural—"the prayers."

With the coming of Jesus, a new form of corporate prayer appeared. Instead of memorized formal prayers recited aloud, the people of God from this time on prayed in their own words as the Spirit led them.

You can see evidence of this type of prayer in 1 Corinthians, a letter to another group some years later. There, Paul insists that prayers spoken in tongues during a gathering must be translated so that people know when to say "amen" (1 Corinthians 14:16). In other words, others' response to prayers (saying "amen") depended on what was prayed. We will see multiple examples of corporate prayer later in Acts where groups gather and take turns praying, praising God and seeking his will in their own words.[3]

Thus another new ministry of the Holy Spirit came as the result of universal indwelling. Paul describes it this way:

> Likewise the Spirit helps us in our weakness; for we do not know how to pray as we ought, but that very Spirit intercedes with sighs too deep for words. And God, who searches the heart, knows what is the mind of the Spirit, because the Spirit intercedes for the saints according to the will of God. (Romans 8:26–27)

In corporate prayer believers aren't simply praying about issues in their private lives. Rather, they come together to seek the mind of the Spirit for the group. That's the significance of Paul's reference to saying "the amen."

3. See Acts 1:14, 24; 4:24–31; 6:4, 6; 9:40; 10:2, 4, 9, 31; 11:5; 12:5; 13:3; 14:23; 16:25; 22:17; 28:8.

Amen means "Yes!" or "True!" Believers praying together verbally affirm prayers they feel are within God's will for that moment.

## Supernatural

> Everyone kept feeling a sense of awe; and many wonders and signs were taking place through the apostles. (v. 43)

When you see God working with your own eyes, it is truly awe-inspiring. You will see people's lives changing in ways you never thought possible: people coming to faith in surprising numbers, prayers being answered, healings—all the marks of true, supernatural power.

Were miracles more common or more extreme during this critical time in the development of the body of Christ?

Certainly, we haven't seen the roaring wind or the glowing fire-like energy blobs going out to new believers. Even at the end of the day of Pentecost, we see no mention of the 3,000 converts receiving the tongues of fire or speaking in tongues like the original believers.

As we go through Acts, we will see that outbreaks of major miracles, including raising people from the dead, show up at key points. It's not a constant feature, always a big surprise. As the church spreads out geographically and in time, eventually encompassing thousands of house churches spread from Jerusalem to Rome and beyond, one must wonder: How many miracles would an average believer in a Philippian group see per year? My guess is not many. Miracles are generally rare, and being rare is part of what makes miracles so impressive. If they were commonplace, people would take them for granted. Also, miracles have historically been relatively ineffective at winning people to true faith, as Jesus' ministry made abundantly clear.

From the biblical point of view, no miracle is as extreme as a spiritually dead God-denier turning into a Spirit-filled child of God, and we see that miracle on a regular basis.

## Extreme Generosity

> And all those who had believed were together and had all things in common; and they began selling their property and

possessions and were sharing them with all, as anyone might have need. (vs. 44-45)

This group adopted a form of common purse where wealthier members provided for the poor. It's not a true community of goods, like a commune, because it was voluntary. Members decided whether and how much to participate, as we will see clearly in chapter 5 when Peter confronts a man named Ananias for giving money from the sale of land and lying about it. Peter said, "While it remained unsold, did it not remain your own? And after it was sold, was it not under your control?" (5:4). In other words, the disowning of property and goods was not a rule, but an ethos in the group.

Theologically, these people believed that "the earth is the Lord's, and all it contains, the world, and those who dwell in it" (Psalm 24:1). That means human owners of property and wealth are really stewards, temporarily entrusted with ownership, but with an obligation to use that wealth not only for their own sustenance but also to care for the poor and glorify God.

Under this stewardship view, those with excess property and wealth who behold poor fellow-believers in their midst will naturally liquidate some wealth to help out. The early believers weren't giving away everything they owned. You can see that they still had houses from verse 46, which (as we saw earlier) says that they "broke bread from house to house."

The statement in 4:32 that "not one of them claimed that anything belonging to him was his own" is a theological position, as true today as it was then. Our homes (and portfolios) belong to God and should be available to the community for the glory of God.

So rather than giving away everything they owned, believers who saw poverty in their group liquidated unneeded property to help the poor. For instance, Barnabas sold a piece of property on Cyprus and brought the proceeds to the apostles in Jerusalem (Acts 4:36-37), but he continued to live in his home in Jerusalem.

Today, American Christians may see no need to liquidate unneeded assets to assuage poverty, because most American Christians are in little difficulty. But if we open our eyes to the worldwide body of Christ, the need is plain enough. And of course, we have an obligation to the non-Christian poor as well.

Poverty probably came to this group in part because many of those visiting Jerusalem for Pentecost ended up receiving the Spirit. Rather than going back home as planned, many of them stayed to learn more about Jesus and his teaching. These people would have had no source of income, so it would be natural for other believers to host and feed them.

The church in this part of Judea continued to suffer from poverty for decades to come (Acts 11:27-30; 2 Corinthians 8, 9). Part of it was the result of persecution when the government later fully turned against the body of Christ.

One frequent punishment was to seize believers' houses and all they owned. Another was imprisonment (Hebrews 10:34; 13:3). Both the Sanhedrin (the governing council in Jerusalem) and the Romans made every attempt to snuff the body of Christ out, and poverty was one of the results. Other groups as far away as Syria and Greece took up collections to help.

When we study other local churches throughout Acts, we notice that they no longer practiced this limited common purse, probably because they didn't need it.

## A Unified Community

> Day by day continuing with one mind in the temple, and breaking bread from house to house. (v. 46)

When true Christian community forms, it brings joy and happiness to those who invest in it. God designed humans to live in community, and the Holy Spirit helps remove many of the barriers that often make deep community nothing but a pipe dream in the secular world.

For instance, growing believers learn to take their eyes off self-gratification and instead practice sacrificial love. That, in turn, allows people to become bold enough to open up with one another, because they know the others in the group aren't on the take.

The believers in Acts were learning the basics of deep community as they hung out with each other and developed relationships. The "sincerity of heart" reminds us that this kind of community can't be faked. Outward, showy displays are no substitute for the real thing. Some modern churches call on their people to turn to each other in the pews and have group hugs, but in reality the people barely know each other. That's far from the picture in Acts.

Luke says they were, "day by day continuing with one mind in the temple, and breaking bread from house to house." The group very much saw themselves as Jews. They felt that Jerusalem was their city, and the temple was their temple. They saw following Jesus not as a departure from Judaism, but as the correct understanding of what Judaism was and always had been.[4]

We saw earlier that Jesus had explained how Moses wrote of Jesus' death and resurrection (Luke 24:44). That means Jesus must also have explained how the sacrificial system and festivals predicted his work. In making that case, he must also have explained that offering atoning sacrifices was no longer appropriate after his resurrection.

But some aspects of temple ritual, like various ways of expressing thanksgiving, may still have been permissible. We later see believers carrying out more questionable rituals like fulfilling vows and rites of purification (Acts 21:23-24).

The Christians weren't actually going *into* the temple. Nobody but priests could enter the holy place itself. Rather, they were meeting in the vast colonnades Herod had built around the temple. Herod the Great had expanded the temple mount and built these outdoor patios surrounded by columns such that they were big enough for thousands to gather there. No other place in Jerusalem could have accommodated such a crowd. Solomon's portico, on the east side, was their usual meeting place (Acts 3:11; 5:12).

## Happy and Authentic

> They were taking their meals together with gladness and sincerity of heart. (v. 46)

I walked down a street at night near the university in my city recently.

---

4. This emphasis on the Jewishness of Christianity consistently appears throughout the book of Acts. Luke also shows that the gospel went first to the Jews in Jerusalem but also in every other city, because Jesus was the fulfillment of Judaism. This order had theological grounding based on God's choosing of Israel, as Paul explains in Romans 9-11. But if it's also true that Acts was part of a legal brief for Paul's defense, this emphasis on the Jewish nature of Christianity played an important part in showing his innocence, because one argument that would carry weight in a Roman court is that Christianity is part of Judaism, making it a *religio licita*—an already legally accepted religion.

I noticed that most houses were dark and quiet, but every block or two were front porches full of people laughing, talking, and making a happy ruckus clearly audible from the street. I stopped by each one and walked up, only to find they were all groups based on house churches in our network. I was so gratified to think of the contrast between these enjoyable gatherings and the darkened houses nearby, many of which were probably occupied by people staring at some kind of screen.

Groups in our fellowship have been accused of being drunk (just like the apostles were), but they're not. They're just enjoying the closeness they have with each other through the Holy Spirit. The laughter and joy come from believers engaged in ministry together and practicing *koinonia*.

The other word here (sincerity) is sometimes translated "simplicity" or "singleness." Sincerity is the most common translation, carrying the sense that "what you see is what you get," or a lack of duplicity, sneakiness, or putting on facades. It means authenticity.

Nothing is more nauseating than a group of people pretending to have something they don't have. Paul says, "Don't just pretend to love others. Really love them" (Romans 12:9). In fact, faking community is a major problem in some churches today.

## Praising God

> They were taking their meals together with gladness and sincerity of heart, praising God. (vs. 46-47)

Praising God is not a fringe part of this description. The thankful heart is an unmistakable sign of meeting, believing, and being indwelt by the Spirit. Growing believers know they need to focus attention on what they appreciate about God—not just what he has done, but also who he is.

Believers in community share their appreciation and thankfulness with each other as they lift up their souls to God in thankfulness. The more appreciation we develop, the more joy we feel.

## Reputation

> And having favor with all the people. (v. 47)

At this time, the followers of Jesus had an excellent reputation within the city. Such a good reputation probably grew out of their loving demeanor and their care for the poor. Peter wrote later that the best way to reduce persecution is to engage in good works (1 Peter 2:15).

This favor with the people wouldn't last. Before long, opinion leaders among the religious rulers would turn much of the city against the believers.

## Outreach

> And the Lord was adding to their number day by day those who were being saved. (v. 47)

The whole description of this community would read so differently without this part. Missions expert Ralph Winter observed that without *bona fide* outreach, the New Testament church might have been nothing more than a self-gratification cult.

Outreach to the lost world is an unmistakable mark of communities that are on-mission and healthy. They know they can't afford to be inwardly focused. Successful outreach signals that people are exerting effort and forfeiting personal comfort to take the gospel to those who don't know it.

In our world, nobody succeeds at gospel outreach but those who long for it with all their hearts. Yet nothing is as exciting as seeing someone who didn't know God at all come to true faith. Attracting transfer believers from other Bible-believing churches is nothing like true outreach.

In the church in Acts, each and every person who came in was a convert to personal faith in Jesus. Not a single transfer came from other Christian churches. And it sounds like a lot of people were coming in. Again, the expression "day by day" means most days, perhaps even daily.

It's important to see that the Lord was the one who was adding new converts. When a person goes from unbelief to becoming a child of God, it's a miracle of the highest order, as stated earlier. Believers who long to see successful outreach know they have to devote time to prayer, and at times they need great patience, especially in our culture. But saying God brought them in doesn't mean the people weren't speaking. The human part of the task is also necessary, as we will see continually in Acts.

# The Big Picture

The time span over this portion of Acts between Pentecost and the persecution under Saul (in chapter 8) may have been less than a year.[5] The evil one saw what was happening in Jerusalem and assembled his crew to attack. But scattering the group took at least a number of months, during which time the group grew to at least 5,000 people. That persecution broke up the cozy picture we see here.

As practicing Jews, this crowd of believers had some things to unlearn, like rabbinic, legalistic thinking. But they would have been free from much of the moral and relational damage evident in later Greco-Roman groups, and in churches today, because intact Jewish families would be healthier. They also had all twelve apostles present as leaders, which would be the last time that happened. An unknown number of female leaders who had walked with Jesus the whole time would also contribute to discipleship and teaching.

So although their time together was short, we can imagine excellent and rapid spiritual growth in the lives of emerging leaders in the early church. These leaders would later fan out across the eastern Mediterranean basin, providing readymade leaders in many cities.

The average members were also important. Only people who have actually lived in an atmosphere like this one are in a position to know deep *koinonia* when they see it. They also know how to achieve that type of fellowship. Others have to advance through trial and error, which is a slow teacher. Church planters can describe in words what good community is like, but that's very different from actually experiencing it.

Is a body like this one impractical in our day? After all, we have careers to pursue. On the other hand, they had careers as well. In fact, they had a six-day work week and much longer work days than most of us do. We have kids to worry about... hmmm, but they probably had more kids than most of us do. The culture was different then... but maybe even more difficult than ours when it came to outreach. The Holy Spirit hasn't changed. God's word hasn't changed, and neither has his will for the

---

5. When all the chronological data are assembled, the best year for Jesus' death is AD 33. Based on key time markers laid down later in the book of Acts and some chronological statements by Paul in the book of Galatians, it's likely that Saul's conversion to Jesus happened in AD 34 or 35. We will study these time markers as they come up in the text.

church. Probably the biggest barrier to having this caliber of church today is our own unbelief.

# 5

# PUBLIC ASTONISHMENT
## ACTS 3

> Now Peter and John were going up to the temple at the ninth hour, the hour of prayer. And a man who had been lame from his mother's womb was being carried along, whom they used to set down every day at the gate of the temple which is called Beautiful, in order to beg alms of those who were entering the temple. (Acts 3:1-2)

The ninth hour was about 3 p.m. There would have been a busy throng of people ascending the steps of the temple for evening prayers. They went up to the so-called Beautiful Gate. This was probably what Josephus called the Corinthian Gate. He said it was fifty cubits tall (75 feet) and forty cubits wide (60 feet), much larger than the other gates. It was overlaid with bronze and decorated with gold and silver inlays—a spectacular work of art.[1]

This man, disabled from birth, couldn't walk. As a result, he was a beggar. Judaism smiled on giving alms to the disabled, which is in harmony with the frequent Old Testament calls to share with the poor.

---

1. Flavius Josephus, Wars of the Jews, 5:204-205.

Jerusalem was a good-sized city for the ancient world, but nothing like today's big cities. The estimates for the population of Jerusalem have risen in recent years, based on the discovery of larger water systems and pools. Recent estimates say as many as fifty to sixty thousand lived in the city at this time. During festivals, the population could swell to over a hundred thousand.

But even at the larger number, virtually everyone in town would have known this man. By having his friends place him there at the Beautiful Gate most days, over his whole life—more than forty years—he had become a fixture at this spot in the city. God was about to use this well-known person to make another strong statement that nobody could deny.

## God Acts

> When he saw Peter and John about to go into the temple, he began asking to receive alms. But Peter, along with John, fixed his gaze on him and said, "Look at us!" And he began to give them his attention, expecting to receive something from them. But Peter said, "I do not possess silver and gold, but what I do have I give to you: In the name of Jesus Christ the Nazarene—walk!" (vs. 3-6)

How did Peter and John know they would be able to heal this man? Somehow, the Spirit prompted them. We will see this happen again later in Acts. People with the gift of healing apparently can sense intuitively when healing is possible. Peter clearly knew what was going to happen; he wasn't guessing.

Healing is a sovereign decision that God alone makes. He cannot be manipulated, and he doesn't leave the decision to people. Most of the miracles we have recorded in Scripture are clearly intended as messages. In this case, the message is that God endorses his spokespeople.

## Walking and Leaping

> And seizing him by the right hand, he raised him up; and immediately his feet and his ankles were strengthened. With a leap he stood upright and began to walk; and he entered the temple with them, walking and leaping and praising God. (vs. 7-8)

This man's leg muscles would have been badly atrophied from a lifetime of disuse. God clearly generated new muscle and connective tissue on the spot. Recall a similar instance when Jesus had a man hold out his "withered" hand so everyone could see it transform before their eyes (Matthew 12:13). These types of miracles were intended to dazzle:

> And all the people saw him walking and praising God; and they were taking note of him as being the one who used to sit at the Beautiful Gate of the temple to beg alms, and they were filled with wonder and amazement at what had happened to him. (vs. 9-10)

"That can't be him."

"Yes, it is! Look at his face. I actually saw him stand up!"

People recoiling from the shock of the seemingly impossible, but gradually realizing it's true.

Word streaked through the crowd on the massive thirty-six acre temple mount, creating so much amazement that people literally ran to see. The sight of adults running toward a certain spot would have caused others to run as well, not wanting to miss out.

There the man was, clinging onto Peter and John.

Peter must have waited a few minutes, but when a sufficient crowd had gathered, he cried out:

> "People of Israel," he said, "what is so surprising about this? And why stare at us as though we had made this man walk by our own power or godliness? For it is the God of Abraham, Isaac, and Jacob—the God of all our ancestors—who has brought glory to his servant Jesus by doing this. This is the same Jesus whom you handed over and rejected before Pilate, despite Pilate's decision to release him. You rejected this holy, righteous one and instead demanded the release of a murderer. You killed the author of life, but God raised him from the dead. And we are witnesses of this fact!" (vs. 12-15)

Was it really necessary to confront the people so harshly? Did the well-documented tendency toward self-righteousness among observant Jews call for such strong conviction of sin? Maybe Peter was blocking a superficial acceptance without grasping the underlying issue of personal sin?

Peter roundly denounced both this crowd and the earlier crowd on the day of Pentecost. That suggests that the number of people who cried "Barabbas!" when Pilate asked whom to release before Jesus' death was not a noisy minority, as some reconstructions imagine (Matthew 27:21). It must have been a large proportion of the city that wanted Jesus dead.

Eyes must have dropped down as the shame struck home. But this wasn't just a man bellowing his opinion. The paralytic was standing right there.

Peter preached faith:

> "Through faith in the name of Jesus, this man was healed—and you know how crippled he was before. Faith in Jesus' name has healed him before your very eyes." (v. 16)

He continued,

> "Repent and return, so that your sins may be wiped away, in order that times of refreshing may come from the presence of the Lord." (v. 19)

Here we find further evidence that the word "repent," when used in the context of personal salvation, means to turn away from unbelief to belief, as discussed earlier.

Peter also sounds the consistent theme of fulfilled Old Testament prophecy:

> "But the things which God announced beforehand by the mouth of all the prophets, that his Christ would suffer, he has thus fulfilled." (v. 18)

Although we don't have the details in this short summary of his speech, Peter probably explained one or more prophecies about the suffering servant. His reference to Jesus as God's "servant" (v. 13) probably points to Isaiah's four prophecies about the anonymous "servant of the Lord" (Isaiah 42-53).

Peter added that Jesus must go to heaven "until the period of restoration of all things about which God spoke by the mouth of His holy prophets from ancient time" (v. 21). This expression "restoration of all things" is not used elsewhere in the New Testament, but it is used in the Greek version of the Old Testament.[2] Most of these passages refer to the regathering of Israel to their land in the last days. For example, Jeremiah 16:15 says, "I will restore them to their own land which I gave to their fathers." So Peter, who would have used the Greek Old Testament like nearly everyone in his day (except rabbis), is probably pointing to a coming Millennium when Jesus returns.

This argues against views that such a kingdom either won't emerge, or that it refers to the church rather than a literal thousand-year period. If it refers to the church, though, why would Peter say "until the period of restoration" when the church was already at hand?

Peter cited Moses' prophecy that God would "raise up for you a prophet like me" (Deuteronomy 18:15, 19). The rabbis applied this passage to the coming Messiah, and based on Peter's words here, they were right. Peter was declaring that belief in Jesus lines up with faith in what Moses wrote. He also reminded them of the penalty for refusing to listen to that future prophet: "Anyone who will not listen to that Prophet will be completely cut off from God's people" (v. 23).

Finally, Peter said,

> "Starting with Samuel, every prophet spoke about what is happening today. You are the children of those prophets, and you are included in the covenant God promised to your ancestors. For God said to Abraham, 'Through your descendants all the families on earth will be blessed.' When God raised up his servant, Jesus, he sent him first to you people of Israel, to bless you by turning each of you back from your sinful ways." (vs. 24-26)

Samuel anointed King David, and David later received the promise known as the Davidic Covenant, which promised that David's throne would be eternal through the Chosen One (2 Samuel 7).

Peter also tied his line of reasoning to the Abrahamic Covenant. That covenant promises that through Abraham's descendants "all the families on earth will be blessed." That promise was being fulfilled in their sight. The Jews were the first family to be blessed by the gospel. This policy of taking the gospel to the Jews first apparently came from Jesus,

---

2. Jeremiah 15:19; 16:15; 24:6; 50:19; Ezekiel 16:55; Hosea 11:11.

who said he had been sent to "the lost sheep of Israel" (Matthew 15:24). Paul also later said he preached "to the Jew first and also to the Greek" (Romans 1:16).

## The Big Picture

As Peter spoke, God's Spirit was completing the work he began with the healing. People all over the temple mount were surrendering to Jesus. Before anything else could happen, they got interrupted.

# 6

# COUNTERATTACK

## ACTS 4

We're not sure how long Peter had been talking, but before he could finish, the priests, the Sadducees (who oversaw the security and business of the temple), and a squad of armed guards burst into the crowd. Luke says they were "greatly disturbed because [Peter and John] were teaching the people and proclaiming in Jesus the resurrection from the dead" (Acts 4:2).

This was a double problem for priests and Sadducees. The first problem was the teaching about "the resurrection from the dead" (v. 2). Sadducees didn't believe in the afterlife (see Matthew 22:23 and Acts 23:8).

The second issue was that they were preaching Jesus. These priests and Sadducees were the same ones who presided over Jesus' trial. They wanted him dead then, and nothing had changed.

This must have been a jostling, shouting, confused scene. What happened to the healed man? The rulers brought him too (4:14). What was the crowd's reaction to the arrest? They must have been shouting out about what had just happened. But these guards were dangerous and well-armed.

"They laid hands on them and put them in jail until the next day, for it was already evening" (v. 3). Jesus' prediction that the disciples would be treated this way had already begun to come true (see, e.g., Mark 13:9).

## Five Thousand?

The priests and Sadducees were too late to blunt the spiritual impact of the miracle and speech. We read, "But many of those who had heard the message believed, and the number of the men came to be about five thousand" (v. 4).

Scholars debate the meaning of this last statement. All agree that the number five thousand is probably cumulative. In other words, the five thousand is not in addition to the earlier three thousand, but includes it.

But Luke also uses the word "men" (*andron*) instead of people, or souls (*pseuchai*), as he did earlier (in 2:41). Are we to understand that this number didn't include women or children? If so, it would mean the total believing community in Jerusalem probably now included fifteen to twenty thousand people!

Luke used the same word (*andron*) when Jesus referred to Nineveh in Luke 11:32. There the word clearly refers to all the people, but later in Acts, he specifies that "multitudes of men and women" were being added. Therefore, the most natural reading is that these five thousand in Acts 4 were men; women and children would be in addition to that number. All we can say with certainty is that the group was at least five thousand strong and perhaps as many as twenty thousand.

Critics argue that there couldn't have been this many Christians in Jerusalem, even granting that (as mentioned earlier) the city's population was larger than previously thought.[1] But in addition, in ancient agrarian societies about ten to fifteen percent of people lived in cities. Most lived in surrounding small villages and homesteads where they worked the land.

They would go into the city for religious events or to take produce to market. In case of war, families would scurry to the city to take advantage

---

1. You can read modern estimates ranging from 80,000. "Estimating the Population of Ancient Jerusalem", Magen Broshi, Biblical Archaeology Review: 4:02, Jun 1978. to 20,000. Hillel Geva, "Jerusalem's Population in Antiquity: A": Harper San Francisco, 1997).

of its fortifications. At such times, the city's population could suddenly swell far above the number who actually lived there.

Viewed this way, the number of people in and around Jerusalem was probably several times the number of people who actually lived inside the city. Jesus had earlier sent the seventy out to prepare towns in the area for his coming (Luke 10:1-12). He also had performed outstanding miracles in nearby towns like Bethany, where he raised Lazarus from the dead (John 11:1-46).

So having 20,000 adults and kids in the group of Jesus' followers would still have been a small minority. People in these towns would have heard about the commotion and gone to Jerusalem to hear more.

Taken together, all of this means the Christian group associated with Jerusalem could easily have included many thousands of people. Since under this model, half of the 20,000 are children, the number of believing adults would have been 10,000. Over twenty-five years later, after extensive persecution and scattering, James would direct Paul's attention to "how many thousands" of people made up this same group (Acts 21:20).

## Before the Rulers

Regardless of the exact number of Christians at this time, such rapid growth in the new movement would have struck fear into the heart of the religious establishment, who viewed Christianity as a false teaching based on a false prophet. After Peter and John spent the night in jail:

> On the next day, their rulers and elders and scribes were gathered together in Jerusalem; and Annas the high priest was there, and Caiaphas and John and Alexander, and all who were of high-priestly descent. (4:5-6)

The Sanhedrin was a body of about seventy members composed of rich lay nobility, large landowners, heads of clans, priests, Pharisees, and Sadducees. Our historical sources are unclear on the exact makeup of the Sanhedrin. The gathering described here sounds like it might have included more than just the usual seventy or so.

The Romans delegated the oversight and control of internal affairs in the province of Judea to the Sanhedrin. They mostly governed over religious matters, including violations of biblical law. No reliable source defines the exact boundaries of their power.

We know they were not authorized to execute anyone without permission (John 18:31), with one exception. Anyone who wrongly entered or defiled the temple—even a Roman citizen—could be executed, as a large sign on the temple gate explained.[2] They could also imprison and beat people, as this story attests.

> When they had placed them in the center, they began to inquire, "By what power, or in what name, have you done this?" (v. 7)

Ancient synagogues (and many modern orthodox synagogues) usually met in a circle, or a semi-circle. At the center was a table where the scrolls could be spread out, or, in the case of a trial, the accused stood to be questioned. Although there were benches, men often stood and wandered around, coming toward the center when speaking. It was a way to argue different interpretations of the scrolls. The hall in this passage is the "Hall of Hewn Stone" where the Sanhedrin held court, according to the *Mishnah*.[3]

> Then Peter, filled with the Holy Spirit, said to them, "Rulers and elders of the people, if we are on trial today for a benefit done to a sick man, as to how this man has been made well, let it be known to all of you and to all the people of Israel, that by the name of Jesus Christ the Nazarene,[4] whom you crucified, whom God raised from the dead—by this name this man stands here before you in good health." (vs. 8-10)

Peter's boldness in this setting is amazing, especially when compared to his cowardice on the night of Jesus' betrayal. The Holy Spirit was filling him, giving him a kind of courage he never had on his own. He went on, citing Old Testament Scripture from Psalm 118:22 but applying it directly to his accusers:

---

2. Josephus describes this policy in Wars VI, 124–28. Two inscriptions have been discovered that hung in the temple, warning non-Jews to proceed no further. Both read, "No stranger is to enter within the balustrade round the temple and enclosure. Whoever is caught will be himself responsible for his ensuing death." The inscription is in The Israel Museum, ID number: IAA 1936-989.

3. This building may have been on the north end of the temple mount area, partly lying on the holy part of the mount, according to the Babylonian Talmud (Yoma 25a). In other words, it was near the Temple, but not touching it.

4. Not Nazarite, as one under a Nazarite vow. *Nazarene* means he was from the city of Nazareth.

"He is the stone which was rejected by you, the builders, which became the chief corner stone. And there is salvation in no one else; for there is no other name under heaven that has been given among men by which we must be saved." (vs. 11-12)

Peter didn't wait for them to come after him; he came after them. *They* were on trial. *They* were the killers, not the believers.

Now as they observed the confidence of Peter and John and understood that they were uneducated and untrained men, they were amazed, and began to recognize them as having been with Jesus. And seeing the man who had been healed standing with them, they had nothing to say in reply. (vs. 13-14)

This thoroughly awkward scene has the leaders recalculating, looking at each other. They hadn't expected a sharp denunciation. Most peasants standing in this court would be shaking in their boots.

"Uneducated and untrained" doesn't mean they were illiterate, as some have claimed. It means they had nothing more than the typical village Hebrew school, where boys studied the Old Testament. What Peter and the other disciples were missing was the advanced rabbinic teaching that made one a scholar.[5]

But when they had ordered them to leave the Council, they began to confer with one another, saying, "What shall we do with these men? For the fact that a noteworthy miracle has taken place through them is apparent to all who live in Jerusalem, and we cannot deny it." (vs. 15-16)

How does Luke know about this discussion? It didn't come from Peter or John, who were out of the room. But later a number of members of the council believed; Nicodemus and Joseph of Arimathea were apparently secret believers (Acts 15:5; John 7:51-52; Matthew 27:57-58). Even the Apostle Paul could have been in this meeting. We know he was a voting member of the Sanhedrin not long after this event. Any of these people could have recounted the discussion to Luke.

The rulers accurately described a New Testament miracle: It was "apparent to all who live in Jerusalem, and we cannot deny it." That's a real

---

5. This question comes up when liberal scholars claim that Peter couldn't have written the letters attributed to him because he was illiterate. We have no proof that Peter was illiterate—and when it comes to his letters, it hardly matters, because he probably dictated to a secretary anyway.

miracle, not the subjective, unverifiable miracles seen in much faith healing today. After sitting through one healing conference for almost a week, I met with some of the charismatic friends who had urged me to attend. I had to admit that after closely observing any number of prayer circles over disabled and sick people, I had not seen a miracle all week. When I asked if they had seen anything, they reported that one person in their group had been healed of a headache, and another had been delivered from insomnia.

You can see the difference between that kind of "miracle" and this New Testament miracle recorded in Acts 4. The results of these modern faith healings were invisible and unverifiable. I really saw no evidence that anything had happened. Without denying the reality of healing in our day, I am only suggesting we need not add fake miracles to God's real miracles.

## The Horns of a Dilemma

The dilemma for the rulers was agonizing. They could declare Peter and John to be false teachers with no authority from God... but then how would they explain the very publicly healed paralyzed man standing with them? Alternatively, they could change their minds about Jesus... Naaah.

Instead, they proposed a compromise:

> "But so that it will not spread any further among the people, let us warn them to speak no longer to any man in this name." and when they had summoned them, they commanded them not to speak or teach at all in the name of Jesus. (vs. 17-18)

They probably accompanied this injunction with severe threats of punishment. This body of rulers wasn't used to people defying them. But Peter and John were different:

> Peter and John answered and said to them, "Whether it is right in the sight of God to give heed to you rather than to God, you be the judge; for we cannot stop speaking about what we have seen and heard." (vs. 19-20)

Again, it would look really bad if the rulers mistreated these men who had just demonstrated God's mighty power to everyone at the temple. So when Peter and John called the rulers' hand, it became clear they were holding nothing:

> When they had threatened them further, they let them go (finding no basis on which to punish them) on account of the people, because they were all glorifying God for what had happened; for the man was more than forty years old on whom this miracle of healing had been performed. (vs. 21-22)

Although the rulers seemed to be all talk and quite impotent in this instance, they would soon show they could deliver powerful blows.

## Celebration

> As soon as they were freed, Peter and John returned to the other believers and told them what the leading priests and elders had said. When they heard the report, all the believers lifted their voices together in prayer to God:[6] "O Sovereign Lord, Creator of heaven and earth, the sea, and everything in them—you spoke long ago by the Holy Spirit through our ancestor David, your servant, saying, 'Why do the nations rage and the peoples plot in vain? The kings of the earth rise up and the rulers band together against the Lord and against his anointed one.'" (vs. 23-26)

This event had been a mismatch between the sovereignty of God and the smallness and weakness of powerful human rulers. The believers' citation of Psalm 2 is so appropriate: "Why do the nations rage... against the Lord and against his anointed one?"[7]

The next verse in Psalm 2 was probably also on their minds: "But the one who rules in heaven laughs. The Lord scoffs at them" (Psalm 2:4). Is God frightened when the nations rage against him? No! He laughs them to scorn. We don't often read about God laughing, but this picture is downright funny: God's tiny creatures raging against him, plotting to destroy his chosen one, the Messiah.

Truly, the disciples were seeing before their eyes, in recent history, an

---

6. Here we have a group praying in specific words. Is Luke making it up, as liberal readers insist? It's not necessary to press this expression literally. The saying means "They prayed along these lines," information Luke could have gotten from anyone who was there, including Peter. At the same time, it's not hard to believe that Psalm 2 came up, because it fits so well.

7. "Anointed" is the relatively rarely used Hebrew word mashiyach, or "Messiah."

example of God's sovereignty ruling over sinful people when they slew Jesus:

> "For truly in this city there were gathered together against Your holy servant Jesus, whom You anointed, both Herod and Pontius Pilate, along with the Gentiles and the peoples of Israel." (v. 27)

But what happened? "They did what your power and will had decided beforehand should happen" (v. 28). What were the chances that Jesus wouldn't be crucified? Zero. But it's not just that he was crucified; it's that his enemies were directly, though unwittingly, contributing to the success of Jesus' mission.

This Spirit-filled prayer says the evil rulers like Pilate and Herod were "predestined" to do what they did. In the case of Pilate, he was reluctant to crucify Jesus, mainly for superstitious reasons, but the crowd pressured him to do it (Luke 23:5, 13-25). This may have been a case where God overruled human free will.

However, it would be a mistake to think he always overrules free will, as some theologians argue. Most of the time he allows people to make their own choices, as Jesus implied when he said to the people of Jerusalem, "How often I wanted to gather your children together, the way a hen gathers her chicks under her wings, and you were unwilling" (Matthew 23:37). God's sovereignty means he *can* enforce his will whenever he wants to. It doesn't *require* that he do so. He may choose to go hands-off in many situations.

## The Outcome

They finished praying:

> And when they had prayed, the place where they had gathered together was shaken, and they were all filled with the Holy Spirit and began to speak the word of God with boldness. (v. 31)

Did the building actually shake, or was this an impression they had? Or is it something metaphorical? The plain sense reading is plausible enough. It's no more farfetched than the wind and flame on Pentecost. If it was a literal shaking from God, it would probably be a form of encouragement for the believers not to be intimidated by the council's threats.

"They were filled with the Spirit," which, as we saw earlier, shows that the filling of the Holy Spirit is different than the once-for-all baptism with the Spirit.

The final outcome of the counterattack was that the believers "spoke the word of God with boldness." This isn't always what happens after persecution. It's unlikely unless the people of God respond in faith. In this case, their courage grew because they interpreted the events in a God-centered way.

## Summary

Luke summarizes the spiritual condition of the massive group in Jerusalem in verses 32-37. He records a remarkable level of unity and love in the group, saying they were "of one heart and soul" (v. 32).

This is also where Luke describes their voluntary pooling of unused wealth to feed the hungry. Based on Peter's words in the next chapter, it's clear that the expression "all who were owners of land or houses would sell them" is hyperbole—a deliberate exaggeration for effect.

We also learn from this passage that the early church handled its funds via the leadership of the apostles, or later, its elders. The point is that the financial and spiritual leadership in the local church should be the same. A church's decisions about how it handles money are some of the most important decisions it makes. That's why a group should entrust such decisions to a group of spiritually qualified, accountable elders.

Finally, Luke introduces us to Barnabas, who will play a key role in the rest of the story in Acts. Already we can see his godly character from his nickname, which means "son of encouragement," and from his willingness to sell family-owned land on Cyprus and give the proceeds to the apostles for distribution.

## The Big Picture

The first collision between God's power and the world's rulers was over, but only for a moment. The exploding Jesus movement in Jerusalem was too powerful for the enemy to relent. From here on, the pattern is escalating persecution.

During these precious months, believers were learning the Bible in light of Jesus' work. They were learning a new way of life as they built into the community. We only get snapshots, and we have to imagine what lay between the high points.

Did they struggle with conflict and selfishness like we do today? Probably. The statements about their unity don't imply that they didn't have to fight for that unity, as we'll see in Acts 6. They were humans just like us, and yet they saw God moving powerfully—just like we can.

# 7

# ATTACK FROM WITHIN

## ACTS 5

The excitement believers feel when experiencing a strong spiritual awakening can be intense. I've had the opportunity to be a part of two significant awakening events, and I absolutely relished the experience.

People in the grip of spiritual excitement may come under different temptations than those you usually think of. Fallen human nature wants attention and self-glorification. And with all the excitement, that urge to be recognized as a key player intensifies. It's not just certain outliers who feel this temptation. Everyone, including the best leaders, feels it.

At the peak of growth and victory in the early church, we saw in the previous chapter that Barnabas, Paul's future companion, sold a family estate and gave the proceeds to the apostles for distribution to the poor. People in the group must have overflowed with praise and admiration for such a selfless act.

In that setting, we read:

> There was a certain man named Ananias who, with his wife, Sapphira, sold some property. He brought part of the money

to the apostles, claiming it was the full amount. With his wife's consent, he kept the rest. (Acts 5:1-2)

The words "with his wife, Sapphira" signify that she was in on it all the way. They conspired to present their gift, saying that it was the full price for the land, even though they knew it wasn't. Then, we are rocked by the text:

> Then Peter said, "Ananias, why have you let Satan fill your heart? You lied to the Holy Spirit, and you kept some of the money for yourself. The property was yours to sell or not sell, as you wished. And after selling it, the money was also yours to give away. How could you do a thing like this? You weren't lying to us but to God!" As soon as Ananias heard these words, he fell to the floor and died. Everyone who heard about it was terrified. Then some young men got up, wrapped him in a sheet, and took him out and buried him. (vs. 3-6)

This story is astonishing! Could it possibly be that God struck this man dead? For what?

## False Reasons

This didn't happen because they hadn't given enough or because they held some back. They were free to give whatever they wanted, or to give nothing at all. Peter's words in verse 4, "The property was yours to sell or not sell, as you wished, and after selling it, the money was also yours to give away," show that their sin had nothing to do with any obligation to give.

It should also be clear that Peter was not the one who struck him down. Peter speaks no command or word that suggests he is striking them dead. He acts as a prophet, speaking for God and predicting what will happen. He defines the issue, probably for the benefit of other observers. God is using Peter as the instrument of his discipline.

## Harsh?

Readers wonder, "Since when does God waste believers?" Actually, this isn't the only case where God killed someone for judicial or disciplinary reasons. Old Testament examples are ambiguous, because being a believer meant something different then. But other cases appear in the New Testament as well. For example, Paul says some people in Corinth had died because of their blatant disrespect for God during meetings (1 Corinthians 11:30).[1]

Remember, these two were almost certainly believers. That means that, although their lives were taken, they immediately found themselves in heaven. That probably led to a rather humorous moment: Ananias looks around at the surroundings in the presence of God, trying to understand. A sheepish look comes over him.... "Sooo... I'm guessing we probably shouldn't have done that, right?"

God is eternal, and he knows every human is fated to die because sin entered the world. If he decides to shorten the length of their few years, that's his prerogative, and it's not the worst thing that can happen to people. This would be especially true when the people involved are believers.

## A Deadly Bacillus

Ananias and Sapphira's sin was lying, and it was a specific kind of lying, much more dangerous than normal deception. This was the lying Jesus warned against, when he said, "Beware of the leaven of the Pharisees, which is hypocrisy."

Hypocrisy—what is it? It's saying one thing, but living another. In the context of the Pharisees, it refers to trying to pretend that you're more spiritual than you really are. Jesus excoriated the Pharisees for showing off their "righteousness" to be noticed by people (Matthew 6:5). They could be so hypocritical that they sometimes foreclosed on widows while crying out long public prayers for show (Mark 12:40).

When a local body begins moving in this direction, it can completely derail what God intends. In an environment where people are competing to show how righteous they are, you don't dare open up about a problem you're having. Honesty disappears when people accept the validity of showing off their devotion and holiness.

Think of Jesus' story of the Pharisee and the tax collector. The Pharisee stood showing off, saying, "I thank you, God, that I am not like other people—cheaters, sinners, adulterers. I'm certainly not like that tax

---

1. No one knows what John's "sin unto death" is (1 John 5:16). But it could possibly be referring to disciplinary, physical death.

collector! (Luke 18:11). This fool actually thought he didn't sin. They had redefined sin in such a shallow and external way that they thought they were avoiding it. Meanwhile, they would smear ash on their faces to show that they were fasting (Matthew 6:16).

One of the grimmest consequences of legalistic duplicity is the disgust non-believers feel when beholding this strange and phony dance. "Holy living" under this definition drives non-believers away, holding their ears. Younger people especially long for authenticity, and easily sense when it's missing.

That offends God. He let all of us know what he thinks about phony holiness through Ananias and Sapphira.

For the thousands of people coming to faith in Jesus at this time, this was their religious background. God knew this self-righteous view could easily invade the body of Christ, carrying them off in a direction that blocks grace and true fellowship. That's why Jesus called it "the leaven" of hypocrisy. It spreads like yeast in a lump of dough. He also warned, "I have come to call, not those who think they are righteous, but those who know they are sinners" (Matthew 9:13).

This is the best way to understand the unusually strong statement God made in this account. With the church just beginning, he wanted to head off any turn toward people hypocritically showing off their super-spirituality. We read in verse 11, "Great fear came over the whole church, and over all who heard of these things." That suggests the statement worked.

## Her Too

> About three hours later his wife came in, not knowing what had happened. Peter asked her, "Was this the price you and your husband received for your land?"
>
> "Yes," she replied, "that was the price."
>
> And Peter said, "How could the two of you even think of conspiring to test the Spirit of the Lord like this? The young men who buried your husband are just outside the door, and they will carry you out, too." Instantly, she fell to the floor and died.

When the young men came in and saw that she was dead, they carried her out and buried her beside her husband. (vs. 7-10)

Her arrival in heaven might have been humorous as well. She looks around and sees Ananias. He nods ruefully, "Yeah."

Peter confirmed in verse 9 that they had conspired together to pull off the scam. Deliberate, prior agreement to lie together makes this act even worse. This was no careless exaggeration. She immediately joined her husband in heaven, but left behind a virulent warning to all: don't go this way.

We can all feel grateful that God made this statement, but has not continued to enforce the standard in the same way, or we would have many empty seats in our meetings today.

## Still Surging

The spiritual surge continued at a white-hot intensity:

> At the hands of the apostles many signs and wonders were taking place among the people; and they were all with one accord in Solomon's portico. But none of the rest dared to associate with them; however, the people held them in high esteem. (vs. 12-13)

In spite of God's gracious gifts of healing and the obvious joy the people of God were experiencing, we already sense a foreboding that the happy times weren't going to last. The neutral people in the city admired the believers, but they sensed that trouble was coming, so they kept their distance. Probably they were hearing a lot of negative commentary and anger in their synagogues.

> And all the more believers in the Lord, multitudes of men and women, were constantly added to their number, to such an extent that they even carried the sick out into the streets and laid them on cots and pallets, so that when Peter came by at least his shadow might fall on any one of them. (vs. 14-15)

The text doesn't say whether the act of lying in Peter's shadow did anything.

This is the zenith of spiritual explosion in the group. The word "multitudes" here means large numbers. And this is all in addition to the earlier estimate of 5,000 men. The Jewish leaders must have been worried to death that they were going to overrun the city.

You would think this growth and supernatural blessing would make outsiders think, "Maybe they're in the right after all? God seems to be moving here." But often, increased growth and success make outsiders more suspicious and hostile—and more jealous.

No one would see this growth as a threat more than stakeholders in the existing religious system. People from their synagogues were now attending meetings of this new group. Rabbis were seeing their congregations diminish. Or were they being asked a lot of awkward questions?

> Also the people from the cities in the vicinity of Jerusalem were coming together, bringing people who were sick or afflicted with unclean spirits, and they were all being healed. (v. 16)

This confirms what we suggested earlier; that the large numbers reported for the body of believers in Jerusalem include many from surrounding towns and villages.

# 8

# OPEN BATTLE

## ACTS 5:17-42

The leaders in Jerusalem had seen enough.

> The high priest and his officials, who were Sadducees, were filled with jealousy. They arrested the apostles and put them in the public jail. But an angel of the Lord came at night, opened the gates of the jail, and brought them out. Then he told them, "Go to the temple and give the people this message of life!"
>
> So at daybreak the apostles entered the temple, as they were told, and immediately began teaching. (Acts 5:17-21)

Again, we can know about what was going on in the council because members of the council at this time, possibly including the future Apostle Paul, heard and saw all of it, and could report it to Luke.

Luke says the leaders were filled with jealousy. That had been a key motivating factor earlier during Jesus' ministry, too. The leadership was jealous because Jesus was so popular. At one point they argued that, "If we let him go on like this, everyone will believe in him, and the Romans will come and take away both our place and our nation" (John 11:48).

That, of course, was just an excuse. The Romans weren't interested in

taking their nation away—they already owned it. The council was coop-
erating with the Romans, and had heard no threat from them. It was
Jesus whom they feared and loathed.

Even Pilate realized "that the leading priests had arrested Jesus out of
envy" (Mark 15:10). How did Luke know what was in Pilate's mind? The
witness for this interaction was Jesus himself. He was standing right there.
He must have told his followers about these interactions with Pilate later,
after the resurrection.

## In Prison

So the apostles were arrested and thrown in jail. Was it all of them? Or
just a selection? We know Peter was there, along with more than one
other apostle (v. 29). It didn't matter, because God wasn't willing to allow
the rulers to imprison the apostles. The angel came and delivered them,
apparently at night. He didn't say, "Get out of town and lay low." Instead,
he said, "Go to the temple and give the people this message of life!" (v. 20)

We know in a later episode Jesus came to Paul at Corinth and reassured
him, urging him with the words, "Do not be afraid any longer, but
go on speaking and do not be silent." That's similar to what the angel
said here. But in that case he added, "for I have many people in this
city" (Acts 18:10).

That was probably the thought here as well. God was building up a base
group from which he would soon launch an assault against the whole
known world. He knew exactly who would still believe, and he wasn't
going to let these rulers derail that progress.

Were the guards cast into a coma-like sleep? When they woke up the
next day, they assumed their prisoners were still in there.

## Discovery

Next comes a hilarious account, as the rulers gather and solemnly send
for the prisoners to be brought before them. The report comes back,
"The jail was securely locked, with the guards standing outside, but
when we opened the gates, no one was there!" (v. 23).

The captain of the temple guard and the leaders "were perplexed, wondering where it would all end" (v. 24). Would they see that their release

was supernatural? Not necessarily. It would probably be easier to think the guards were in on it.

At that moment, a man came running in crying out, "The men whom you put in prison are standing in the temple and teaching the people!" (v. 25). They look at each other in confusion. Incredulity. "Well, go get 'em!" someone finally ordered.

The captain takes a troop of armed guards with him and picks his way carefully through the crowd. The situation is tense. If anyone begins throwing stones, the whole crowd could light up. But the early Christians had a strong ethos against violence. In all the attacks on believers we see in the New Testament, the Christians never fight back with anything stronger than prayer or public argumentation. There was one case earlier when Peter cut off a servant's ear with a sword. But Jesus rebuked that action (Matthew 26:51-52). Arguing and rebuking opponents is another thing. We see plenty of that.

When Peter and the others stood before the council, he again insisted that they must follow God rather than men. And he again got in their face, reminding them it was Jesus "whom you had put to death by hanging him on a cross." He also declared that "God put him in the place of honor at his right hand as Prince and Savior" (v. 31).

## Gamaliel

The council was so infuriated they wanted to kill them illegally. But we read "a Pharisee named Gamaliel, a teacher of the Law, respected by all the people, stood up in the Council and gave orders to put the men outside for a short time" (v. 34)

Gamaliel was a renowned rabbi who was mentioned here in Acts, but also in the Mishnah and the Talmud.[1] He was the grandson of the great rabbi Hillel and his leadership role in the Sanhedrin is confirmed by extra-biblical sources.

He also has another interesting connection that comes up later in Acts when the Apostle Paul reveals that he was "educated under Gamaliel, strictly according to the law of our fathers" (22:3). So this man discipled

---

1. He is mentioned briefly in *Mishnah* Sotah 9:15. He is recorded to have acted to protect women who had been divorced in Yevamot 16:7. He also comes up in the *Talmud*. Sanhedrin 2:6; 11b; 18d; and Shabbat 30b.

Paul, at that time Saul, before we meet him. Saul must have broken from his teacher when he went ballistic in persecuting Christians.

In this scene, Gamaliel is portrayed as moderate and wise. He cautioned the leaders:

> "I say to you, stay away from these men and let them alone, for if this plan or action is of men, it will be overthrown; but if it is of God, you will not be able to overthrow them; or else you may even be found fighting against God." (vs. 38-39)[2]

His counsel prevailed, but not completely: "They took his advice; and after calling the apostles in, they flogged them and ordered them not to speak in the name of Jesus, and then released them" (v. 40).

This public beating was brutal and agonizing. Thirty-nine lashes was the tradition based on Deuteronomy 25:2-3. They would have come out bruised and bleeding profusely.

The encounter ends with the most stirring verse in the chapter: "The apostles left the high council rejoicing that God had counted them worthy to suffer disgrace for the name of Jesus" (v. 41). I remember reading that as a new believer and looking up from the page, stunned. Are you kidding? Worthy to suffer disgrace? I knew I had a long way to go.

## The Big Picture

The governing council was raising the temperature. Now they imprisoned, threatened, and beat the apostles. The apostles weren't deterred.

The chapter wouldn't read the same without the last verse: "And every day, in the temple and from house to house, they continued to teach and preach this message: 'Jesus is the Messiah'" (v. 42). Utterly undeterred, not intimidated in the least, they pressed the offensive.

---

2. Gamaliel also made some historical claims that have led to confusion. He refers to a revolutionary "Judas of Galilee" who led a tax revolt in 6 AD. He also mentions Theudas, who according to Josephus, died between AD 44 and 46—far later than this account in AD 33-34. Josephus, *Antiquities of the Jews*, Book 20, chapter 5. Many think Gamaliel and Josephus are talking about two different people with the same name. Their careers don't match at all. Gamaliel's Theudas had 400 men, while Josephpus' Theudas was a magician with a huge following.

# 9

# DIVISION
## ACTS 6:1-7

At this point, the scene shifts to the inner life of the group:

> Now at this time while the disciples were increasing in number,
> a complaint arose on the part of the Hellenistic Jews against the
> native Hebrews, because their widows were being overlooked
> in the daily serving of food. (Acts 6:1)

This passage refers to Hellenistic and native Hebrews, who are some-times called Hebraic Jews. This division predated Christianity.

The division grew out of the fact that many Jews had formed communi-ties in other countries, or later, provinces in the Roman Empire. There, they tended to assimilate to local culture in language, dress, diet, and other cultural features. They were more tolerant of Gentiles and their ways. These were the Hellenistic Jews.

"Hellenistic" comes from *Helene*, meaning Greek. Although they were Greek-influenced and Greek-speaking, they were still practicing Jews. And not all Jews who lived abroad from Judea were Hellenistic. Some families held firm to strict, traditional Judaism.

The Hebraic Jews took pride in being native Hebrews. They avoided going into a Gentile's house or even conversing with them. They thought physical contact with a Gentile was defiling. And they looked down on Hellenistic Jews, considering them too liberal. Hebraic Jews didn't converse in Hebrew. They spoke Aramaic. But many of them knew some Hebrew, mainly used for interpreting and reciting Scripture.

Paul considered himself to be among the *Hebraioi* ("Hebrews," 2 Corinthians 11:22) and a "Hebrew of the Hebrews" (Philippians 3:5), though he was also fluent in Greek and came from a diaspora city. His parents probably sent him to Jerusalem for his education to keep him from slipping into Hellenistic Judaism.

This division comes up here, but also permeates the entire book of Acts.

## The Daily Serving of Food

Here, in Acts 6, the conflict appears in connection with the charitable feeding of widows and poor people. It's clear the believers had organized a daily disbursement of food. In the ancient world, when a family lost their male provider through death or divorce, they were in big trouble.

Women were normally not trained in trades and would not be hired for labor. Women could try selling handiwork, sewn garments, or garden produce if they were left with land. Often they had no land and were ruthlessly exploited by the propertied class. They might become prostitutes, beggars, or virtual slaves.

Some were fortunate enough to have an extended family large enough to shelter them. Most widows and their "orphaned" kids went back to their families of origin and worked for income as part of the family team.

But even in these cases, the rule was poverty. Most people in Judea at this time were poor, even if they weren't widowed. Widows were very poor. And it's clear that the believers felt morally obligated to help. Old Testament Scriptures are full of calls to care for widows and orphans. Here are some examples:

> **Isaiah 1:17** "Learn to do good. Seek justice. Help the oppressed. Defend the cause of orphans. Fight for the rights of widows."

> **Exodus 22:22** "You must not exploit a widow or an orphan."

> **Psalm 82:3-4** "Give justice to the poor and the orphan; uphold

the rights of the oppressed and the destitute. Rescue the poor and helpless; deliver them from the grasp of evil people."

**Deuteronomy 10:18** "God ensures that orphans and widows receive justice. He shows love to the foreigners living among you and gives them food and clothing."

You can see from these samples that God's heart is to protect the poor and the helpless, and widows and fatherless children were high on that list.

So the gifts flowing into the apostles went in part to this daily feeding ministry.

# Delegation

So the twelve summoned the congregation of the disciples and said, "It is not desirable for us to neglect the word of God in order to serve tables. Therefore, brethren, select from among you seven men of good reputation, full of the Spirit and of wisdom, whom we may put in charge of this task. But we will devote ourselves to prayer and to the ministry of the word." (vs. 2-4)

Some people read the Acts 2 description of the earliest church thinking that the whole thing might have happened without any human leadership. Wrong. You see here that the apostles weren't just teaching and hoping for the best. They were decision makers. They didn't want to micro-manage, but when a decision was needed, they had the authority.

Many in the group probably wanted to see the apostles take over this feeding ministry so they wouldn't have to worry about bias. But the answer was no. The leaders set the priorities and time allocations as they saw God's will. And their priority at this point was the ministry of the word and prayer. Modern preachers could learn from that priority list.

Instead of taking over, they delegated the feeding ministry to the seven men selected.

The decisions being made here had to do with the ordering of the ministry, and that lies directly under the authority of church leadership. Church leaders are not to speak to issues in people's private lives with any more authority than any other believer. But when it comes to how the ministry is going to operate, they have the say (Hebrews 13:17).

## Leading a Movement

The apostles said, "But we will devote ourselves to prayer and to the ministry of the word." So they must have met together and spent time praying. Can you imagine how baffling the whole situation in Jerusalem was? None of them had ever seen anything like this. It was truly unprecedented.

What should they do? What should they call for? They certainly must have had other leaders heading up house churches and other meetings. We soon meet two of those junior leaders (Philip and Stephen) and they are very impressive in their capabilities. So training leaders must have been a big concern.

There must have been thousands of children. Probably, they didn't need as much supervision as kids in modern cities. And older kids could watch over younger kids. But we don't know what they did.

They must have had a leadership council of some kind. How could they select these seven men if thousands of people were trying to make the decision? We can sense the presence of multiple features in the group that we aren't told about.

## The Ministry of the Word

They wanted to give themselves to the ministry of the word of God. What did that look like? People didn't carry Bibles around at this time. Normal Jews didn't have even one copy of the Old Testament in their homes.

These hand-copied scrolls were huge, and would be fabulously expensive. Just think of how long it would take for a scribe to copy the Old Testament using a crude quill pen that didn't work easily, like our ballpoint pens. Our sources say it usually took a scribe working six days a week about fifteen months to copy the Old Testament once. In addition to the skilled labor was the substantial cost of the vellum itself.[1] So, to

---

1. Vellum, or parchment, is prepared from animal skin, especially calf skin. The skin is cleaned, stretched on a frame, scraped, and treated with chemicals to add flexibility and help it receive ink. Squares or rectangles of vellum were sewn together to make a scroll. So even before a single word was written on it, a vellum scroll was quite expensive.

buy a copy in equivalent modern buying power would cost tens of thousands of dollars.

A complete Old Testament Bible was made up of a collection of ten to fifty vellum scrolls, depending on how long the scribe made them. People didn't carry them around. Rather, they shared the collection by keeping it at the synagogue, covered in a large protective cloth sleeve. The rabbis held daily readings in the synagogue but could also get out a specific passage if someone asked.

Christians made popular the "codex"—an early version of a book. These were far cheaper to produce, but still expensive. If made from sheets of vellum, they could be just as expensive as scrolls. But most popular codices began with a stack of blank papyrus sheets that were fastened together on one side, like a book. They also had a cover.[2]

After the codex was fashioned, the scribe began copying. They had to estimate how many sheets would be needed to copy a given book, so they usually added some extra sheets to avoid running out of space. After the book was copied, depending on how many blank pages were left at the end, they would typically copy another, smaller book that would fit.

Codices were smaller, lighter, and less expensive than scrolls. Another advantage was the ability to turn to a passage in the middle of a book without having to laboriously unroll a lengthy scroll. They could also be produced by common people who weren't scribes. Our evidence shows that Christian groups usually owned some codices. Papyrus codices didn't hold up as long as vellum, because papyrus would become brittle and begin to crumble after some years, but some have survived, usually in fragments.

So only the rich could own their own Bible, but this group had some rich people in it, and they had a large body giving donations. They must have had most or all of the Old Testament that they kept somewhere (in the upper room?). The apostles and other leaders could gather there to read, study, pray over, and discuss what they were finding. They could also produce additional copies of sections or even complete books.

---

2. Papyrus was made from a reed. The reed was shredded lengthwise before being laid out, typically in two layers, crisscrossed, forming a mat. They then beat the mat with water, causing a slimy film to appear. That slime when dried, was like glue, holding the mat together and forming a surface suitable for writing

Their copy would be in Greek—the so-called *Septuagint* translation—rather than in Hebrew. In the New Testament writings, they constantly quote the Old Testament using the words and phrases from the Septuagint, just like we quote English versions today. The Septuagint reads differently from some passages in the Hebrew text, but most are just different wording that means the same thing. Translation always involves some variation.

The reason we have thousands of early copies of the New Testament is the early Christians' view of Scripture. They were a people of the Book, and that stands out clearly throughout the book of Acts. They knew that God's Spirit works through his word. That's why the apostles wanted to devote themselves to the ministry of the word, but also to prayer. They had Jesus' promise that the Spirit would guide them "into all truth" as they studied Scripture and prayed over it (John 16:13).

Once they secured copies for the group, they continued to copy the Old Testament, and later, the gospels and epistles written by apostles. According to our earliest sources, a central part of a typical house church meeting was reading a segment of Scripture and discussing it.[3] That meant every house church kept busy growing their collection of biblical texts.

These leaders had to reread and rethink the entire Old Testament in light of Jesus' life. Much of the Old Testament would carry over, but almost never without manifesting new dimensions. Jesus had given them the outline and some examples, but he certainly didn't go through the whole Old Testament in one afternoon. That task was left to these men.

They were scrambling to comprehend the vast story, the prophets, and the Psalms. Much of the insight Stephen displays in chapter 7 was probably part of what they were distilling during these months.

No wonder they didn't want to turn aside to run the widow feeding ministry.

## Public Preaching

Once they acquired their new understanding of God's word, they needed

---

3. Justin Martyr, in his "First Apology" says that once people are gathered, "the memoirs of the apostles or the writings of the prophets are read, as long as time permits." Then a leader would teach based on that text.

to assign one or more of their own to organize it and prepare a teaching. They had an immense, hungry crowd dying to learn more.

They must have broken the group up into segments, perhaps holding teaching at several venues at one time (which could easily be done on the temple mount). Or they may have had different parts of the group gathering on different evenings.

However they did it, these leaders must have been in constant danger of exhaustion. That means their decision to delegate was wise.

## The Seven

The representatives came back with their picks of the seven men.

> The statement found approval with the whole congregation; and they chose Stephen, a man full of faith and of the Holy Spirit, and Philip, Prochorus, Nicanor, Timon, Parmenas and Nicolas, a proselyte from Antioch. And these they brought before the apostles; and after praying, they laid their hands on them. (vs. 5-6)

Interestingly, none of these names are Hebraic. They apparently selected Hellenistic Jews in order to remove any doubt about bias in favor of the Hebraic segment of the group.

Three names stand out. Stephen, as we will see in the ensuing account, was an amazing spiritual and biblical heavyweight.

Philip went on to spark an awakening that led most of an entire city to faith. That story will come up in chapter 8.

Nicolas is said to be "a proselyte from Antioch." He is the only one called a proselyte, although all of them would have been recent converts to Jesus. The proselyte tag refers to his earlier conversion to Judaism. He was not Jewish by birth, but by conversion. Later, he also converted to faith in Jesus.

It's intriguing that he came from Antioch. That city would soon become the center of a spiritual explosion, finally penetrating the gentile community, and from there to the rest of the empire. And Nicolas was a Gentile!

## Were These Men Deacons?

Traditional interpretation of Acts 6 holds that these were the first deacons. The word *diakonos* means a servant or a minister. In later, large, local bodies they appointed elders, as overseers, and deacons, who served under the elders. Nobody is sure what deacons did in the early church, but the most common answer comes from this passage.

In verse 2, the apostles said it wasn't right for them to neglect the word in order to serve (*diakoneo*) tables. So, many readers conclude that here we have a job description for deacons.

But the problem is that the apostles also refer to themselves as engaging in the ministry *diakonia* of the word. So the concept of ministry is not just serving tables, or as modern readers often take it, overseeing issues of practical service, like taking care of buildings and grounds, serving the poor, and other benevolences, and perhaps serving as ushers—a vision far distant from the New Testament.

While these seven might have been deacons, they were also strong in the ministry of the word, as seen from Stephen and Philip. When considering the exacting requirements for deacons given in 1 Timothy 3, it seems likely that deacons could serve in a wide range of ministry roles, including as under-shepherds. This passage doesn't warrant any limitation of deacons to physical service.

## The Big Picture

Thanks to the apostles' wisdom, they had avoided division within the young group. Through this short episode, we gain a glimpse into the thinking and priorities governing their leadership. Peter later calls himself an elder (1 Peter 5:1), and the office of elders in later churches is clearly embodied here in the apostles.

The leaders were busy studying and spreading the word of God, already developing a strong second tier of leaders. When the group was scattered soon after this incident, they would need all the leaders and copies of Scripture they could get.

The final verdict on this period comes in verse 7:

> The word of God kept on spreading; and the number of the

disciples continued to increase greatly in Jerusalem, and a great many of the priests were becoming obedient to the faith.

After all the descriptions of the vast size of the Jerusalem body, now we hear this. It continued to surge! But God's enemy was ready to raise the stakes.

# 10

# STEPHEN

## ACTS 6:8-14

At this point, Luke introduces us to Stephen:

> And Stephen, full of grace and power, was performing great wonders and signs among the people. (Acts 6:8)

God was validating Stephen by working miracles through him. His speech was empowered too. He went and argued at a local synagogue:

> But some men from what was called the Synagogue of the Freedmen, including both Cyrenians and Alexandrians, and some from Cilicia and Asia, rose up and argued with Stephen. But they were unable to cope with the wisdom and the Spirit with which he was speaking. (vs. 9-10)

Stephen's arguments were too powerful for these rabbinic scholars to cope with. What was he saying? We have to read between the lines of Luke's description.

> Then they secretly induced men to say, "We have heard him speak blasphemous words against Moses and against God." (v. 11)

Stephen was probably arguing that the New Covenant had replaced the covenant of Moses. That could constitute blaspheming Moses—a serious crime that could bring harsh punishment. The charge of blasphemy against God could easily have resulted from Stephen teaching the deity of Christ. Even though it comes straight from the Old Testament (e.g., Isaiah 9:6-7), the rabbis' extreme view of God's transcendence made it impossible for them to accept the idea of God putting on humanity.

> And they stirred up the people, the elders and the scribes, and they came up to him and dragged him away and brought him before the Council. They put forward false witnesses who said, "This man incessantly speaks against this holy place and the Law; for we have heard him say that this Nazarene, Jesus, will destroy this place and alter the customs which Moses handed down to us." (vs. 12-14)

Luke says they were false witnesses, but any good lie has to have some truth in order to be persuasive. They claimed he spoke against "this holy place" which was probably the temple and perhaps the holy city of Jerusalem, or even the promised land. Stephen's words later bear this out. It wasn't that he was actually speaking against them, but that he was teaching their true place in God's plan.

They dragged him before the council for judgment. But before he speaks, we hear the curious comment, "All who were sitting in the Council saw his face like the face of an angel" (v. 15). This description of his face doesn't advance the story, but it has all the feel of a personal memoir. We later learn that the Apostle Paul was there that day. In fact, it later emerges that Paul (still going by his Hebraic name, Saul) was Stephen's main accuser.

Saul was from Tarsus, a city in the province of Cilicia. Notice in verse 9 that the Synagogue of the Freedmen, where this story began, was populated by foreign, immigrant Jews from several provinces, including Cilicia.

Saul was there. He was one of the ones arguing and being bested by Stephen. Saul was the one that described Stephen's teaching as blasphemy, as we see later in the story when the rulers lay their garments at his feet.

Since Paul and Luke were working together to write this book, Paul is probably Luke's primary source for the whole story. The impression recorded here that Stephen's face looked like an angel was probably what Paul vividly and painfully remembered as he recounted that day to Luke, now twenty-five years later.

## Strange Content

In the speech that follows, Stephen seems to ramble, bringing up details that don't advance the narrative, and seem to distract. These strange details often baffle readers, including scholars. New Testament scholar Howard Marshall says,

> The purpose of this speech is still much disputed. In form it is a lengthy recital of Old Testament history, discussing in detail what appear to be insignificant points and culminating in a bitter attack on the speaker's hearers. What is the speaker trying to do?[1]

Later he complains, "It is not clear what the theological point of the details is."

These are striking statements, coming, as they do, from one who demonstrates keen insight throughout the text of Acts. Yet, they are hardly unusual. Dibelius is much stronger,

> The irrelevance of this speech has for long been the real problem of exegesis. It is, indeed, impossible to find a connection between the account of the history of Israel to the time of Moses (7:2-19) and the accusations against Stephen.... The major part of the speech shows no purpose whatever.[2]

These interpreters have badly missed the point in this brilliant speech. To understand Stephen's argument, all you have to do is look at the charges brought against him from the perspective of a first century Jew.

Here are the points to look for:

1. Stephen's opponents would argue that if the Messiah showed up, nobody would be more qualified to recognize him than the learned rabbis and leaders. But Stephen shows that Israel's history reveals

---

1. Howard I. Marshall, *The Acts of the Apostles* (Leichester, England: Inter-Varsity Press, 1980), 131.
2. Cited in Richard N. Longnecker, *The Acts of the Apostles*, in The Expositor's Bible Commentary, Frank Gabelein, Ed. (Grand Rapids MI: Zondervan Publishing House, 1978), 337-338.

that the Jews (and especially their leaders) have consistently failed to recognize the hand of God or his agents—just as they were again with Jesus.

2. Stephen charges that although the Jews have shown hyper-reverence for the temple and its rituals, they have misunderstood both the whole time.

3. He also argues that now that the temple and ritual system have been fulfilled, they should be set aside.

4. Stephen shows that not only the temple, but the sacred city and sacred land have never been necessary to God's work in history. He rejects the importance of sacred space and shows how God often worked apart from it. This is why his "strange details" often have to do with geography.

   Stephen and the rest of the Christians knew about the great commission and the implication from it—that God was now going to move out to the rest of the world.

5. At the heart of ethnic-religious worldviews are the twin values of "race and space," or to put it differently, "blood and soil." These values are hardly unique to first century Judaism, but are common themes for most religions, including much of western Christianity.

   But such values can be dangerous substitutes for real spirituality, and may act as barriers to a truly universal, loving following of Jesus. Throughout Acts, these blood and soil values battle with God's agenda for his people. And Luke, the only gentile author of a biblical book, follows that battle carefully.

   Stephen rejected the blood and soil approach to spirituality, thus infuriating his hearers.

With these points in mind, we are ready to go through Stephen's speech one section at a time. As we do, remember that this speech is not verbatim. It only takes a couple of minutes to read the whole thing. Luke is giving us the salient points raised, and we have to fill in the rest of the content.

# 11

# STEPHEN'S DEFENSE

## ACTS 7

## Abraham

Stephen begins with Abraham:

> Then the high priest asked Stephen, "Are these accusations true?"

> This was Stephen's reply: "Brothers and fathers, listen to me. Our glorious God appeared to our ancestor Abraham in Mesopotamia before he settled in Haran." (Acts 7:1-2)

Everyone agreed that God had personally called Abraham. The important point to Steven is that He did so "while [Abraham] was still in Mesopotamia, before he lived in Haran" (v. 2). So Stephen immediately reminds the council that this story doesn't begin in Israel, but in pagan Ur of the Chaldees. Score one for point 4 from the list in the previous chapter—that God often works outside the Holy Land.[1]

And what did God say to Abraham? "Leave your native land and your

---

1. The first call we have recorded in Genesis 12 came while Abraham was in Haran. But God later reminded him, "I am the Lord who brought you out of Ur of the Chaldeans to give you this land as your possession" (Genesis 15:7). So this original call in Ur is not recorded.

relatives, and come into the land that I will show you" (v. 3). So Stephen admits God guided Abraham to the promised land, but that also involved him leaving his own country and people, just as God was now going to call his people to leave their land and people again. Score 1 for point 5, against blood and soil religion.

> "Abraham left the land of the Chaldeans and lived in Haran until his father died. Then God brought him here to the land where you now live." (v. 4)

So God did ordain the promised land, and it was a key part of the Abrahamic covenant.

> "But God gave him no inheritance here, not even one square foot of land. God did promise, however, that eventually the whole land would belong to Abraham and his descendants— even though he had no children yet." (v. 5)

Abraham, the great father of faith, traveled around in the land, but never owned any of it. He was a foreigner in the land throughout his life.

"God also told him that his descendants would live in a foreign land, where they would be oppressed as slaves for 400 years" (v. 6). That means for over 400 years, the locus of God's work was entirely outside the Holy Land. Score again for point 4, against the need for sacred space. If the sacred land was so important, why did God take his people out of it for centuries? We now know God used the situation in Egypt to grow his people from a family to a nation without the danger of assimilation into pagan culture.

## The Patriarchs

Stephen acknowledged that God gave Abraham circumcision, a mark of the covenant, and that they continued the practice down to the time of the patriarchs—a term referring to the twelve sons of Abraham's grandson, Jacob, later renamed Israel. So this ethnic distinction was of God.

But, he suggests, as long as we're talking about the patriarchs, did you notice? "These patriarchs were jealous of their brother Joseph, and they sold him to be a slave in Egypt. But God was with him and rescued him from all his troubles" (vs. 9-10).

How similar to the present situation! Here, in Genesis, the revered patriarchs saw nothing of what God was doing and attacked Joseph, just like the current leaders failed to see who Jesus was and attacked and killed him. And a big part of their motive was also the same—jealousy—as we saw earlier.

For decades, the patriarchs believed Joseph was dead or gone and only then did they finally learn that God was with Joseph the whole time. None of the patriarchs recognized God's hand, just like the leaders in Jesus' day who didn't recognize him.

But contrary to their beliefs, God was raising Joseph up to a supreme position of power in Egypt. Score for point 1—the Jewish leadership consistently failed to recognize what God was doing. Also point 4—God working with his people in Egypt, not in the Holy Land. The center of action moved with Joseph. "God was with him," affirms Stephen (v. 9).

In verses 11-16, Stephen recounts how God used the pressure of a famine to bring the disobedient patriarchs into Egypt, where they all died. Again, God's people were far away from the Holy Land.

## Moses

Blasphemy of Moses was one of the charges brought against Stephen, so his analysis of this period in salvation history is important.

Stephen recounts the miraculous way God was able to infiltrate Moses into the palace of the Pharaoh. God was clearly setting Moses up to be the deliverer. But did his own people recognize God's hand? No.

Stephen reminds them, "Moses assumed his fellow Israelites would realize that God had sent him to rescue them, but they didn't" (v. 25). Instead, they challenged him, "Who made you a ruler and judge over us?" (v. 27). Score another point for argument 1, failure to recognize God's man.

Next, Moses "fled to Midian, where he settled as a foreigner" (v. 29). So it was in Midian, not in Palestine, that he saw the burning bush. Score for point 4—God working outside of sacred space.

Stephen goes on, "Forty years later, in the desert near Mount Sinai, an angel appeared to Moses in the flame of a burning bush" (v. 30). Here is real sacred space. Stephen reminds them, "Then the Lord said to him, 'Take off your sandals, for you are standing on holy ground'" (v. 33).

But interestingly, nobody knew then or now where this holy ground is. Shouldn't Moses have marked the spot so people could get back there? Why didn't he ever organize a search party to find the place of the burning bush? He never set up a shrine there; never apparently showed any further interest in it.

That's because it was only holy when God was doing something there. Holy means distinct, or special; not common. Later, when God's presence had departed, the place was no longer holy. It was like any other patch of ground. It would have been a serious mistake to stand around at this site waiting for God to act when he had already moved on to other work.

Now, in Stephen's day, God was moving out again—this time from the temple and from Jerusalem. The new temple is the people of God—Jesus' own body. We're not clear how much the believers understood about the body of Christ at this early time. Jesus had hinted at it when he said, "Destroy this temple, and in three days I will raise it up," and John added, "He was speaking of the temple of His body" (John 2:19, 21). Jesus also referred to the mystical union of believers with himself in the upper room. But we don't see the full doctrine of the body of Christ until almost twenty years later, in 1 Corinthians.

Stephen's point is that believers in his own day were going to have to realize God was moving on again. They considered that blasphemy, but it was true.

Stephen proceeded to discuss Moses' return to Egypt and his successful deliverance of the Jewish people from slavery. He not only points out that Moses did wonders, but he also reminds them of the venue for those works: "in Egypt, at the Red Sea and for forty years in the desert" (v. 36). So once again, God did some of his greatest work outside of the Holy Land. Moses also "received life-giving words to pass on to us" (v. 38). Here is argument 4 again, that God does some of his greatest works outside the boundaries of the Holy Land.

The punch line follows: "But our ancestors refused to listen to Moses. They rejected him and wanted to return to Egypt" (v. 39). So again, it's point number 1—that the leadership usually failed to recognize God's agents.

Stephen covered the people's disloyalty during the golden calf incident (vs. 40-41) and then moved to their even more revolting ongoing worship of "the stars of heaven... Molech... Rephan... and the images they made" (vs. 42-43). He backed up his claims by quoting from the prophet Amos, who exposed these sins. So argument 1 is proven again—any claim that the Jewish people or their leaders were discerning and faithful to God's servants is belied by history.

## The Tabernacle

Finally, Stephen discusses God's "portable sacred space" known as the tabernacle.

> "Our ancestors carried the tabernacle with them through the wilderness. It was constructed according to the plan God had shown to Moses." (vs. 44-45)

The tabernacle was prescribed by God in every detail. That was God's way of signifying that he alone specifies the way people can approach him. Allowing any innovation would suggest works. In the tabernacle, God was saying, "You can come to me, but I'll determine how." Also, the tabernacle had critical types and symbols that predicted the work of Jesus. In the full version of Stephen's speech, he may have covered some of these.

To Stephen, a key feature of the tabernacle was the absence of any tie to a geographical location. It sat in some farmers' back yards for centuries after the conquest (v. 45). Then, David proposed building the temple. We don't have Stephen's citation of God's reply in this abridged version, but he probably referred to it, as his later words imply. God's reply to the temple suggestion came through Nathan the prophet:

> "I have not dwelt in a house since the day I brought up the sons of Israel from Egypt, even to this day; but I have been moving about in a tent, even in a tabernacle. Wherever I have gone with all the sons of Israel, did I speak a word with one of the tribes of Israel, which I commanded to shepherd my people Israel, saying, 'Why have you not built me a house of cedar?'" (2 Samuel 7:6-7)

Of course not. How ridiculous. Stephen cries out the obvious:

"However, the Most High does not dwell in houses made by human hands." (v. 48)

Then he cites the very similar passage from Isaiah:

> "Heaven is my throne,
> and the earth is my footstool.
> What kind of house will you build for me?
> says the Lord.
> Or where will my resting place be?
> Has not my hand made all these things?" (vs. 49-50 citing Isaiah 66:1-2)

The Jewish people knew God didn't actually live in the temple, even though they called the temple the house of God. That meant it *stood for* the house of God.

Solomon himself, when dedicating the temple, prayed:

> "But will God indeed dwell on the earth? Behold, heaven and the highest heaven cannot contain you, how much less this house which I have built!" (1 Kings 8:27)

The temple and its rituals were for teaching. In a day when many of the people were illiterate, these rituals acted out principles like God's holiness, humans' sinfulness, the need for atonement, and the need for intercession.

Religious people in Israel sometimes failed to comprehend the true nature of the temple and rituals. They came to view the temple as being the literal dwelling place of God. To them, Stephen's cry, "The Most High does not dwell in houses made by human hands," was an outrage. In fact, Stephen's whole talk was an outrage.

## The End

By this time, Stephen probably knew he had signed his own death warrant. So he cut loose:

> "You men who are stiff-necked and uncircumcised in heart and ears are always resisting the Holy Spirit; you are doing just as your fathers did. Which one of the prophets did your fathers not persecute? They killed those who had previously

announced the coming of the Righteous One, whose betrayers and murderers you have now become; you who received the law as ordained by angels, and yet did not keep it." (vs. 51-53)

The reaction was explosive. They didn't bother trying to refute any of Stephen's arguments. Instead, they erupted into a hysterical state of fury, "gnashing their teeth at him" (v. 54). The picture, vividly remembered by Paul, is one of complete breakdown of self-control.

Stephen made no effort to cool things down. Instead,

> But being full of the Holy Spirit, he gazed intently into heaven and saw the glory of God, and Jesus standing at the right hand of God; and he said, "Behold, I see the heavens opened up and the Son of Man standing at the right hand of God." (vs. 55-56)

Stephen must have been dazzled by what he saw. It was as if the violent crowd around him didn't exist. It's fascinating that he sees Jesus standing at God's right hand. Did Jesus stand up to welcome Stephen home?

He refers to Jesus as the Son of Man. This is the only use of this title outside the Gospels. This reference to Daniel 7:13-14 would have been instantly recognized by this gathering of Bible scholars. Jesus had often used this title for himself, and it's entirely possible that Stephen had earlier listened to Jesus teach.

## The Rush

The rulers broke and ran screaming at Stephen, literally holding their hands over their ears as though they couldn't stand to hear anymore. Seizing him, they drove him out of the chamber. Then,

> When they had driven him out of the city, they began stoning him; and the witnesses laid aside their robes at the feet of a young man named Saul. (v. 58)

Getting outside the city didn't take long. Their chamber was very close to the eastern gate. There, out of public view below the temple mount, they hurled their wrath at Stephen.

Laying their robes at Saul's feet showed that he was the plaintiff or accuser; the winner of the trial. Our first glimpse of this man shows him in the act of proudly killing a Christian.

They went on stoning Stephen as he called on the Lord and
said, "Lord Jesus, receive my spirit!" Then falling on his knees,
he cried out with a loud voice, "Lord, do not hold this sin
against them!" Having said this, he fell asleep. (vs. 59-60)

As Saul's unblinking eyes stared, his opponent, bleeding profusely, cried
out to God not to hold this sin against them. We have good reason to
believe that Saul was haunted by this scene for the rest of his life. He
repeatedly recounts his persecution and killing of Christians, of which
Stephen was the first. The shock he must have felt when he later learned
he had been in the wrong is hard to imagine.

## The Aftermath

The fact that the counsel stoned Stephen without Roman approval was
a clear breech of Roman law, even if the crimes of blasphemy were capital offenses. They were going by the old dictum that it's easier to be
forgiven than to get permission. The police wouldn't do anything—the
council owned the police: the temple guard. If any Romans came asking
questions, they could simply deny they had anything to do with it. Some
angry mob must have killed him.

The church lost a great light on the day Stephen died. Stephen's thinking
was ahead of many of the other leaders in the Jerusalem church. This
becomes evident later in the book, as we will see. His understanding of
how the gospel related to the issues of race, sacred space, and the radical change in God's program from the Old Testament surpassed his
contemporaries.

Stephen was one of the Hellenistic Jews in Jerusalem chosen to help heal
the friction between the Hellenistic and Hebraic groups. That suggests
he was probably less encumbered with the ethnocentricity, ritualism,
and traditionalism of the "Hebraic" group in the Jerusalem church.[2]

---

2. F. F. Bruce says, "Stephen's attitude to the Temple betokens a much clearer appreciation of the
incompatibility of the old order with the implications of the teaching of Jesus than appears to have
been common among the early disciples in Jerusalem." F. F. Bruce, *New Testament History* (NY:
Random House, 1973), 223. Marshal agrees: "It would seem likely that Steven went much farther
than the twelve in emphasizing this teaching [on the temple]." Howard I. Marshall, *The Acts of the
Apostles* (Nottingham, UK: SPCK Publishing, 1983), 128.

# The Big Picture

It must have seemed like an unmitigated tragedy to lose a visionary like Stephen, with such a depth of understanding and so much courage. Stephen was a thought leader who would have been a key player in the training of hundreds of new leaders. Instead, he lay there dead.

Believers had seen the mass lynching. But they had to stay back until the attackers left. After the frenzied mob departed, they came and stood around Stephen's bloody corpse, weeping and holding each other for support. Then, "Some devout men buried Stephen, and made loud lamentation over him" (8:2).

Although they had no way of knowing it, God was already at work with his plan to replace Stephen's lost brilliance. The attackers laid their cloaks at the feet of one who would later demonstrate every bit as much radicalism as Stephen: Saul of Tarsus!

# 12

# FIRST BREAKOUT

## ACTS 8

## Persecution

Stephen's death was not the end, but the beginning of lethal attacks. His death was like a bursting dam unleashing a flood of hatred and persecution.

> Saul was in hearty agreement with putting him to death.... And on that day a great persecution began against the church in Jerusalem, and they were all scattered throughout the regions of Judea and Samaria, except the apostles.
>
> Saul began ravaging the church, entering house after house, and dragging off men and women, he would put them in prison. (Acts 8:1-3)

Luke only mentions imprisoning believers, but later Paul made it clear that he also executed a number of people. "I persecuted this Way to the death, binding and putting both men and women into prisons" (Acts 22:4).

The expression "to the death" might only refer to Stephen if it weren't for a later confession in another setting.

> "And this is just what I did in Jerusalem; not only did I lock up many of the saints in prisons, having received authority from the chief priests, but also when they were being put to death I cast my vote against them. And as I punished them often in all the synagogues, I tried to force them to blaspheme; and being furiously enraged at them, I kept pursuing them even to foreign cities." (Acts 26:10-11)

The statement "when they were being put to death I cast my vote against them" is in the plural. So Stephen was not the only one. Unlike with Stephen, where they mindlessly attacked, Paul says they voted. That suggests they had worked out some arrangement with the Romans by then that made killing followers of Jesus legal.

Another reference to Paul killing believers comes in chapter 9, where Luke describes him as "breathing threats and murder against the disciples of the Lord" (9:1). Being imprisoned under this government was close to death, and often resulted in death, because of the harsh conditions.

This persecution is another reason for the lasting poverty in the Jerusalem group, still evident twenty years later. According to the book of Hebrews they had their homes and possessions seized (10:32-34). They never fully recovered.

The expression "I punished them often in all the synagogues and tried to force them to blaspheme" probably refers to torture. Torture was common in that day and culture, and we know of cases where Christians were tortured unless they cursed Jesus. The Mishnah confirms that people were sometimes whipped in synagogues.[1] They were also tortured to make them give up the identities of other Christians.[2]

---

1. Mishnah, *Makkoth* 3:10–15. This lengthy discussion explains that synagogue whippings were done with a thick leather strap. Both men and women were punished. The whipping was on the naked torso, one third on the chest and two thirds on the back. If the victim soiled him or herself with feces, the whipping was suspended.

2. For instance, Pliny, Governor of Bithinia's "Letter to Trajan" discusses the use of torture on Christians. He was much later, but still early, writing in about AD 112. https://christianhistorinstitute.org/study/module/pliny. (We earlier saw Peter and other apostles publicly whipped in chapter 5).

## Fleeing the Nightmare

The temple guards were bursting into houses and seizing men and women (v. 3). What happened to their children? They didn't care. They weren't seizing the kids. The children may have been abandoned, but other believers and family would have moved in to give them shelter.

How terrifying this persecution must have been, especially to those with families! The instinct was natural—Let's get out of here! Anyone who had friends or family living outside Jerusalem would have fled there for shelter. So we read, "They were all scattered throughout the regions of Judea and Samaria, except the apostles" (v. 1).

That last phrase is important, because it clarifies that the Philip in the rest of this passage is not the Philip in the Twelve. Instead, this is Philip, one of the seven men chosen in Acts 6, along with Stephen.

Satan used the persecution to break up the big group in Jerusalem, but it didn't work as well as he hoped. We read, "Therefore, those who had been scattered went about preaching the word" (v. 4).

These fleeing believers had amazing stories to tell in the Jewish communities to which they fled. Eyewitness accounts of amazing miracles would have carried far more weight in an age that accepted the supernatural and was far less skeptical than people today.

One of the fleeing believers was a man named Philip.

## Philip's Awakening

Luke recounts in this context a spiritual awakening in Samaria, led by Philip.

> Philip went down to the city of Samaria and began proclaiming Christ to them. The crowds with one accord were giving attention to what was said by Philip, as they heard and saw the signs which he was performing. For in the case of many who had unclean spirits, they were coming out of them shouting with a loud voice; and many who had been paralyzed and lame were healed. So there was much rejoicing in that city. (vs. 5-8)

Where did Luke get this story about Philip the Evangelist, as he became known? Interestingly, Luke and Paul had recently stayed at Philip's house in Caesarea (Acts 21:8; notice this is in one of the "we" passages). So they got this detailed account from Philip himself, along with the next story about the Ethiopian eunuch, more than twenty years later.

Although Samaria is north of Jerusalem, the Jews always referred to leaving Jerusalem as "going down" and entering it as "going up" because of Jerusalem's altitude. It's a mountaintop city.

Luke's account refers to "crowds" accepting Philip's gospel "with one accord." So the numbers must have been impressive—not just a few dozen. A big reason they believed were the miracles God performed through Philip (v. 6). Of course, the other reason people believed was the drawing action of the Holy Spirit bringing life to the proclamation of the gospel. Jesus' promise that "If I am lifted up, I will draw all men to myself" was coming true (John 12:32).

Luke also adds, "As many who had unclean spirits, they were coming out of them shouting with a loud voice" (v. 7). This is one of the rare mentions of delivery from demon possession after Jesus' ministry.[3] It's even more surprising that demon possession is never mentioned in any of the epistles. No instructions are ever given for exorcism.

This doesn't prove that possession no longer exists, but it does suggest that exorcism is not an important component in Christian ministry. If it were important, surely we would have at least one passage explaining how and when to do it. We have the examples of Jesus and Paul casting out demons, so we should follow those examples as needed. But we are far more likely to meet Satan in his more undercover work—temptation, accusation, deception, and infiltration.

## Simon

They also encountered an occult practitioner:

> Now there was a man named Simon, who formerly was practicing magic in the city and astonishing the people of Samaria, claiming to be someone great; and they all, from smallest to greatest, were giving attention to him, saying, "This man is

---

3. The only other mentions are in Acts 16:16ff and Acts 19:12. Although rare, this passage proves MacArthur and similar commentators are wrong when they say nobody but Jesus or the apostles ever had authority to address an evil spirit. Philip was not one of the apostles. MacArthur, *Standing Strong: How to Resist the Enemy of Your Soul,* (Colorado Springs: Victor, 2006).

what is called the Great Power of God." And they were giving him attention because he had for a long time astonished them with his magic arts. (vs. 9-11)

You can already tell from the text that Simon is a bad player. His "signs" were the product of "magic arts." Probably this refers to sleight-of-hand trickery, but could include actual supernatural power.

We're not sure how much Satan can do when it comes to miracles. Demonic miracles are sometimes called "false wonders," suggesting they aren't real (2 Thessalonians 2:9). We know Satan can't tell the future, even though occult practitioners claim they can.[4] On the other hand, Satan caused a whirlwind that destroyed the homes of Job's kids (Job 1:18-19), but only with permission from God.

Simon had impressed the people in Samaria, so much that they called him "the Great Power of God." But his own mind was blown when he saw real miracles. We read, "Even Simon himself believed; and after being baptized, he continued on with Philip, and as he observed signs and great miracles taking place, he was constantly amazed" (v. 13).

Was it that he really believed? Or was it that he claimed to believe? Was it that he believed Philip had something special, which was obvious? It's possible to believe that Jesus is real without believing *in* him, in the sense of entrusting yourself. He got baptized, so it looked to others like he had believed.

## Peter and John Arrive

Word got back to Jerusalem that something big, but also strange, was happening in Samaria:

> Now when the apostles in Jerusalem heard that Samaria had received the word of God, they sent them Peter and John, who came down and prayed for them that they might receive the Holy Spirit. For he had not yet fallen upon any of them; they had simply been baptized in the name of the Lord Jesus. Then they began laying their hands on them, and they were receiving the Holy Spirit. (vs. 14-17)

---

4. We know that demons can't tell the future because of several passages where God declares that he is the only one who can (e.g., Isaiah 42:8-9; 44:24-25).

The apostles immediately sent Peter and John. Why? The messengers must have told them what was happening. It was something they had never seen before. People were coming to faith in Jesus, but the Holy Spirit wasn't indwelling them.

Who better to send than Peter and John, who God had used so powerfully already? They gathered the new believers together and prayed over them. As they laid hands on them, something happened that they understood to be evidence of the Holy Spirit—probably speaking in tongues, and perhaps prophesying.

The word for prophesying means to speak forth. It doesn't necessarily imply predicting the future, like it usually does in secular English. It means speaking under the direct inspiration of God. Paul considered it one of the greater spiritual gifts (1 Corinthians 14:1).

He explains that "one who prophesies speaks to men for edification and exhortation and consolation" (1 Corinthians 14:3). So if you've been to a Bible study where people pray and share what's on their heart, you have probably heard prophecy.

Prophecy was common in the early church (Acts 11:27-28; 13:1; 15:32; 21:9-10; 1 Corinthians 11:4-5; 13:9; 14:5, 24, 31-32, 39; Ephesians 4:11; 1 Timothy 4:14; 1 Thessalonians 5:20). It disappeared sometime during the second century, along with many other biblical traits of the early church. The second century leaders' more high-control mindset and the increasingly sharp division between clergy and laity doomed this and other gifts to the ash heap of history.

Today, the Pentecostal and charismatic movements have resurrected prophecy (as some earlier movements temporarily did). However, the majority of churches reject prophecy and argue that God no longer sanctions it. In fact, we have no reason to reject prophecy or speaking in tongues based on any sound exegetical finding.[5]

Instead, we should follow the rules Paul gave for practicing tongues and

---

5. "Ceasationists" deny the validity of so-called "sign gifts" like tongues, healing, and prophecy. Their most common argument is that Paul says in 1 Corinthians 13:8-10, "Love never fails; but if there are gifts of prophecy, they will be done away; if there are tongues, they will cease; if there is knowledge, it will be done away." But in the context, Paul adds "for we know in part and we prophesy in part; but when the perfect comes, the partial will be done away."
Ceasationists argue that the canon of New Testament Scripture is "the perfect." As the canon was completed and disseminated around the end of the first century, these gifts were no longer needed. But in the context "when the perfect comes" means the second coming of Jesus (v. 12).

prophecy in assembly.[6] We should also discard showy displays like lapsing into King James English—"Thus saith the Lord...!" There's no reason to believe that God, who easily spoke in Hebrew, Aramaic, and Greek, would get stuck in old time English.

# The Role of Race

Jews and Samaritans were racially prejudiced against each other. This is a well-documented problem. John simply comments, "Jews have no dealings with Samaritans" (John 4:9). Jews used the word "Samaritan" like a cuss word. In John 8:48, we read: "The Jews answered and said to him, 'Do we not say rightly that you are a Samaritan and have a demon?'" Being demon-possessed and being a Samaritan were on the same level in their view.

Jesus, of course, rejected the prejudice and reached out to the Samaritan woman in John 4. He also stayed in the Samaritan city of Sychar several days, and "many of the Samaritans believed in him" (John 4:39). When he told a parable to rebuke the provincialism of a questioner, he made the hero a Samaritan (Luke 10:30-37).

Samaritans were part Jewish ethnically. They grew out of a population of Jews left in Israel in the eighth century BC. Most Jews from that area had been deported by the Assyrians.

The rabbis called Samaritans "Cuthites" or "Cutheans," from the city Cuthah in Iraq from which the new immigrants came. Josephus agrees.[7] 2 Kings 17:24 explains that the king of Assyria sent thousands of settlers to live in Samaria around 720 BC. These foreigners inter-married with the remaining Jews that escaped exile, resulting in the Samaritans. So Samaritans were of mixed race. They viewed themselves as descendants of the tribes of Ephraim and Manasseh. But the Jews viewed them as non-Jewish.

Initially, the Cuthites didn't know anything about Judaism, and they superstitiously concluded that they were having problems, including

---

6. Paul moved to block the chaos and selfishness in Corinthian assemblies. They were emphasizing the gift of tongues too much and all talking at once. To correct the situation he instructed them: 1) to have no more than two or three tongues spoken, 2) they must speak one at a time and 3) only if they are translated into the vernacular. He also restricted prophecy to one speaker at a time, and that the other members should judge whether it was an authentic message from God. All of these rules are regularly ignored in many charismatic and Pentecostal groups.
7. Josephus, *Wars of the Jews* 2:6. Also Josephus, *Antiquities* 9.277–291.

being attacked by lions, because they weren't honoring the local god of the land in which they lived. When they explained this to the Assyrian king, he sent back a captured Jewish priest to teach them about the local god—Yahweh. So they learned some about the Old Testament, but they also continued to worship the gods from their homeland. This is all explained in 2 Kings 17:24-35.

Ezra 4 recounts the struggle against the Samaritans when Zerubbabel was rebuilding the temple. The Samaritans were able to delay the work with letters to the Persians and threats of military action. The villain Sanballat was a Samaritan (see Nehemiah 4).

Jews and Samaritans fought battles during the intertestamental period. Bin Sirah says, "My whole being loathes [them]... The foolish people who dwell in Shechem." He says they are "not even a people" (Sirach 50:25–26). In 128 BC, the Jewish leader John Hyrcanus led an armed company and destroyed Shechem.

By the time of Jesus, the Samaritans' religion had morphed into a form of distorted Judaism. They read the Old Testament, but they only accepted the first five books. The name "Samaritan" comes from "Shamerim," a Romanized version of a word meaning "Guardians" [of the Torah].

They differed from Judaism on where the holy mountain was located and where the temple should be. Samaritans held that it was Mt. Gerizim in Samaria, not Mt. Zion, where Jerusalem is. They actually built their own temple there. So there was a religious component to the alienation between the two peoples.

But again, the Jews didn't consider Samaritans Jewish. They were a different race, an unclean race, and they didn't belong in the Promised Land.

## Overthrowing Racism

The primary reason why this scene unfolds the way it did is racism. Racism is very human and grows naturally from humans' selfish, fallen nature. Holding one group, often one race, as superior delights our thirst for identity. Of course, any suggestion that humans are not equal is a direct denial of clear biblical teaching, beginning in Genesis 1, where humans were created in God's image.

In this period of Acts, God knew his people had not yet fully grasped a vision of world Christianity. They had been raised believing that godly people don't talk to or hang out with sinful foreigners. The rabbis taught that Gentiles and Samaritans were unclean. Close contact with them was defiling.

God knew he was going to have to work on his people to correct this devastating view. They already knew Jesus didn't follow the racist thinking. He went to dinner parties with tax collectors; he talked to Gentiles and expressed willingness to enter their homes (Matthew 8:5-7). But if they had merely heard that people in Samaria had believed, doubts would have arisen.

They needed unimpeachable proof that the wall between Jews and Samaritans was now demolished. Earlier, Jesus had designated Peter to be the leader of the apostles. He also said, "I will give you the keys of the kingdom of heaven; and whatever you bind on earth shall have been bound in heaven, and whatever you loose on earth shall have been loosed in heaven" (Matthew 16:19).[8]

What does it mean?

In the first place, keys are used to open or lock doors. In Acts, Peter was front and center to open each of the three doors Jesus mentions in chapter 1: "You shall be my witnesses both in Jerusalem, and in all Judea and Samaria, and even to the remotest part of the earth" (v. 8). So Jerusalem was first, and Peter preached at Pentecost.

Next comes Samaria. Peter wasn't there at the time Philip launched the movement. This is the most plausible explanation for why God hesitated to send the Holy Spirit to these new believers. He was waiting for Peter to come and bear personal witness to what was happening. Nothing less would overthrow the loathing for Samaritans in which they had been raised.

Soon, Peter would be present for the official opening of the third door—this time the door to the Gentiles.

---

8. This passage about binding and loosing refers to rabbis who would render decisions about the law by saying one was bound or loosed in a particular situation. Here in Matthew and elsewhere when discussing the apostles' binding and loosing, Jesus uses an unusual tense—the future perfect. It means that in the future when you bind something, it will already have been bound in heaven. NASB captures that with "shall have been bound." It means that the apostles weren't making something true or false, right or wrong. Rather, they were authorized to delare what truth or falsehood was. This authority to define the boundaries of Christian teaching gave the apostles the ability to create an authoritative canon of Scripture. Books needed apostolic authority to be accepted as Scripture.

## Not a Second Act of Grace

Modern Pentecostal and some charismatic groups point to this several-day gap between when the Samaritans believed and when they received the Spirit as proof that the baptism of the Spirit is a second act of grace.

They argue that people first believe and are spiritually reborn. They are also indwellt by the Spirit at that time. Then, subsequently, believers can pray for the baptism of the Holy Spirit and he comes, usually with the laying on of hands, and signified by speaking in tongues, just like in this story.

But the careful reader sees that this story does not fit the Pentecostal scenario. These believers didn't first receive the Spirit for salvation and then for baptism. The text is clear; they had not received the Spirit *at all.* Romans 8:9 says, "But if anyone does not have the Spirit of Christ, he does not belong to him." So these Samaritans were technically neither indwelt nor baptized with the Spirit.

These Samaritans were experiencing a unique exception. In order to confirm his move into Samaria, God deliberately delayed sending the Holy Spirit—not just for spiritual baptism, but in any sense. That means this passage cannot be used to confirm the second act of grace theology.

## Peter and John's Hands

Only when Peter and John put their hands on the Samaritans did the Holy Spirit fall. That's a graphic way to give authority and credibility to these apostles. God was saying, "Listen to them."

The Samaritans didn't need to receive all this explanation. They just saw whose hands the Spirit moved through.

## Simon Reappears

Simon the Magician, mentioned earlier, was watching the apostles and the evident power of the Holy Spirit.

> Now when Simon saw that the Spirit was bestowed through
> the laying on of the apostles' hands, he offered them money,

saying, "Give this authority to me as well, so that everyone on whom I lay my hands may receive the Holy Spirit." (vs. 18-19)

The desire to be able to bring the Holy Spirit to people wasn't necessarily wrong. The bizarre part here was offering the apostles money in exchange for that power. The money offer clearly signaled that Simon had no comprehension of what was going on. Specifically, he clearly didn't know God. The thought that a material gift could alter what was happening is so absurd that it's offensive to all that was going on.

Simon's name was later enshrined in a new word: "simony." Simony is when someone tries to buy a church position with money. It became a widespread practice during the medieval period, when wealthy nobles could buy a bishopric for one of their sons. Then, the tithing from that area (collected like a tax, not voluntarily) would be a lasting source of income for the family.

The new bishops sometimes had no training in anything theological and might not even live in the district in question. This was one of the outrages that led to a number of dissident groups and finally to the Reformation.

The Catholic Church eventually ruled against simony and prescribed punishments, but in many lands, assigning of bishoprics was up to secular nobles, not the church. That made it hard to enforce rules against simony.

## Simon Magus

Post-apostolic church fathers tell a number of stories about Simon, calling him Simon Magus, which means Simon the Magician, or Simon the Sorcerer. These authors include Irenaeus, Justin Martyr, Hippolytus, and Epiphanius. They often described him as the founder of Gnosticism—a prominent heresy, mainly in the late second century. That is quite implausible.

Justin Martyr claims that Simon visited Rome at the time of the emperor Claudius (AD 41–54) and was declared to be "god" because of his miracle working.[9]

---

9. Justin Martyr, *The First Apology*, ch. 26.

In one legend from the third century, Simon fell to his death from atop the Roman Forum in an attempt to demonstrate his occult ability to fly. [10]

All of these accounts are nonsense. The real story of Simon is right here in Acts 8. Historians discount the much later, fanciful stories.

Back to Acts, Peter let him have it:

> But Peter said to him, "May your silver perish with you, because you thought you could obtain the gift of God with money! You have no part or portion in this matter, for your heart is not right before God. Therefore repent of this wickedness of yours, and pray the Lord that, if possible, the intention of your heart may be forgiven you. For I see that you are in the gall of bitterness and in the bondage of iniquity." But Simon answered and said, "Pray to the Lord for me yourselves, so that nothing of what you have said may come upon me." (vs. 20-24)

Such a firm rejection should have served as a warning to later generations against putting a monetary value on ministry. But if that was the intent, it didn't work. Ministry has been monetized, not only by medieval bishops but also modern day preachers making millions for their often false preaching.

Simon's reaction is ambiguous. He may have been repentant, but he still doesn't seem to understand how God relates to believers. We don't know what happened to him after this.

The apostles apparently stayed on, imparting some teaching. Then, on their way home to Jerusalem they "were preaching the gospel to many villages of the Samaritans" (v. 25). So the door to Samaria really had been unlocked and the apostles correctly followed the implications of recent events.

## Desert Encounter

Philip wasn't with them. Instead, we read: "But an angel of the Lord spoke to Philip saying, 'Get up and go south to the road that descends from Jerusalem to Gaza.' (This is a desert road.)" (v. 26).

Imagine Philip, in the midst of a mass spiritual movement unlike

---

10. See a good collection of the early church tales about Simon in *Encyclopedia Britannica*: www. britannica.com/biography/Simon-Magus.

anything he had ever seen. Suddenly, an angel comes, telling him to walk away from it all and head down a hundred miles into the desert. Did he argue? Did he say anything? Did this make any sense at all?

It's an incredible example of how God's direction often seems to defy common sense. It's not always the case. Philip had earlier used common sense when he saw the quandary in the Samaritans believing but not receiving the Spirit, and he sent to the apostles for help. That makes sense.

This call makes no sense to the human eye, but God knows things we can't possibly know.

> So he got up and went; and there was an Ethiopian eunuch, a court official of Candace, queen of the Ethiopians,[11] who was in charge of all her treasure; and he had come to Jerusalem to worship, and he was returning and sitting in his chariot, and was reading the prophet Isaiah. (vs. 27-28)

Who knew that an Ethiopian official was on the road to Gaza, struggling to understand the Bible? God! Nobody else. So in the end, this move was not nonsense at all. But if you limit common sense to what we humans know, it seems like nonsense. Servants of God need to leave space for that which God knows and we don't.

God had sovereignly arranged this meeting, and that becomes crystal clear when we note what passage the official was reading:

> The Holy Spirit said to Philip, "Go over and walk along beside the carriage." Philip ran over and heard the man reading from the prophet Isaiah.

> Philip asked, "Do you understand what you are reading?"

> The man replied, "How can I, unless someone instructs me?" And he urged Philip to come up into the carriage and sit with him. The passage of Scripture he had been reading was this:

> "He was led like a sheep to the slaughter.
> And as a lamb is silent before the shearers,
> he did not open his mouth.

---

11. In Greek, Candice, *Kandak*, was not the name of a specific queen, but a title for queen mothers. There are at least ten during the 500 years between AD 260 and 320 BC. Read the Wikipedia article for a solid coverage.

He was humiliated and received no justice.
Who can speak of his descendants?
For his life was taken from the earth." (vs. 29-33)

He's reading Isaiah 53! That's arguably the clearest Old Testament prediction of the atoning death and resurrection of Jesus! And he wants help:

The eunuch asked Philip, "Tell me, was the prophet talking about himself or someone else?" So beginning with this same Scripture, Philip told him the good news about Jesus. (vs. 34-35)

How would you like to walk into a situation like this? The red carpet has been rolled out. All Philip has to do is stride down it.

Although this case is extreme, the basic picture of God working both ends against the middle isn't unusual. Believers active in evangelism must learn to ask God to set up divine appointments with non-believers. It's an unmistakable sign that God is at work, as we will see repeatedly later in Acts.

The Ethiopian was all ears. He believed word by word everything Philip said.

Then, there was a puddle or stream—unusual for this arid location. And it's doubtful that it was deep enough to immerse. It's probably a justification for using sprinkling for baptism under conditions where immersion isn't available.

## Teleportation?

Then comes a startling verse:

When they came up out of the water, the Spirit of the Lord snatched Philip away. The eunuch never saw him again but went on his way rejoicing. (v. 39)

Seriously? He disappeared? And then appeared further north at Azotus (usually called Ashdod)? Yes. It isn't the first time God snatched someone. This is actually less spectacular than when he sucked Elijah or Enoch up into heaven (2 Kings 2; Genesis 5:24), or the ascension of Christ.

Obadiah referred to Elijah being snatched away (1 Kings 18:12 see also Ezekiel 3:12).

The more important point is that in Philip, God had a powerful evangelist. He preached in Azotus and right up the Mediterranean coast town after town. Finally, "he came to Caesarea" (v. 40). That's where we meet him again more than twenty years later. Luke was there, along with Paul, and Luke refers to him as "Philip the Evangelist" (21:8). It would be hard to imagine a more appropriate name.

# 13

# SAUL

## ACTS 9

## The Pursuit

Back in Jerusalem, Saul was savagely pursuing his campaign of terror.

> Now Saul, still breathing threats and murder against the disciples of the Lord, went to the high priest, and asked for letters from him to the synagogues at Damascus, so that if he found any belonging to the Way, both men and women, he might bring them bound to Jerusalem. (Acts 9:1-2)

Damascus is about 200 miles from Jerusalem. It contained a large Jewish community, and Saul was not mistaken in thinking there were followers of Jesus there. He probably extracted information on them from his torture victims. We later meet Ananias and some unnamed "brothers." This is the first time we hear followers of Jesus called "the Way." It's a name that stuck in Jerusalem for decades. So Saul had his target in the crosshairs.

## Countermanded

It wasn't going to go the way Saul thought.

As he was traveling, it happened that he was approaching Damascus, and suddenly a light from heaven flashed around him; and he fell to the ground and heard a voice saying to him, "Saul, Saul, why are you persecuting Me?"

And he said, "Who are You, Lord?"

And he said, "I am Jesus whom you are persecuting." (vs. 3-5)

We could imagine Saul seeing the blinding light and hearing Jesus' words and saying, "So you're Jesus, right?" No. To Jesus' question, "Why are you persecuting me?" He says, "Who are you, Lord?"

A paradigm shift happens when you realize everything you've been thinking in some area is wrong. Most of us can think of a time when we underwent such a shift; maybe at the time of our conversion. But hardly ever on this level. Saul's entire blackboard was instantly erased. He lay dazzled by the light, but even more so by his utter wrong. He has been killing and imprisoning people and now suddenly he realizes they were in the right!

The wheels in Saul's mind were grinding as smoke came out of his ears. He couldn't think coherently. He would have been staring in confused dismay. Did he expect to be struck dead? That would be befitting. But Jesus doesn't come at him with fury and fire. Instead, he asks a question. It's a question Saul can't answer.

How long did Jesus leave him lying there? Not long, it seems. Jesus already knows what's in Saul's mind. It was a rhetorical question. He immediately tells him where to go.

## The Missing Text

But Luke's text here is selective. Later, we find that Jesus also said:

"But get up and stand on your feet; for this purpose I have appeared to you, to appoint you a minister and a witness not only to the things which you have seen, but also to the things in which I will appear to you; rescuing you from the Jewish people and from the Gentiles, to whom I am sending you, to open their eyes so that they may turn from darkness to light and from the dominion of Satan to God, that they may receive forgiveness of sins and an inheritance among those who have been set apart by faith in me." (26:16-18)

This was apparently in response to Saul's question, "What shall I do, Lord?" (22:10).

Luke wanted to move on with his narrative in chapter 9, so he gave the short version. Only by gathering details from all three times Paul told the story do we get a full picture.

From chapter 26, it's clear that Jesus announced what Saul's future would be. Paul didn't volunteer, he was drafted. To the Galatians he said, "God, who had set me apart even from my mother's womb and called me through his grace, was pleased to reveal his Son in me so that I might preach him among the Gentiles" (Galatians 1:15-16).

Jesus announces that he is appointing Saul to be a minister. He doesn't use the usual words for minister, or servant (*diakonos* or *doulos*). This is the word *huperates*, an under-rower. It's a term for a galley slave. They were chained to a bench in one of the many large, oar-driven warships operated by the Romans. Often, people convicted of crimes were sentenced to be a galley slave for a number of years, or for life.

He also says Paul would be a "witness," or *martus*, from which we get "martyr." It didn't imply dying then, like it did later in history. At this time the word simply meant he would tell what he had seen, like someone giving testimony in court. That included everything up to the present day plus more "things in which I will appear to you" (26:16).

Paul described one of those subsequent visitations in 2 Corinthians 12. He says he was taken to the third heaven and saw and heard things so far out that he wasn't allowed to say what they were (vs. 1-4).

Jesus also said he would rescue Saul from both Jews and Gentiles, and that he was sending Saul specifically to the Gentiles (26:17).

When he gets there, he will "open their eyes so that they may turn from darkness to light and from the dominion of Satan to God, that they may receive forgiveness of sins and an inheritance among those who have been set apart by faith in me" (26:18). This is a significant description of Christian outreach, coming, as it does, from Jesus himself. He says Saul (and, by inference, us) will open people's eyes. So human agency, in conjunction with the Spirit's ministry of enlightenment, will enable people to comprehend the gospel.

Then, they can turn "from darkness to light and from the dominion of Satan to God." That confirms the true nature of spiritual warfare. Jesus sees two kingdoms in conflict. He pictures believers attacking Satan's fortresses and releasing the prisoners held there.

Jesus also says the people Saul reaches will receive the forgiveness of sin and an inheritance, that is, a place as God's adopted children in heaven (26:18).

## On to Damascus

For more detailed instructions, Jesus told Saul to go on to Damascus, a far safer place than back to Jerusalem. There, "You will be told what you must do" (v. 6).

> The men with Saul stood speechless, for they heard the sound of someone's voice but saw no one![1] Saul picked himself up off the ground, but when he opened his eyes he was blind. So his companions led him by the hand to Damascus. He remained there blind for three days and did not eat or drink. (vs. 7-9)

Was Saul lying in a bed? Or sitting and staring at nothing? We know he was praying from verse 11. No doubt, he had a lot to think and pray about.

## Saul's Theological Revolution

What was he thinking? We can draw some hints from the book of Galatians. Saul, renamed Paul, said years later,

> The gospel which was preached by me is not according to man. For I neither received it from man, nor was I taught it, but I received it through a revelation of Jesus Christ. (Galatians 1:11-12)

---

1. Later, we read that Paul's traveling companions fell down also (26:13), but apparently stood back up while the vision was still in progress as described here in chapter 9. Another point of confusion is what they saw and heard. In Acts 22:9 Paul says, "Those who were with me saw the light, to be sure, but did not understand the voice of the one who was speaking to me." He doesn't say they couldn't hear the voice, but that they couldn't understand it. Here in chapter 9 he says, "The men who traveled with him stood speechless, hearing the voice but seeing no one" (v. 7) So they couldn't see Jesus, but they could hear him. Read side by side, there are no contradictions in these three accounts.

But here in Acts 9, Luke says a believer named Ananias and some other brothers came and announced the gospel to him. How can he say he wasn't taught it by man?

In all probability, Paul had already inferred much of this gospel before Ananias got there. Just based on his meeting Jesus on the road, he could infer at least ten critical components of his later letters.

## 1. Jesus Is the Messiah

He knew Jesus was dead. But here he was, alive. So he must have been raised from the dead, and therefore, he must be the Messiah after all. He later said that Jesus, "was declared the Son of God with power by the resurrection from the dead" (Romans 1:4).

## 2. Jesus' Atonement on the Cross

Paul knew and cited Deuteronomy 21:23, which says in part, "He who is hanged is accursed of God" (c.f. Gal. 3:13). That was one thing that made it unthinkable to Jews that Jesus could be God's Messiah. But now he had appeared in blinding light. The implication was that he must not have died for his own sins. Therefore, he must have been cursed *for us!*

There can be no doubt that Paul had been confronted with Isaiah 53 by the Christians he interrogated and tortured. There is the clear claim:

> But he [the Servant of the Lord] was pierced through for our transgressions, he was crushed for our iniquities; the chastening for our well-being fell upon him, and by his scourging we are healed... the Lord has caused the iniquity of us all to fall on him. (Isaiah 53:5-6)

Paul by now knew that Jesus was the servant of the Lord in this passage.

## 3. Rejection of His Prior Belief System

Paul now had to realize that so many of his beliefs were clearly wrong, and for all he knew, *everything* he believed might be wrong. Where did the wrongness end? The only thing he could be sure of at this point was that everything he believed had led him to a conclusion that was flat wrong. His entire existing belief system had to be jettisoned or reevaluated.

### 4. God Accepts Even the Worst Sinners

Saul now realized he had been killing and torturing true followers of God! Yet Jesus was apparently willing to accept him as a follower. Why hadn't Jesus struck Paul dead? Why was he speaking in a kind way? The conclusion was unavoidable that forgiveness and salvation were possible for even the worst sinner.

### 5. Grace

Based on the previous point, if acceptance was not based on avoiding sin, what was it based on? He saw that if salvation isn't based on good works it must be a gift—an undeserved gift! And that's what grace is.

### 6. Reinterpreted Old Testament

Saul had been schooled in the Pharisaic view of the Old Testament. That view went against each of the previous points. With his vast knowledge of Old Testament Scripture, he was able to sit in darkness without reading, and completely reassess scores, even hundreds of texts from memory. He had listened to, and debated Stephen, so he must have reflected on the points Stephen made. And how many others under interrogation pointed out messianic passages?

Obviously the rabbinic view of the role of the law must be completely changed. Was he able to realize what he later wrote: "Sin shall not be master over you, for you are no longer under law but under grace" (Romans 6:14)?

### 7. Even Gentiles?

We know from the larger version of this confrontation in chapter 26 that Jesus mentioned in passing "Gentiles, to whom I am sending you." If people are saved apart from the law, it probably follows that even Gentiles could be rescued. The entire basis for excluding Gentiles was the law, so as Stephen had argued, under the New Covenant, all are welcome. Paul knew passages like Isaiah 42:6, where God says to the Servant of the Lord:

> "I am the Lord, I have called you in righteousness, I will also hold you by the hand and watch over you, and I will appoint

you as a covenant to the people, as a light to the nations [i.e. the Gentiles]."

Had he already heard that the Christians were accepting Samaritans? Probably yes, because as the chief investigator of the new sect, word of such developments would have quickly traveled to Saul.

## 8. The Mystical Union of Believers with Jesus

He must have pondered Jesus' saying, "Why do you persecute me?" He had never met Jesus. Otherwise, he would surely have mentioned it at some point. And he would have recognized him here instead of asking who he was. Anyway, he wasn't persecuting Jesus; he was persecuting Jesus' followers. But that's not how Jesus said it. He was clear- "You are persecuting me." How odd!

So Jesus made no distinction between himself and his followers, as though they were fused together. He surely had heard his victims talk about receiving the Spirit. This mystical union is the basis for: 1) the Body of Christ (Romans 12:5 says "We, who are many, are one body in Christ, and individually members one of another.") and 2) our new identity in Christ (e.g., Romans 6:1-11).

## 9. Jesus' Second Coming

The Messiah is to reign as King, and that hadn't happened yet. So, Jesus must be coming back. No doubt he had heard this claim from believers he interrogated. Now he realized it was true.

## 10. The Deity of Christ

Paul knew passages like Isaiah 9:6 where the Messiah is called "Mighty God" and "Eternal Father." He knew Micah said of the Messiah, "His goings forth are from long ago, from the days of eternity" (Micah 5:2). And he had just seen Jesus in a dazzling light. Again, his victims had no doubt claimed Jesus was divine. Did Saul comprehend the Trinity? Maybe not, but he was already struggling with it.

So based on these ten inferences from his vision on the road, Paul could correctly say that he didn't get his gospel from any human, but directly from Jesus in a vision. That's what he told the Galatians.

## Still in Damascus

We left Saul blind and neither eating nor drinking.

Meanwhile:

> Now there was a believer in Damascus named Ananias. The Lord spoke to him in a vision, calling, "Ananias!"
>
> "Yes, Lord!" he replied.
>
> The Lord said, "Go over to Straight Street, to the house of Judas. When you get there, ask for a man from Tarsus named Saul. He is praying to me right now. I have shown him a vision of a man named Ananias coming in and laying hands on him so he can see again."
>
> "But Lord," exclaimed Ananias, "I've heard many people talk about the terrible things this man has done to the believers in Jerusalem! And he is authorized by the leading priests to arrest everyone who calls upon your name."
>
> But the Lord said, "Go, for Saul is my chosen instrument to take my message to the Gentiles and to kings, as well as to the people of Israel. And I will show him how much he must suffer for my name's sake." (vs. 10-16)

What courage it must have taken for Ananias to walk up to that door and knock!

## Why so long?

Why did Jesus leave Paul sitting for three days blind? He could have sent Ananias over earlier.

There are several likely reasons:

- In his blinded state, Saul had no distractions. He could do nothing but sit, think, and pray.

- It must have taken some time to reach the realizations we just went through above.

- The blindness would have been a good block from any thought to the effect, "Maybe I hallucinated that?" The blindness was real enough, and showed that the encounter was real.

- The three days were evidence enough that the blindness wasn't just a momentary reaction to light. Three days in, it was crystal clear that this condition was going nowhere. That led directly to the importance of Ananias.

When Ananias arrived:

> He laid his hands on him and said, "Brother Saul, the Lord Jesus, who appeared to you on the road, has sent me so that you might regain your sight and be filled with the Holy Spirit." Instantly something like scales fell from Saul's eyes, and he regained his sight. Then he got up and was baptized. Afterward he ate some food and regained his strength. Saul stayed with the believers in Damascus for a few days. (vs. 17-19)

The laying on of hands had the same effect we've seen earlier. God was telling Saul, "This guy speaks for me."

What an exciting conversation must have ensued! He stayed with Ananias and his buddies for several days, questions pouring out, probably taking notes. Were Saul's traveling companions there? We don't know, but there's a good chance they were converted too after seeing the light and hearing the voice, even if they didn't understand it.

The result of these talks was that Saul felt the urge to preach. Anyone who has a preaching gift knows exactly what it's like to learn deep things from God and then feel the overwhelming urge to get that truth out where people can believe it.

At the synagogue, Saul's hearers were stunned: "Is this not he who in Jerusalem destroyed those who called on this name?" (v. 21). And as time went by with more study and growing comprehension, we read, "But Saul kept increasing in strength and confounding the Jews who lived at Damascus by proving that this Jesus is the Christ" (v. 22).

"Proving" here is possible only because his hearers were Bible believers. The form of proof was fulfilled prophecy. This is why God set up the prophetic message so many centuries earlier. To Bible believers, one passage after another becomes impossible to explain unless Jesus is real.

# Three More Years

Altogether, Paul stayed in Damascus for three years. At one point he had to flee to Arabia. But the trip to Arabia wasn't three years long, as some claim. Rather, "I went away to Arabia, and returned once more to Damascus" (Galatians 1:17). The short-term flight to Arabia was apparently to let things cool down in Damascus. His enemies were losing it, just like Paul had with Stephen when he was confounded.

Finally, Saul's enemies went for murder. A group conspiracy to kill Saul had them watching the gates of the city day and night in case he tried taking another trip to Arabia again.

> But Saul was told about their plot, and his disciples took him by night and let him down through an opening in the wall, lowering him in a large basket. (vs. 24-25)

Notice who lowered him: "his disciples." NIV calls them "his followers," but that really misses the point. They weren't followers of Saul; they were his disciples. A disciple is a *mathetes*, a student. It's improper to call them Paul's followers. They were followers of Christ. It's also important to see that Saul was already discipling young believers. That's the primary New Testament method for raising up leaders.

The NLT calls them "the other believers," again missing the point. But they also add a footnote, admitting that the Greek actually says "his disciples." Then why not put that in the text? It's probably because most of the modern church has rejected disciple-making.

The modern western church in general doesn't believe in or practice personal disciple-making. Instead, they use classes, and for those interested, Bible colleges and seminaries. Classes and seminaries are fine. But without personal disciple-making, something is lost.

Mentoring a younger believer in the context of actual ministry and interactions in community takes equipping beyond the mere transfer of theological information. Many character issues only become evident when living together in community. That is the venue for New Testament disciple-making.

The word for disciples here is in the plural. In only three years, Saul had won probably several young men and won them into discipleship. When

Saul left Damascus, he left behind trained, competent leaders to continue the work. Leaders today should follow his example.

## The Big Picture

After the loss of Stephen and the murderous persecution that followed, God now had his man. He knew Saul inside and out, and he knew that Saul would never quit or back down. His theological training was second to none. The fact that he was a Pharisee and a rabbi would prove quite handy in the coming years. Saul would eventually account for far more positive for God than the damage done by his ferocious persecution.

# 14

## TRIP TO JERUSALEM
### ACTS 9:26-43

As Saul faced south toward Jerusalem, what was he thinking? The persecution in Jerusalem had apparently cooled off after three or more years. But Saul was a special case. He was a maximum traitor in the view of the powerful leaders in Jerusalem. If they caught him, his life would be on the line. Indeed, his enemies did eventually develop a plot to kill him.

So why go there? He later said of this move that he did it "to become acquainted with Cephas," another name for Peter (Galatians 1:18).

Luke gives us more detail:

> When he came to Jerusalem, he was trying to associate with the disciples; but they were all afraid of him, not believing that he was a disciple. (Acts 9:26)

The word "disciples" here doesn't necessarily mean the Twelve. Luke sometimes used the word disciple to refer to all believers. The believers in Jerusalem suspected that Paul was an infiltrator, pretending to be a believer in order to discover who the believers were and where they could be found. Nobody would talk to him except for one of the true heroes of Acts—Barnabas. He must have overcome his fear and talked to Saul.

Barnabas came from Cyprus, so he may have been a member of the Synagogue of the Freedmen where Saul and Stephen originally collided. Perhaps they had been friends before the Stephen event. We know it was Barnabas who reached out and got Paul's story:

> Then Barnabas brought him to the apostles and told them how Saul had seen the Lord on the way to Damascus and how the Lord had spoken to Saul. He also told them that Saul had preached boldly in the name of Jesus in Damascus. (v. 27)

Based on Barnabas' endorsement, the other apostles accepted him. Apparently, they had not heard Paul's story before. According to Saul's later letter, he "stayed with him [Peter] fifteen days" (Galatians 1:19). How exciting this must have been for Saul! To sit with the leader of Jesus' disciples, to hear living accounts of what Jesus said and did.

This would be the same material we have in the Gospels. We can well imagine Saul taking notes. We know he later refers to a written source in his possession, as we saw earlier. He may have taken notes on Peter's personal accounts, or he may have spent much of the time copying a written account already compiled by the apostles.

Saul wasn't afraid of being captured by the authorities, probably because he knew, based on what Jesus said—that he had a mission for Paul that was not yet complete:

> And he was with them, moving about freely in Jerusalem, speaking out boldly in the name of the Lord. And he was talking and arguing with the Hellenistic Jews; but they were attempting to put him to death. (vs. 28-29)

The statement that Saul argued with the "Hellenistic Jews" sounds like he may have gone back to his old Synagogue of the Freedmen. It would make sense because he would be going as the accuser of Stephen, now back saying, "I was wrong!" And he would have told his amazing story about meeting Jesus. But it didn't work very well. Maybe some believed, but the rest, unable to refute him, planned to kill him.

> But when the brethren learned of it, they brought him down to Caesarea and sent him away to Tarsus. (v. 30)

Caesarea is a port city run by the Romans, not the Jews. Getting away with murder there would be significantly more difficult. Tarsus is a city in the province of Cilicia, several hundred miles north of Jerusalem. He probably landed in Antioch of Syria and went overland from there to Tarsus. At this point, Saul disappears from the story in Acts for at least eight, and possibly eleven years. But he was still active. He explained:

> After that visit [to Jerusalem] I went north into the provinces of Syria and Cilicia. And still the churches in Christ that are in Judea didn't know me personally. All they knew was that people were saying, "The one who used to persecute us is now preaching the very faith he tried to destroy!" (Galatians 1:21-23)

So Paul preached his way through Syria to Cilicia. Later, we will see evidence that he was successful in planting multiple churches during this period.

## Mapping out the Timeline

In Galatians 1 and 2, Saul, now called Paul, recounts his first two visits to Jerusalem. The first visit was after three years in Damascus (Galatians 1:18). That's the visit we've been studying here in Acts 9.

He goes on to say, "Then after an interval of fourteen years I went up again to Jerusalem with Barnabas, taking Titus along also. It was because of a revelation that I went up" (Galatians 2:1-2). This second visit to Jerusalem is described in Acts 11:27-30.

Paul says the reason for the second visit was "because of a revelation." That perfectly fits with the prophecy by the Agabus that there would be a famine in Judea (11:28). Paul went with Barnabas and Titus to bring a financial gift for the famine. He did not go to Jerusalem because of a dispute over circumcision, as in Acts 15. That was later.

Some commentators miss this point and mistakenly claim that Paul's second visit to Jerusalem was for the Jerusalem council described in Acts 15. The main reason readers take this view is Paul's statement, "after an interval of fourteen years." Adding the initial three years in Damascus to fourteen years here gives a total of seventeen years between Paul's conversion and the second visit. That won't fit within the boundaries of Jesus' death in AD 33 and the Jerusalem council in AD 49. Seventeen years after AD 33 would be AD 50. In fact, as we will see later, this second visit after fourteen years could have happened no later than AD 48.

The solution is simple: The fourteen years are not counted from Paul's first visit, resulting in a total of seventeen years. Rather, the fourteen years are counted from his conversion in about AD 34 and the 3 years are not consecutive.

This isn't clear in English translations like the NASB, which reads "Then, after an interval of fourteen years..." That makes it sound like the fourteen years are *after* ther thee years in Damascus. But the words "an interval of" are not in the Greek text. It just says, "after fourteen years," that is, fourteen years as a believer. The three and the fourteen are concurrent, not consecutive.

So the interval between the first and second visit would have been at most eleven years (14-3=11). And it could be less, considering the ancient tendency to count any part of a year as the whole. That means it could be as few as nine or ten years. The best dates would be about AD 34 for Paul's conversion. Then, fourteen years later, in AD 48, he visited the Jerusalem for the second time. This question becomes important later, as it affects the interpretation of Galatians.[1]

## Still Growing

Before going on with the story, Luke lets us know how the body of Christ throughout Israel was doing:

> So the church throughout all Judea and Galilee and Samaria enjoyed peace, being built up; and going on in the fear of the Lord and in the comfort of the Holy Spirit, it continued to increase. (v. 31)

The persecution had subsided, and they were enjoying a respite.

---

1. Another reason Paul's second visit in Galatians cannot refer to the Jerusalem council is that it would contradict Acts 11. The Jerusalem council was not Paul's second visit. It was his third, and this is admitted by late date interpreters. They argue that the second visit wasn't important enough to mention. Or, of course, in the view of liberal interpreters, either Paul or Luke lied.

Finally, the second visit is not the Jerusalem council because if it was, it's inconceivable that Paul wouldn't mention that the elders and apostles had agreed that circumcision was unnecessary for salvation. That's one of the main points in the book of Galatians. But under the late chronology, the council already happened, yet Paul failed to mention it.

# Peter Hits the Road

After meeting with Saul, Peter began to travel.

> Now as Peter was traveling through all those regions, he came
> down also to the saints who lived at Lydda. There he found
> a man named Aeneas, who had been bedridden eight years,
> for he was paralyzed. Peter said to him, "Aeneas, Jesus Christ
> heals you; get up and make your bed." Immediately he got up.
> (vs. 32-34)

Lydda is modern-day Lod, lying between Jerusalem and Tel Aviv. Already,
a group of believers had sprung up. As with the man healed at the temple earlier, a man like Aeneas, who had been paralyzed for eight years,
would have been known to this whole small village. The impact would
have been stunning. The gospel, already known in this town, no doubt
received a whole new hearing. Luke says, "And all who lived at Lydda
and Sharon saw him, and they turned to the Lord" (v. 35). It sounds like
most of the people in these villages believed.

He continued down to the coast at the southern edge of Tel Aviv, which
now encompasses ancient Joppa. There he raised to life a believing woman named Tabitha, or Dorcas. Again, she was well known in the town as
a doer of good, so the impact was immediate and powerful: "It became
known all over Joppa, and many believed in the Lord" (v. 42). Here we
have a case of an apostle raising someone from the dead. Old Testament
prophets did the same thing (2 Kings 4:32-35).

Peter sent the mourners out before he raises her. Was there too much
noise? Did he need quiet to pray?

The final verse takes us to the next story. "And Peter stayed many days
in Joppa with a tanner named Simon" (v. 43). "Many days" sounds like
a year or more. We can't say where this account or the next story about
Cornelius stand in the chronology of Acts. Luke probably got this material from a direct interview with Peter many years later. It seems likely
that he interviewed Peter during Paul's imprisonment at Caesarea.

The next date post comes in Acts 11, when the Antioch church took a gift
to Jerusalem in the care of Paul and Barnabas. That was in about AD 46.
So this collection of accounts about Peter's ministry in Lydda and Joppa
could be anywhere between Paul's departure for Cilicia (about AD 37)

and the famine mentioned in Acts 11:27ff (about AD 48). I'm inclined to see it earlier in that span.

## The Big Picture

Luke gives slight coverage to this ten-year gap, but he does cover key events, like the raising of Tabitha, and the striking healing of Aeneas. And in both cases, the response of people was substantial. Peter must have spent some time consolidating and training this new outburst of faith. But there was still a major flaw in the pattern of ministry in the church at this time. They weren't reaching out to Gentiles.

# 15

# THE THIRD BARRIER FALLS

## ACTS 10

The next account in Acts is one of the most important in advancing God's plan. The third door, the door to the Gentiles, was still unopened. That was about to change, but it wouldn't be easy.

> In Caesarea there lived a Roman army officer named Cornelius, who was a captain of the Italian Regiment. He was a devout, God-fearing man, as was everyone in his household. He gave generously to the poor and prayed regularly to God. (Acts 10:1-2)

Cornelius was a "God fearer" in the language of Acts. These are Gentiles who had realized the truth of the Old Testament, and monotheism, but who had not undergone circumcision and the other steps in becoming a full Jewish convert, or "proselyte."

We will run into these "God fearers" repeatedly in Acts. They were often responsive to the gospel, having less inclination to hang onto traditional Judaism. As such, they provided a bridge between traditional rabbinic Judaism and the rest of the Gentile community.

In almost every city where Paul and his team spread the gospel, they began with the synagogue. But in almost all synagogues they found both Jews and God-fearing Gentiles.

God reached out to this believer, Cornelius:

> One afternoon about three o'clock, he had a vision in which he saw an angel of God coming toward him. "Cornelius!" the angel said.
>
> Cornelius stared at him in terror. "What is it, sir?" he asked the angel.
>
> And the angel replied, "Your prayers and gifts to the poor have been received by God as an offering! Now send some men to Joppa, and summon a man named Simon Peter. He is staying with Simon, a tanner who lives near the seashore."
>
> As soon as the angel was gone, Cornelius called two of his household servants and a devout soldier, one of his personal attendants. He told them what had happened and sent them off to Joppa. (vs. 3-8)

Meanwhile, God was also working on Peter:

> The next day as Cornelius's messengers were nearing the town, Peter went up on the flat roof to pray. It was about noon, and he was hungry. But while a meal was being prepared, he fell into a trance. He saw the sky open, and something like a large sheet was let down by its four corners. In the sheet were all sorts of animals, reptiles, and birds. Then a voice said to him, "Get up, Peter; kill and eat them."
>
> "No, Lord," Peter declared. "I have never eaten anything that our Jewish laws have declared impure and unclean."
>
> But the voice spoke again: "Do not call something unclean if God has made it clean." The same vision was repeated three times. Then the sheet was suddenly pulled up to heaven. (vs. 9-16)

Several things stand out in this account. First, God lowers a sheet with animals forbidden under kosher rules. According to the Old Testament, reptiles were definitely unclean, and some birds were, especially raptors and scavengers. So this collection was not made up of animals that had only later become non-kosher under rabbinic teaching. They included animals named in Scripture as prohibited.

That's why Peter had so much trouble accepting the offering. They were prohibited under the Mosaic Covenant, but that was all changing. He answered the voice saying, "No Lord," so he knew the vision came from Jesus. Yet he ironically refused it. This is a clear case of a follower of Jesus refusing to follow where Jesus led if it meant breaking with the past.

That's not unusual. Arguably, you could walk into most traditional churches in the west and see features on every side that come from hundreds of years ago. And many of those features are distasteful to modern people. They should have been discarded.

This section in Acts documents the difficulty God had getting his people to accept a radical departure from the Old Covenant, and just as much from traditional, rabbinic teaching.

Amazingly, the vision is repeated three times and Peter stubbornly still refuses the offering each time!

## Changing the Law?

How could God change his law? Isn't his moral nature fixed and unchangeable?

First, the dietary laws in the Old Testament weren't moral laws. They were for teaching. Some symbolized the distinctiveness between the people of God from other people. Some of them, like prohibiting pork, could have been partially for health reasons. Others reminded people of symbolic connections, like scavengers, and their connection to death. Touching any dead body made one ritually unclean. It's a way of expressing that the problem is sin, leading to death—something that shouldn't have ever happened.

But although the dietary laws were non-moral, the Jews of Peter's day didn't view it that way. They thought eating a forbidden food was just as bad as lying, stealing, or other violations.

The same goes for other rabbinic restrictions. In this story, God wants Peter to preach the gospel to Gentiles in their home—something the rabbis forbade. They would strenuously resist entering a Gentile's home, arguing that it made one unclean. Of course, the Bible contained no such teaching.

Peter was a loyal Jew, as were almost all believers at this time. They really believed it was God's will to continue practicing the religion of their fathers. But Jesus came to bring change. The disciples should have known this because Jesus already signaled it when he wouldn't follow the rabbinic customs, such as the ritual hand washing before meals.

He also rejected their view that evil entered people from the outside through what you eat or what you touch. He said, "There is nothing outside the man which can defile him if it goes into him; but the things which proceed out of the man are what defile the man." Mark later saw the implication: "Thus He declared all foods clean" (Mark 7:15, 19).

Even when the rules come from Scripture, when God says it's time to change, his people have to be ready to follow. God wasn't changing his nature; he was changing direction to a new covenant. As the book of Hebrews explains, this was always the plan. The Mosaic Covenant was only temporary.

## Answer the Door

> Peter was very perplexed. What could the vision mean? Just then the men sent by Cornelius found Simon's house. Standing outside the gate, they asked if a man named Simon Peter was staying there.
>
> Meanwhile, as Peter was puzzling over the vision, the Holy Spirit said to him, "Three men have come looking for you. Get up, go downstairs, and go with them without hesitation. Don't worry, for I have sent them."
>
> So Peter went down and said, "I'm the man you are looking for. Why have you come?"
>
> They said, "We were sent by Cornelius, a Roman officer. He is a devout and God-fearing man, well respected by all the Jews. A holy angel instructed him to summon you to his house so that he can hear your message." (vs. 17-22)

The Spirit needed to say, "Don't worry," because these could have been persecutors hunting for the Christian leader. Instead, it turned out to be God working both ends against the middle, just as we've seen before with the Ethiopian eunuch. When you see this kind of synchrony, it's a sure sign that God is at work. This is no coincidence.

## At Cornelius' House

> They arrived in Caesarea the following day. Cornelius was waiting for them and had called together his relatives and close friends. As Peter entered his home, Cornelius fell at his feet and worshiped him. But Peter pulled him up and said, "Stand up! I'm a human being just like you!" So they talked together and went inside, where many others were assembled. (vs. 24-27)

What a setting! Anyone with a heart for evangelism would view this gathering with zeal and terrific excitement. As they gather and take seats, what will Peter's first line be?

> Peter told them, "You know it is against our laws for a Jewish man to enter a Gentile home like this or to associate with you." (v. 28)

That's great! Are you kidding? That's your opening pitch? Mercifully, he went on:

> "But God has shown me that I should no longer think of anyone as impure or unclean."

Better, but still rather patronizing.

Peter declared the main point: "There is peace with God through Jesus Christ, who is Lord of all" (v. 36). Then he went on to recount the life of Jesus: "You know what happened throughout Judea, beginning in Galilee, after John began preaching his message of baptism" (v. 37). In the full version, of which this is a summary, he probably included John the Baptist's endorsement of Jesus as the coming one. John had terrific credibility with the people.

"And you know that God anointed Jesus of Nazareth with the Holy Spirit and with power" (v. 38). This probably refers to Jesus' baptism, where the Spirit came down in public.

"Then Jesus went around doing good and healing all who were oppressed by the devil, for God was with him" (v. 38). Everyone in Judea and Galilee knew about Jesus' miracles. The Gospels are clear that his renown spread far and wide. Peter is confident that they had already heard about it. He probably told some specific stories.

Then, "They put him to death by hanging him on a cross" (v. 39). He must have explained the significance of the cross. The atoning role the cross played is essential.

"But God raised him to life on the third day" (v. 40). The resurrection is also an essential part of the gospel.

"We were those who ate and drank with him after he rose from the dead" (v. 41). He must have told some stories about how they were so astonished that they thought he was a ghost.

"He is the one all the prophets testified about" (v. 43). Peter definitely went through some key messianic prophecy. This is what he has done in every previous sermon. It was the standard way to demonstrate Jesus' authenticity.

"Everyone who believes in him will have their sins forgiven through his name" (v. 43). Here is the punch line: Salvation by faith alone.

Cornelius and the room full of people had been believing Peter line by line as he spoke. At this point, we read, "Even as Peter was saying these things, the Holy Spirit fell upon all who were listening to the message" (v. 44). How did they know the Spirit fell? "They heard them speaking in other tongues and praising God" (v. 46).

Peter didn't even get to finish his speech. At the point where he explained salvation by faith, their faith reached a critical mass. There was nothing to wait for. How different from the Samaritan experience! There, they had to wait until Peter, the carrier of the keys, showed up. But in this case, Peter was already present. So the suddenness of the Spirit's arrival here tends to confirm the view that Peter's presence was key to whether the Spirit delayed.

Notice that, "The Jewish believers who came with Peter were amazed that the gift of the Holy Spirit had been poured out on the Gentiles, too" (v. 45). They were amazed! Even after all that had happened with correlated visions, they still couldn't believe God would accept Gentiles. This shows the level of racial prejudice God was dealing with.

Then Peter asked, "Can anyone object to their being baptized, now that they have received the Holy Spirit just as we did?" So he gave orders for them to be baptized in the name of Jesus Christ. Afterward Cornelius asked him to stay with them for several days. (vs. 47-48)

What a wonderful chance to fill in a group of new believers on everything Jesus did and taught. We already saw how this passage proves that conversion comes before baptism, and that baptism does not confer salvation.

## The Big Picture

The Cornelius event was an outstanding victory for Jesus. Peter and his friends were probably anxious to get back to their other believing friends to recount what had happened. Surely, they would be excited and full of joy at the news?

No.

Their eyes went right past the spectacular work of God to their own prejudice.

# 16

# GIVE AN ACCOUNT
## ACTS 11:1-19

Word spread about what happened in Caesarea. Eventually, Peter and his crew went back to Jerusalem. They must have been ecstatic when they heard about such an incredible movement of the Holy Spirit, right? Not exactly.

> But when Peter arrived back in Jerusalem, the Jewish believers criticized him. "You entered the home of Gentiles and even ate with them!" they said. (Acts 11:2-3)

That's it? That's what they got out of the story of Cornelius' household coming to faith?

This failure to comprehend what God is doing combined with a fixation on legalistic rules makes for a very sick outlook. Part of their problem was that they didn't have the full story. But God often has to deal with this kind of view, even up to this day.

"Hey, thirty people came to faith this month!"

"Yeah, well, I heard there was a lot of cussing going on there. And they were vaping."

It's hard to know how to respond. You're wondering, does that really matter? Did you hear what we said?

Peter was ready, and had the answers. His reply becomes a classic explanation of how we can know the will of God. He explains eight distinct elements that made the case.

## Prayer

He begins his answer, "While I was praying" (v. 5). The leading of the Holy Spirit doesn't come to the heedless or the preoccupied. If you want to hear from God's Spirit, you have to devote some time to prayer. Coming before God, you need to present yourself and ask if he has anything for you. And you need to listen. God does speak, but it's not usually in words and sentences. He causes you to know what he's saying. The voice of the Spirit is not usually loud, but subtle, and insensitive believers could easily miss hearing him.

## Vision

Next, he says, "I went into a trance and saw a vision" (v. 5). Direct visions are unusual. One could go decades without seeing a vision. Or, one might come when you least expect it, just like in this case.

Most visions that we see in Scripture have to do with furthering God's program, perhaps by reassuring one of his workers to press on. Or he may reveal more about his nature. You see that clearly in this case. God was giving Peter a vision in order to reassure him about breaking through to the Gentiles.

People who aren't working for God and his purposes have little likelihood of seeing a direct vision. But we have no reason to be cynical about the reality of visions. God speaks. We could hardly claim we have a personal relationship with God if he never said anything.

On the other hand, Paul warns us not to base our beliefs on one who is "taking his stand on visions he has seen" (Colossians 2:18). People who claim God is talking to them need to be carefully examined. What is their way of life? Do they "profess to know God, but by their deeds deny him?" (Titus 1:16). And is the content of the vision biblical? Peter's vision passes these tests.

# Correlated Leading

"Just then three men who had been sent from Caesarea arrived at the house where we were staying" (v. 11). God frequently confirms his direction by giving the same leading to more than one person.

Particularly when leading correlates in the absence of any prior contact (like in this case), it lends added credibility. People who spend time together may have talked about the very things the vision communicates. That could bring in the power of suggestion. But how could these three men at the door know that Peter was on the roof having a vision at that very moment? Correlated leading is a way God often gives his people more assurance that he is the one speaking.

# Inner Spiritual Prompting

Peter went on, "The Holy Spirit told me to go with them and not to worry that they were Gentiles" (v. 12). The Holy Spirit can speak to our spirits. Although people often recount the Spirit's leading in full sentences, the actual leading often, but not always, bypasses formal language. It's a sudden awareness of what to do that comes through direct thought. To spiritual beings, it's not always necessary to encode a message in words. God thinks to us.

Many believers today are suspicious of this idea because it leaves too much to subjective feeling. That is a valid fear. Anyone who has worked long with people has seen foolish ones blaming their foolishness on God. "It's okay, God told me he wanted me to be happy," declared one woman who had left her husband and kids to move in with another lover. That's an extreme case, but lesser examples abound.

Inner prompting is reliable when coming to mature, biblically based believers. When hearing a false message, such believers know God would never say something like that. That makes it hard for the evil one or a person's own flesh to counterfeit God's voice. Young believers, however, are in danger if they put too much reliance on inner promptings.

I had an experience that illustrates the inner voice of the Holy Spirit. A friend and I were having dinner at some other friend's home. As they were preparing the meal, I went into the living room to pray for the Bible study I was giving that night. As I stood staring out the big window at an early snow flurry, the phone rang. (This was before cell phones).

I looked back at the door into the kitchen where the phone was, with a sudden clear thought: that call is for me. That seemed strange, because nobody knew where we were. The idea of dinner came up suddenly, and we hadn't told anyone where we were going. Sure enough, seconds later one of our hosts came to the door and said, "It's for you."

I strode over and picked up the house phone. The call was from a believer I respected, who said she had guessed where I might be. She had a message that isn't important for this story. We agreed to talk about it later, because what she was saying had major implications for my life.

I went back into the living room, marveling that I somehow knew that call was for me. As I stood again before the window, another sense came to me to the effect of, "Did you get my message?" I suddenly knew with certainty that the message was real.

## Discerning in Community

Peter explained, "These six brothers also went with me" (v. 12). This is a significant detail. Peter didn't go off on his own. By bringing along a team, he removed any possibility that he was wrongly reading into the situation. It also sounds like they made a corporate decision to baptize the new Gentile believers (10:47).

This principle is also the basis for plurality of eldership in each local church. More on that later.

## Providential Circumstances

Again, when Peter and his friends arrived at Cornelius' house, they heard the story about the angel visiting him and giving directions. This is further detail about correlated leading. But a related concept is that God may arrange circumstances as part of his leading.

Believers should be careful when concluding that God has arranged a situation as a way to guide them. The Law of Moses forbids divination or reading of omens (Deuteronomy 18:10). Also, the Old Testament use of lots was discontinued under the New Covenant, as was the practice of "fleecing" God. Fleecing is when a believer like Gideon spells out a sequence of actions in advance, which will signify God's will (Judges 6:36-40). These methods of determining what God wanted are from an earlier time when people were not indwelt by the Holy Spirit.

The main usefulness of circumstances is in providing negative leading. That is, when a given course of action is *not* God's will. For instance, if you're planning on speaking at a conference and your plane has to land because of mechanical problems, and you are unable to find any other way to get there in time, you can safely assume that speaking there was not God's will.

Positive circumstances, on the other hand, usually tell us little, because the positive circumstance could be one of many positive outcomes. For instance, a student applies to Harvard and gets accepted. Does that mean it's God's will to go there? What about the ten other colleges that also accepted him or her? Being rejected by Harvard would, on the other hand, be a good indication that God is not leading the student to go there.

## Spiritual Fruit Borne

Next, Peter recounts, "And as I began to speak, the Holy Spirit fell upon them just as he did upon us at the beginning" (v. 15). Any time God uses a given course of action to win people to faith in Jesus, that's a strong argument that the action was within his will.

This is a general maxim, because it's not always true. For example, corrupt preachers profit exorbitantly from their ministry or even use their influence to get sex from people. Yet, God may use that corrupt preacher to win people over to faith. It doesn't mean the whole situation is God's will. God is more interested in seeing people won than in insisting on perfection.

When you assess the fruit being borne, you are really assessing "spiritual expediency." You can see Paul using this approach in 1 Corinthians 16:8-9: "But I will remain in Ephesus until Pentecost; for a wide door for effective service has opened to me, and there are many adversaries."

Here, he's not saying the Spirit told him to stay. Rather, the reason (signified by the word "for") is that in his judgment, more spiritual fruit will result from his staying there longer. This kind of leading is common for Christian workers. The worker assesses the situation and selects the option that will probably result in the maximum spiritual fruit being born. Of course, these judgments are made while praying and will usually make sense to the rest of the team you're on.

## Scripture

Peter concludes, "And I remembered the word of the Lord, how he used to say, 'John baptized with water, but you will be baptized with the Holy Spirit'" (v. 16). Remembering the words of Jesus here is the same as remembering Scripture. Most communications from God come through the word. Even when God uses other subjective channels, it's usually confirmed by the word.

Here, Peter remembered what Jesus said and how it came to pass when they received the baptism by the Holy Spirit on Pentecost. He also remembered that it included speaking in tongues and other inspired utterances. Peter drew the natural inference: "Therefore if God gave to them the same gift as he gave to us also after believing in the Lord Jesus Christ, who was I that I could stand in God's way?" (v. 17).

## Their Response

The leaders were satisfied with Peter's rationale. "When they heard this, they quieted down and glorified God, saying, 'Well then, God has granted to the Gentiles also the repentance that leads to life'" (v. 18). So God made his point and everything came out well.

No.

Luke, the Gentile, adds the most pertinent comment: "So then those who were scattered because of the persecution that occurred in connection with Stephen made their way to Phoenicia and Cyprus and Antioch, speaking the word to no one except to Jews alone" (v. 19).

What an astonishing aftermath! Had they heard what happened? Probably, but the power of habit and tradition was too strong. After all God had done to make his point, his people didn't connect it with actual deeds.

## The Big Picture

By this time in history, God had put his own stamp of approval, and really his insistence, that outreach to Gentiles go forward. But that work would not go forward until some believers dared to break out of their cultural and religious straitjacket. It was time.

# 17

# GENTILE BREAKOUT
## ACTS 11:20-30

Finally, it happened!

> But there were some of them, men of Cyprus and Cyrene, who came to Antioch and began speaking to the Greeks also, preaching the Lord Jesus. And the hand of the Lord was with them, and a large number who believed turned to the Lord. (Acts 11:20-21)

This is the breakthrough God had been after. It was believers from Cyprus and Cyrene who crossed over to reach out to Gentiles, so they were probably Hellenistic Jews—those more assimilated to Greco-Roman culture. God immediately validated their efforts by drawing large numbers of Gentiles to faith.

In the context of what large numbers are in Acts, what would it take to make Luke say, "a large number who believed turned to the Lord?" We can safely assume that hundreds or maybe even more believed. This became a spiritual awakening that overwhelmed the local leaders.

> The news about them reached the ears of the church at Jerusalem, and they sent Barnabas off to Antioch. Barnabas

was a good man, full of the Holy Spirit and strong in faith. And
many people were brought to the Lord. (vs. 22, 24)

Normally, leaders in New Testament churches raised up new leaders
from within the local group. But there are cases where growth becomes
so intense that bringing in outside help makes sense.

They sent Barnabas, whom the text extols for his godly character. Again,
Luke says, "And many people were brought to the Lord" (v. 24). This is
*after* the earlier "many." Such language could hardly describe less than
hundreds of people. Antioch was a large city at this time in history.

From this point on, the spiritual epicenter of God's outreach shifted from
Jerusalem to Antioch. The Jerusalem leadership failed to embrace God's
heart for all people. Even much later in the book of Acts we find many of
them still resistant to God's direction in accepting Gentiles as they were
and discarding the Old Covenant.

## Saul Reappears

Barnabas was discerning enough to realize the exploding movement in
Antioch needed more leaders. He went in person northward to Tarsus to
find Saul and recruit him to come to Antioch. The year is AD 47.

We will later see evidence that Saul had been busy the whole time he was
in Syria and Cilicia, including planting multiple churches between AD
37 and 47. We don't know if he had undergone his own revolution in
reaching out to Gentiles. He was still using his Hebraic name, Saul. He
certainly underwent a full paradigm shift when he got to Antioch and
saw what God was doing there.

Luke says, "Both of them stayed there with the church for a full year,
teaching large crowds of people" (v. 26). Again, we see the emphasis
on large numbers in this city. Their ministry is described as "teaching"
rather than evangelism. That makes sense in a setting where vigorous
evangelism is already happening. The need of the hour was to ground
new believers in the word and to train leaders.

Luke also comments that here in Antioch is where believers were first
called Christians. The word "Christian" is the Greek word *Christos*
(anointed one, or messiah) joined to a Roman suffix "ian," meaning
a supporter or imitator. Scholars believe it was not a word created by

Christians, but rather by their enemies. It was a derisive term, also meaning "little Christs." The believers apparently thought the title fit and accepted it. However, we don't see it used much in the New Testament. The more popular name was "The Way."

## Famine in Judea

During this year in Antioch, a famine occurred.

> During this time some prophets traveled from Jerusalem to Antioch. One of them named Agabus stood up in one of the meetings and predicted by the Spirit that a great famine was coming upon the entire Roman world. (This was fulfilled during the reign of Claudius.) (vs. 27-28)

A number of famines are well-attested between AD 44 and 48, but it doesn't appear that they all happened at the same time. This was more of a rolling famine in different areas of the empire. Josephus confirms there was a severe famine in Judea lasting two to three years at this time.[1]

> So the believers in Antioch decided to send relief to the brothers and sisters in Judea, everyone giving as much as they could. This they did, entrusting their gifts to Barnabas and Saul to take to the elders of the church in Jerusalem. (vs. 29-30)

While the famine was spread over a lengthy period, we can confidently place this trip to Jerusalem in AD 47 or early AD 48. That's because Luke says Saul was only in Antioch for a year, and the first missionary journey followed immediately. For reasons we will see later, the first journey must go from spring to fall of AD 48.

This event also demonstrates the apostles' view that distant churches in need should not be ignored, just because they are far away. Paul consistently saw the needs of the poor in Judea as a problem for the whole body of Christ. He taught new churches as far away as Greece to give generously to the needy in Judea.

Today, the western church is awash in money, including wasted money, while much of the body of Christ lives near starvation. We should be following the example of the apostolic church in prioritizing ministry to the poor in developing countries.

---

1. Flavius Josephus, *Antiquities* 20.2.5.

# Second Journey to Jerusalem

So the three leaders journeyed to Jerusalem with the gift. This is also the same visit to Jerusalem Paul mentions in Galatians 2 where he met with some apostles:

> I submitted to them the gospel which I preach among the Gentiles, but I did so in private to those who were of reputation, for fear that I might be running, or had run, in vain. But not even Titus, who was with me, though he was a Greek, was compelled to be circumcised. (Galatians 2:2-3)

Luke didn't mention Titus in Acts 11, probably because it was the elders, Paul and Barnabas, who were entrusted with the gift. Titus just came along as a friend.

John, Peter, and James (Jesus' half-brother) were those "of reputation" in the meetings with Paul, as becomes clear later. When he met with them, he went over what he was preaching, probably with the main focus on the Gentile question. He may have also presented new information he had about the body of Christ, eschatology, radical grace, or end times prophecy.

It's possible that Saul had new information from Jesus that came through his vision taking him to the "third heaven." He says to the Corinthians that the vision was "fourteen years ago" (2 Corinthians 12:2). That puts it in the late 30's during the "silent years" when he was in Syria and Cilicia—before this meeting in Jerusalem. Saul had not been in touch with the Jerusalem apostles since then. It makes sense that if he had new material he would want to compare notes with the Jerusalem apostles.

The meetings went well. Paul says,

> Those who were of reputation contributed nothing to me. But on the contrary, seeing that I had been entrusted with the gospel to the uncircumcised, just as Peter had been to the circumcised (for he who effectually worked for Peter in his apostleship to the circumcised effectually worked for me also to the Gentiles), and recognizing the grace that had been given to me, James and Cephas and John, who were reputed to be pillars, gave to me and Barnabas the right hand of fellowship, so that we might go to the Gentiles and they to the

circumcised. They only asked us to remember the poor—the very thing I also was eager to do. (Galatians 2:6-10)

Nothing that Paul had to show them was problematic. On doctrine, they all agreed. And in addition, they agreed to specialize, with Paul taking the lead in outreach to Gentiles while Peter led further outreach to Jews. Remembering the poor was a consistent New Testament norm.

## The Big Picture

By the end of this chapter, all the conditions are right for launching the international mission spearheaded by Saul and Barnabas. During their first journey, Saul drops the use of Saul and goes under his Hellenistic name Paulos.

# 18

# MORE ATTACKS IN JERUSALEM

## ACTS 12

At this point, Luke goes back in history a few years to fill in some key events involving the other apostles.

## The Death of James

> About that time King Herod Agrippa began to persecute some believers in the church. He had the apostle James (John's brother) killed with a sword. (Acts 12:1-2)

Killing with a sword probably means beheading. An earlier, but related Herod had beheaded John the Baptist for his blood thirsty niece and second wife. The kingdoms of the Herods operated under different rules than the rest of Judea, and they could apparently kill at will.

Herod Agrippa I reigned as king of Judaea from AD 41–44. He was able to make friends with the Roman imperial family, including the bloody, insane heir of Tiberius, Caligula, who granted him the kingdom of his grandfather—Herod the Great—yet another Herod, who tried to kill Jesus as a baby.

# Peter's Turn

> When Herod saw how much this pleased the Jewish people, he also arrested Peter. (This took place during the Passover celebration.) Then he imprisoned him, placing him under the guard of four squads of four soldiers each. Herod intended to bring Peter out for public trial after the Passover. But while Peter was in prison, the church prayed very earnestly for him. (vs. 3-5)

How did Luke know Herod's intentions? The most likely source is Peter himself. He was probably brought in and was standing there as Herod set the schedule.

As we saw earlier, it's highly likely that Luke interviewed Peter at length during Paul's later two-year imprisonment at Caesarea. In all the Peter stories, we hear him described in the third person, yet the perspective is from Peter himself. We see through his eyes, including things nobody else saw, like his three visions on the rooftop, this event, and the coming of the angel later. Luke already said he had material from those "who from the beginning were eyewitnesses" (Luke 1:2). One of them was probably Peter.

Imagine being a believer in Jerusalem at this time. After all the persecution, they already killed one of your top leaders, James Zebedee, in a gory public show, as the crowd cheered. Now they have Peter, your top leader! Where is God? How far is he going to let this murderous persecution go?

# God Intervenes

God overruled Herod:

> The night before Peter was to be placed on trial, he was asleep, fastened with two chains between two soldiers. Others stood guard at the prison gate. Suddenly, there was a bright light in the cell, and an angel of the Lord stood before Peter. The angel struck him on the side to awaken him and said, "Quick! Get up!" And the chains fell off his wrists. Then the angel told him, "Get dressed and put on your sandals." And he did. "Now put on your coat and follow me," the angel ordered.

So Peter left the cell, following the angel. But all the time he thought it was a vision. He didn't realize it was actually happening. They passed the first and second guard posts and came to the iron gate leading to the city, and this opened for them all by itself. So they passed through and started walking down the street, and then the angel suddenly left him. (vs. 6-10)

This part of the story has as much detail as one of Luke's "we" passages. We have everything, step by step, including the words spoken and what Peter was thinking inwardly. It has all the marks of an eyewitness account from Peter.

At the end, there is Peter, standing on the cobblestone street in the dark. They didn't have street lights like today. He originally thought it was a vision, and you can imagine right when you wake up, and are somewhere between waking and sleep, things can seem unreal. At this point, the full realization must have settled in. What a dazzling event! Now what?

He decided to seek out fellowship. "He went to the home of Mary, the mother of John Mark" (v. 12). This is Mark, the author of the Gospel, a cousin of Barnabas, who later joined in the first missionary journey with Paul and Barnabas. Peter called him his son (1 Peter 5:13), probably meaning his spiritual son.

This could well be the same house mentioned repeatedly in Acts, and in the Gospels, where they had the last supper. It was good sized, as "many" believers were gathered there praying for Peter's safety.

# Rhoda

There follows an amusing account, bearing all the earmarks of a real event:

> He knocked at the door in the gate, and a servant girl named Rhoda came to open it. When she recognized Peter's voice, she was so overjoyed that, instead of opening the door, she ran back inside and told everyone, "Peter is standing at the door!" (vs. 13-15)

One can imagine a girl doing this. But no doubt when she told the believers he was there, they responded, "Finally! We knew God would answer our prayers.

No.

"You're out of your mind!" they said. When she insisted, they decided, "It must be his angel" (v. 15). So it certainly wasn't their expectancy in faith that resulted in God's miraculous intervention. Apparently, even after she kept insisting, they refused to go see. Did they go on praying?

"Meanwhile, Peter continued knocking. When they finally opened the door and saw him, they were amazed" (v. 16). There must have been a spontaneous outburst of astonishment.

> He motioned for them to quiet down and told them how the Lord had led him out of prison. "Tell James and the other brothers what happened," he said. And then he went to another place. (v. 17)

The other place he went to was probably out of town. He would now be a fugitive and had to hide out until Herod was gone. That didn't take long.

## Aftermath

> Now when day came, there was no small disturbance among the soldiers as to what could have become of Peter. When Herod had searched for him and had not found him, he examined the guards and ordered that they be led away to execution. Then he went down from Judea to Caesarea and was spending time there. (vs. 18-19)

Herod's fury was as dangerous as possible. He "examined the guards," which probably refers to torture. Then he had them executed. Did he ever wonder if it might be something supernatural? Perhaps Peter's disappearance did frighten him a bit, because he stopped attacking believing leaders.

## Death of Herod Agrippa

At several points, the book of Acts crosses pathways with other ancient historical narratives, making it possible to assess the historicity of the book. This is one of them and frankly, it's outstanding.

We read,

> On an appointed day Herod, having put on his royal apparel,

took his seat on the rostrum and began delivering an address to [people in Caesarea]. The people kept crying out, "The voice of a god and not of a man!" And immediately an angel of the Lord struck him because he did not give God the glory, and he was eaten by worms and died. (vs. 21-23)

It's an odd story, especially the last part about being eaten by worms. That usually happens after you die. It so happens that this very incident is also described by Jewish historian Flavius Josephus.

The first thing to note is that these two authors had not read each others' accounts. Luke couldn't have read Josephus because Josephus didn't write until thirty years later. It's equally clear that, although Josephus agreed with several key details in Acts, the differences are such that scholars are convinced that Josephus never read Acts.

That means the two accounts are completely independent—the best condition for comparing sources in a parallel account of the same event.

Josephus' account is longer, going on for four or five times the length of Luke's. So, we're not going to reproduce it here. But you can read it for free if you Google the passage.[1]

Luke mentions Herod putting on "his royal apparel," which seems like a strange detail to include. But we learn from Josephus that the robe he put on was made from "silver thread." This robe shimmered in the morning sun, dazzling the crowd.

That's why they cried out, according to Luke, saying "The voice of a god and not of a man!" Herod was glowing as he reflected the sun onto the crowd. So Josephus' detail perfectly explains something from Luke.

Josephus says they cried out, "Be merciful to us; for although we have hitherto reverenced you only as a man, yet shall we henceforth own you as superior to mortal nature." So, although the account is wordier, the meaning is the same, even to this level of detail.

Praising humans, especially kings and emperors, as being gods was common in the ancient world. But Herod was supposed to be a monotheist. Josephus thought that by accepting this praise and not rebuking it he was smitten with "intense agony in his bowels." Herod's death took several days, according to Josephus.

---

1. Flavius Josephus, *Antiquities of the Jews* XIX, 343–50.

Readers of Acts may see it more as judgment for what he did to James and almost did to Peter. Josephus adds that Herod was 54 when he died.

Today, we know round worms, a parasite common in ancient times, often form balls in the host's intestines, completely blocking them. The victim begins to vomit up worms, explaining how they knew worms were the problem. But the ball usually can't be removed that way and death is not uncommon. So this perfectly explains Luke's statement that he was eaten by worms and then died.

Round worm eggs are usually ingested from untreated water containing a low level of feces. In the ancient world, all water fits this description.

Josephus goes on to include other features of the death, including an owl, which was a bad omen. He doesn't mention the delegation from Tyre and Sidon who were visiting at the time (v. 20). These are the kind of differences that show independence.

## Why Not James?

God powerfully intruded into history to free Peter, and protect his church. But why didn't he intervene to save James Zebedee? He was also an important leader, and a close personal friend to Jesus. Surely the church prayed earnestly for him too?

Of course, we don't know the answer to this question, so painful to James' family and friends. God didn't save Stephen either. What are we to conclude about these inconsistencies?

At base is the sovereignty and the omniscience of God. As finite, limited humans, we must accept God's choice to intervene in one case, but not in another. He knows things we don't know. He doesn't dread physical death like we do because he knew exactly where James would be one moment after his death—right with Jesus in heaven.

The default is that God does not intervene to prevent death. The death rate for believers is the same as that for non-believers—100%. Age at time of death is also about the same. It's only in special cases where God isn't done with a believer that he may prevent death.

Paul told the Philippians that he was pretty sure he would not die when tried before the emperor because he was still needed (Philippians 1:25). Yet, he accepted the possibility that he might die, and was ready for that

(Philippians 2:17). We too need to respect God's decision on whether to intervene or not, and realize he cannot be manipulated.

## The Big Picture

Luke finishes chapter 12 with the comment, "The word of the Lord continued to grow and to be multiplied" (v. 24). Although his narrative will now move to the international outreach to the Gentiles, he makes it clear that God had not abandoned the Jewish church in Judea. They continued to reach people for Jesus.

The final line jumps forward to AD 47 or 48 and really belongs in the next chapter. "And Barnabas and Saul returned from Jerusalem when they had fulfilled their mission, taking along with them John, who was also called Mark" (v. 25). He's referring to the trip they took at the end of chapter 11 to relieve the poor from famine. They have picked up another traveler, Barnabas' cousin, John Mark. They return to Antioch.

# 19

# THE WORK TO WHICH I HAVE CALLED THEM

## ACTS 13

After the brief retrospective on persecution in Jerusalem, Luke snaps back to real time in chapter 13. We earlier saw that Antioch was the scene for a spiritual explosion based mainly on outreach to Gentiles. Now he adds:

> Now there were at Antioch, in the church that was there, prophets and teachers: Barnabas, and Simeon who was called Niger, and Lucius of Cyrene, and Manaen who had been brought up with Herod the tetrarch, and Saul. (Acts 13:1)

Here we meet the leadership in Antioch. Barnabas and Saul we already know. In addition, we now meet "Simeon who was called Niger." Niger is a loanword from Latin, meaning "black," so he was probably African. Could he be the Simon of Cyrene who was pressed into service to carry Jesus' cross? Some early Christian writings say it's him, and Cyrene was in eastern Libya in Africa.

Mark 15:21 says, "They pressed into service a passer-by coming from the country, Simon of Cyrene (the father of Alexander and Rufus), to bear his cross." Mark mentions his sons as if his early church readers would know who he was talking about. According to tradition, Rufus and Alexander became missionaries, and Paul extols a man named Rufus in Romans 16:13: "Greet Rufus, a choice man in the Lord."

Is Lucius of Cyrene yet another member of this family? He, too, was from Cyrene in Africa, so it's possible. We have no reason to identify him with the Lucius in Romans 16:21 and Lucius was a common name.

Manaen is said to have been brought up with Herod the tetrarch. That could mean he was part of Herod's household, possibly the son of servants that Herod owned. Or, as the NLT takes it, that he was a childhood friend of Herod Antipas.

This leadership team is diverse, but with more Hellenized Jews or even Gentiles rather than Hebraic Jews. Saul may be the only Hebraic Jew there, and even he had greater than usual knowledge of Greek and Gentile culture.

## Serving and Fasting

The leadership team was gathered together when it happened.

> While they were ministering to the Lord and fasting, the Holy Spirit said, "Set apart for me Barnabas and Saul for the work to which I have called them." (v. 2)

The word for "ministering" here means serving. It's also the word for a priest's service in the temple, so they may have been interceding in prayer for their people.  ·

They were also fasting. We see Paul and Barnabas fasting here and one other time later when commissioning elders for several newly planted churches (Acts 14:23). That's it. Of course, Jesus fasted for forty days, but that seems rather special.

In the Old Testament, fasting was associated with mourning, and Jesus seemed to confirm that when he explained to John the Baptist's disciples why he and his disciples didn't fast. It wouldn't be appropriate to do something associated with mourning when the bridegroom was present (Matthew 9:14-15). But we don't sense mourning in this narrative. Jews fasted on the Day of Atonement, but it's not part of the day in the Old Testament. It was a later addition.

So fasting is barely mentioned in the New Testament, especially after Pentecost. And crucially, we have no explanation of what fasting is or why to do it. We find no imperative calling on us to fast, but we have this and one other example.[1]

We can rule out any idea that fasting puts more *oomph* into our prayers as a way to invoke an answer from God. God cannot be manipulated, and he doesn't need self-abuse from us to persuade him to answer (like the prophets of Baal in 1 Kings 18).

The best suggested meaning of this kind of fasting is either that they were too intense into prayer to take time out to eat, or that fasting might sharpen people's concentration.

## The Commission

The Holy Spirit spoke. Was it through a word of prophecy given to one of the men? Probably. But it could have been combined with a correlated word given to another for confirmation that God was speaking. The message probably went on to give instructions.

Barnabas was from Cyprus, so he may have had some contacts there. It's to the island of Cyprus they go first.

## The Sending

Luke condenses his account into very few words, and we are suddenly on the ship:

> "Then, when they had fasted and prayed and laid their hands on them, they sent them away. So, being sent out by the Holy Spirit, they went down to Seleucia and from there they sailed to Cyprus" (vs. 3-4).

The fact that Luke repeats his claim that their commission comes from the Holy Spirit shows how adamant he is that this is a work of God. A core early church assumption was that Jesus, not humans, is the leader of the church, mediated through the Spirit. He had earlier promised that

---

1. The early church later became fascinated with fasting, and it signaled a growing asceticism (the belief that self-caused suffering results in deeper spirituality). That probably explains the false insertion of fasting as instrumental in exorcism (Mark 9:29). It's not found in the earliest manuscripts. The Pharisees, who were also ascetic, fasted twice a week (Luke 18:12).

"upon this rock I will build my church" (Matthew 16:18). The church belongs to Jesus, and he never has given it to anyone else.

When the elders laid hands on the church planters, it was a way of expressing solidarity with them. It's a form of pledge that the sending church is going to support the mission with their prayers and funds. The physical contact signifies that they will go along with the team in spirit.

## The Cyprus Outreach

The three workers sailed about 130 miles, probably upwind. Then, landing in the south-east end of the island, they debarked at the port city of Salamis. Their first order of business would be the pattern for all subsequent cities—they went to the synagogue.

We saw earlier that Paul believed the gospel should go "to the Jew first and also to the Greek" (Romans 1:16). He never explicitly explains why he held this view, but various statements he makes in Romans 9 imply that he felt the Jews' history and the task they accomplished (like recording the Old Testament Scriptures and keeping the temple ritual) entitled them to hear first.

Later in this trip we read that when the Jews in Antioch of Pisidia began smack talking the church planters,

> Paul and Barnabas spoke out boldly and declared, "It was necessary that we first preach the word of God to you Jews. But since you have rejected it and judged yourselves unworthy of eternal life, we will offer it to the Gentiles" (Acts 13:46).

Why was it "necessary" that the Jews hear first? Paul must have had direction from God to that effect. They were here first, so they get to hear first.

At the same time, most or maybe all of the synagogues they spoke in contained both Jews and "God fearing" Gentiles. So from a strategic point of view, these people were already prepared to hear the gospel, based on their knowledge of the Old Testament.

The word "synagogues" is in the plural here, so Salamis had a significant Jewish community. We don't know how the preaching in Salamis went in terms of responsiveness. Maybe not so well, because they soon move on.

## To the West

Cyprus is about 140 miles long and the team would travel most of that distance on their way to Paphos, the provincial capital at the west end of the island.

There, just as happened earlier in Samaria, they encounter an occult sorcerer, a false prophet named "Bar-Jesus." Later, he goes by the name "Elymas" (vs. 6, 8). In typical fashion, Satan has his player there, ready to oppose God's work.

Jesus had warned this would happen in his parables of the kingdom in Matthew 13. Whether it was birds snatching the word from people's hearts, or someone sowing tares among the wheat, the owner's intent to raise a harvest is constantly opposed. Why did he have tares in his field? He said simply, "An enemy has done this" (v. 28).

So having enemies attacking God's work and his people is normal. Believers need to expect opposition and not be rattled by it.

## Before the Governor

Sergius Paulus was a well-educated Roman governor. He must have heard about the mission team being in town, because he invited them to visit him and explain what they were teaching. Luke says, "He wanted to hear the word of God" (v. 7).

Had someone from the synagogue relayed to Sergius what they were saying, perhaps with that excitement that makes others want to hear? Or was this the drawing action of the Holy Spirit that the team recognized in retrospect? Either way, successful evangelism depends on believers coming into contact with heart hungry people whom God has prepared to hear the gospel.

Somehow, we end up with the mission team, Sergius Paulus, and Elymas all in the same place. Was Elymas an acquaintance or even an advisor to Sergius? What is he doing there? We don't know. But he isn't a passive listener.

As they explained the gospel, Elymas "interfered and urged the governor to pay no attention to what Barnabas and Saul said. He was trying to keep the governor from believing" (v. 8). Suddenly,

Paul was filled with the Holy Spirit, and he looked the sorcerer in the eye. Then he said, "You son of the devil, full of every sort of deceit and fraud, and enemy of all that is good! Will you never stop perverting the true ways of the Lord? Watch now, for the Lord has laid his hand of punishment upon you, and you will be struck blind. You will not see the sunlight for some time." (vs. 9-11)

God acted in exactly the way Paul said he would. Instantly, mist and darkness came over the man's eyes, and he began groping around, begging for someone to take his hand and lead him.

Of course, it was God, not Paul, who struck him blind. Paul merely announced what God was going to do when he said, "the Lord has laid his hand of punishment upon you" (v. 11). And the blindness was temporary. Having Paul announce it in advance unmistakably showed that Paul was speaking for God.

When the governor saw what had happened, he became a believer, for he was astonished at the teaching about the Lord. (v. 12)

Sergius' eyes locked onto Elymas, groping in darkness, and then swung back over to Paul. He must have instantly known that whatever followed from Paul was true. He became a believer.

We don't know what happened in the rest of Paphos. Did they succeed in planting a new group? There's a good chance they did, and having a proconsul on their side would keep them safe for a while.

## Saul Becomes Paul

Notice Luke refers to Saul as Paul, and for the rest of the book that's his only name. Paulos was a Greek name, while Saul was a Hebraic name. Had Paul more fully embraced his mission of reaching Gentiles and Hellenistic Jews? Or was he just learning about contextualizing in mission work? We will consider Paul's view on contextualizing (fitting in with cultural features of the group you're trying to reach) later.

In this journey, they kept moving, sometimes because they were driven out of town, and other times because it seems to be their strategy to sow broadly and let the new groups take care of themselves.

Arguably, Paul changed his pattern in later trips. In the second journey he stayed a year and a half at Corinth, building up the church. He couldn't stay in Philippi, Berea, or Thessalonica because he was driven out of town there. But he sent Silas and Timothy up to these cities to do follow-up work, grounding them in the word (17:15; 18:5; Macedonia is where these cities were located).

Then, in the third journey, he made a base at Ephesus where he preached and taught for over three years. He did take some side journeys during that time, but not to plant new churches. Instead, he was strengthening the existing groups.

It seems likely that after the first journey, Paul laid more importance on building in deeper with new groups. Probably he was taking longer to train and raise up leaders. Paul expressed shock at the theological instability of the groups they planted on this first journey. He wrote them not long after this journey, crying out "I am amazed that you are so quickly deserting him who called you by the grace of Christ, for a different gospel" (Galatians 1:6). That experience may account for his slower and more deliberate pattern in later journeys.

## Perga

They decide to move on:

> Now Paul and his companions put out to sea from Paphos and came to Perga in Pamphylia; but John left them and returned to Jerusalem. (v. 13)

Luke quietly announces that John Mark left the band and returned to Jerusalem. Reading between the lines, we can imagine a significant quarrel in connection with his leaving. Later, when they were launching the second missionary journey, Paul described Mark as a deserter (Acts 15:38), so they probably had a significant scrap over his departure.

# 20

# PISIDIAN ANTIOCH
## ACTS 13:14-43

But going on from Perga, they arrived at Pisidian Antioch, and on the Sabbath day they went into the synagogue and sat down. After the reading of the Law and the Prophets the synagogue officials sent to them, saying, "Brethren, if you have any word of exhortation for the people, say it." Paul stood up, and motioning with his hand said, "Men of Israel, and you who fear God, listen..." (Acts 13:14-16)

This city of Pisidian Antioch is different from the Antioch they left earlier. That was Antioch of Syria. In this city, we get an inside look at what Paul was doing when he went to synagogues. We notice it was on the Sabbath. Paul and Barnabas simply sat down with the other men (the men sitting separately from the women) and listened to the traditional reading of Moses and the Prophets.

People in the synagogue knew each other; this was not a large crowd. The presence of the two strangers would have been obvious, especially that one of them was a rabbi. It's not unlikely that during social chatting before the meeting Paul had introduced himself as a Jerusalem rabbi.

Some think Paul wore his distinct garment reserved for Jerusalem Pharisees and rabbis. These are said to have had a special tassel around the bottom. It was based on a passage in Numbers:

> Throughout the generations to come you are to make tassels on the corners of your garments, with a blue cord on each tassel. (15:38)

Jesus criticized the practice, saying the Pharisees "do all their deeds to be noticed by men; for they broaden their phylacteries and lengthen the tassels of their garments" (Matthew 23:5). Jesus was saying that these tassels were deliberately showy, proclaiming how holy their owners were. They were supposed to be a reminder to self. The point for us is that, as a Jerusalem Pharisee and a rabbi, Paul would have owned one of these tasseled robes and it's not unlikely that he used it to get speaking opportunities at synagogues.

## Paul's Sermon

As Paul rises to speak, we are about to hear Luke's summary of his speech, recounted to him directly by Paul, about ten years later. The argument seems to jump from point to point, but by reading between the lines, it's not hard to guess what the missing material would have been. While this recounting is shorter than the original, it is very likely to include the main elements he preached. We can see eight specific topics.

### Historical Background

> "The God of this people Israel chose our fathers and made the people great during their stay in the land of Egypt, and with an uplifted arm he led them out from it. For a period of about forty years he put up with them in the wilderness. When he had destroyed seven nations in the land of Canaan, he distributed their land as an inheritance—all of which took about four hundred and fifty years." (vs. 17-19)

His narrative goes back before Moses' time to the point where the patriarchs entered Egypt. That means his rough estimate of 450 years is accurate enough. The Exodus and conquest were touchstones of Jewish identity. This is when God revealed himself like never before, not just to an individual, but to the whole nation.

"After that, God gave them judges to rule until the time of Samuel the prophet. Then the people begged for a king, and God gave them Saul son of Kish, a man of the tribe of Benjamin, who reigned for forty years. But God removed Saul and replaced him with David, a man about whom God said, 'I have found David son of Jesse, a man after my own heart. He will do everything I want him to do.'" (vs. 20-22)

His added details about Saul could have been a note of humor, pointing out that he, too, was Saul from the tribe of Benjamin. He seems to be moving quickly toward his next section on David.

## Messiah Promised

The survey moves up to David, who received the Davidic Covenant (2 Samuel 7:8-17). In David's covenant, God promised him an eternal throne. That took Paul directly to the fulfillment in Jesus.

"And it is one of King David's descendants, Jesus, who is God's promised Savior of Israel! Before he came, John the Baptist preached that all the people of Israel needed to repent of their sins and turn to God and be baptized. As John was finishing his ministry he asked, 'Do you think I am the Messiah? No, I am not! But he is coming soon—and I'm not even worthy to be his slave and untie the sandals on his feet.'" (vs. 23-25)

He stops to cover John the Baptist, who identified Jesus as the one he came to announce. By using nearly identical wording to that found in John 1:27, Paul shows that he probably had access to a gospel source book of some kind—not the Gospel of John—that wasn't written until much later.

According to Josephus, John's fame extended to every Jewish community, even hundreds of miles distant from Judea, like this one. Luke will confirm that later in Acts.[1] First century Jews were excited about John because they hadn't seen a true prophet for four hundred years. Jews

---

1. Josephus also tells the whole story of John the Baptist's conflict with Herod over his incestuous marriage to his half sister, Herodias, and subsequent execution. He gives far more detail than the Gospels on some parts, but Josephus apparently didn't know the part about how Herodias forced Herod's hand to kill John (Matthew 14:1-12). That shows that the accounts are independent. Flavius Josephus, *Antiquities*, 18:109-119.

visiting Jerusalem in a pilgrimage would see or hear about John and the excitement people felt and then take word back to their home cities.

Paul either assumed, or may have been tipped off, that some in his audience knew about John. If so, it would make sense to include his witness about Jesus.

## Jesus' Death

> "Brothers—you sons of Abraham, and also you God-fearing Gentiles—this message of salvation has been sent to us! The people in Jerusalem and their leaders did not recognize Jesus as the one the prophets had spoken about. Instead, they condemned him, and in doing this they fulfilled the prophets' words that are read every Sabbath. They found no legal reason to execute him, but they asked Pilate to have him killed anyway." (vs. 26-28)

Here we notice again that both Jews and Gentiles were present.

In this section, Paul rolls out the story of the cross, and the standard New Testament apologetic for Jesus—fulfilled prophecy. They had their own copy of the Old Testament and could easily check on what he said. Paul probably gave them some examples at this point in his original talk that are not included in this summary. It would have been easy to roll out the scroll of Isaiah to the Servant Songs and invite them to read and reflect.

Interestingly, he claims the Jerusalem leaders didn't have grounds to kill Jesus, and didn't realize that they were fulfilling prophecy until it was too late. Paul often refers to the "messianic secret" that resulted in people unknowingly fulfilling prophecy (e.g., Ephesians 3:8-10; Romans 16:25; 1 Corinthians 2:6-8).

## The Resurrection

> "When they had done all that the prophecies said about him, they took him down from the cross and placed him in a tomb. But God raised him from the dead!" (vs. 29-30)

The resurrection is an essential part of the gospel message. This sequence of affirmations matches the sequence in 1 Corinthians 15:1-8.

> "And over a period of many days he appeared to those who had

gone with him from Galilee to Jerusalem. They are now his witnesses to the people of Israel." (vs. 31)

Did Paul give his own amazing testimony about meeting the risen Christ here? It certainly would fit. Did he tell some of the stories about other resurrection encounters? We don't know if Barnabas ever saw Jesus after his resurrection. If he did, we can be sure he added his account.

## Incarnation

Paul went on, "It is also written in the second Psalm, 'You are my Son; today I have begotten you'" (v. 33). Psalm 2 is definitely a messianic psalm. It even refers to God's "anointed," the word *mashiyach*, or "Messiah." But Paul zeros in on the part that talks about God begetting, or giving birth, to the Messiah. Had they noticed that this psalm predicts the incarnation?

It's not only the work of Jesus, but also his nature that people must comprehend and believe as part of the gospel.

It would have been very difficult for orthodox Jews to accept the incarnation where God put on human flesh. Although it is predicted in several Old Testament passages (e.g., Isaiah 9:6-7), their view of God was exclusively transcendent; far too transcendent to become a man.

## Resurrection Predicted

Next, Paul gives the same argument Peter used on the day of Pentecost— that Psalm 16 refers to God's Holy One, whose body would not see decay, and really is referring to Jesus. Had he already covered Isaiah 53:10, which also predicts his resurrection? He might have covered it here.

## Invitation

Finally, he gave a direct gospel invitation to believe:

> "Brothers, listen! We are here to proclaim that through this man Jesus there is forgiveness for your sins. Everyone who believes in him is made right in God's sight." (vs. 38-39)

He gives the clear terms for personal salvation: "Everyone who believes in him." In other words, salvation is by faith, apart from works.

# Not By Law

And he includes an antithesis—that this is "something the law of Moses could never do" (v. 39). It sounds like he went into the ultimate purpose of the law—to convince everyone that they fall short of God's righteous standards and are in need of grace (e.g., Romans 3).

That antithesis would be important in this setting. He is really arguing that the Pharisaic or rabbinic take on the law as the path to salvation is wrong. Jesus' work wasn't just an add-on to the tail of the law. He "is the end of the law for righteousness to everyone who believes" (Romans 10:4).

This part, the radical grace, would be hard for lifelong law-livers, like many in his audience, to accept. Did he remind them of God's promise in Jeremiah that he would one day establish a "new covenant" that was "'not like the covenant which I made... when I took them by the hand to bring them out of the land of Egypt... this is the covenant which I will make with the house of Israel after those days,' declares the Lord, 'I will put My law within them and on their heart I will write it'" (Jeremiah 31:31-33, see also Hebrews 8:7-13)?

This was another "unforeseen partial fulfillment." Rabbinic teaching had no category for any partial fulfillment of this passage in Jeremiah. They saw it only as applying to the world takeover by King Messiah (and that is also true). It was part of the messianic secret that Jesus would bring in a new covenant of the Spirit, not of the law.

Paul's last citation comes from Habakkuk 1:5:

> Be careful! Don't let the prophets' words apply to you. For they said, 'Look, you mockers, be amazed and die! For I am doing something in your own day, something you wouldn't believe even if someone told you about it.' (vs. 40-41)

Was he getting push-back or heckling from some? Is the focus on not being mockers or not being unbelievers? Or is he focusing on God doing something that is hard to believe? We can't be sure, but it appears that most of the audience was responsive.

> As Paul and Barnabas left the synagogue that day, the people begged them to speak about these things again the next week. Many Jews and devout converts to Judaism followed Paul and

Barnabas, and the two men urged them to continue to rely on the grace of God. (vs. 42-43)

This must have been a thrilling follow-up session. They probably adjourned to someone's home for further discussion, implied by the comment that some "followed" them. The word "many" in this context must be at least dozens.

The Holy Spirit was at work. Excitement spread, until we read that "The following week almost the entire city turned out to hear them preach the word of the Lord" (v. 44).

# The Big Picture

The fact that Luke gave so much detail about this sermon suggests it's a template or a typical speech Paul gave in synagogues. In most of the visits to follow, we have little or no information on what he said. But we can assume it was something like this, with modifications as needed. The response sounds amazing. It looks like Paul and Barnabas are ready to win this whole city!

# 21

# BACKLASH

## ACTS 13:44-52

### Not So Fast

> On the next Sabbath almost the whole city gathered to hear the word of the Lord. When the Jews saw the crowds, they were filled with jealousy. They began to contradict what Paul was saying and heaped abuse on him. (Acts 13:44-45)

The entire city is probably hyperbole, but it may have seemed like it. We can be sure it was standing room only.

When leaders see other leaders gaining more following, jealousy is often the result. It's also likely that the leadership couldn't stand the idea that Paul and Barnabas were offering the gospel to Gentiles without any need to convert to Judaism first.

The synagogue leaders could have joined in the excitement and raised honest questions. But Luke is clear that this was militant unbelief. Any point Paul raised in answer to one question only led to a different question. No answer was satisfactory. Soon the questions turned to accusations.

Believers who share the gospel are familiar with this scenario. Unresponsive people raise questions as smoke screens to obscure the point, but with no interest in truth. When a sharing episode reaches this point, it's usually best to break off the conversation. Continuing only creates more hostility.

But because it was a public situation, they couldn't quietly break away. They needed to declare what was happening for the sake of the other listeners—mostly the God-following Greeks.

> Then Paul and Barnabas answered them boldly: "We had to speak the word of God to you first. Since you reject it and do not consider yourselves worthy of eternal life, we now turn to the Gentiles. For this is what the Lord has commanded us: 'I have made you a light for the Gentiles, that you may bring salvation to the ends of the earth.'" (vs. 46-47)

The passage they quoted from, Isaiah 49:6, is in one of the Servant Songs, where Isaiah described the life and ministry of Jesus 700 years before he lived. This key passage makes it clear that God's plan of redemption includes the Gentiles. So if the Jews were unresponsive, Paul and Barnabas were content to continue working with these monotheistic Gentiles and their idol worshiping friends.

## Were Inclined

> When the Gentiles heard this, they were glad and honored the word of the Lord; and all who were appointed for eternal life believed. The word of the Lord spread through the whole region. (vs. 48-49)

They must have stayed in town for a number of weeks if the word spread throughout the whole region. People must have been inviting friends and family from the surrounding areas to come and hear the good news. Only the Holy Spirit could generate such a spiritual awakening.

Some theologians seize on the expression "all who were appointed for eternal life believed" (v. 48) to prove the Calvinistic doctrine of "unconditional election." This doctrine teaches that God chooses who will have eternal life without any reference to the chosen one's beliefs or actions. Saving faith is not a condition under this view. In fact, non-believers are incapable of believing and must be made to believe as a gift. According to this reading (from the NLT), you can see that election comes first, and only those elected believe.

However, this is not the only way to read the verse. The verb here, *tasso*, is in the "middle-passive" voice. That means it's either passive, "they were appointed," or middle, "they appointed themselves," or "they were inclined." The spelling is identical for middle and passive, so only the context and common sense can determine which is intended.

In this passage, Luke is contrasting the responsiveness of the Gentiles to that of the synagogue leaders. Paul told the leaders, "Since you have rejected (middle voice) the word..." Then, to match the comparison, the Gentiles "inclined themselves (middle voice) to eternal life." It's a parallel contrast.

Besides, Paul already explained, "Everyone who believes in him is made right in God's sight" (v. 39). It would be disingenuous to claim anyone can believe if only the elect are able to do so.

It is true that Jesus said, "No one can come to me unless the Father who sent me draws him; and I will raise him up on the last day" (John 6:44). But he also said, "And I, if I am lifted up from the earth, will draw all men to myself" (John 12:32; see also John 16:7-9). In other words, if God didn't draw people, nobody would believe. But even with his drawing action, it doesn't mean everyone will respond.

# Counterattack

> Then the Jews stirred up the influential religious women and the leaders of the city, and they incited a mob against Paul and Barnabas and ran them out of town. (v. 50)

Just when it seems like the believers are headed toward an outstanding time of victory, the enemy strikes. Even though this pattern is so consistent in Acts, we find ourselves surprised when it happens to us today. I tend to wonder, "What did I do wrong to bring this upon us?" Or, "Why doesn't God protect us from these attacks?"

But the answer is right here before us. Spiritual warfare includes Satan's ability to energize and direct people to attack, and he knows where to strike. We don't know what all the rules governing spiritual warfare are, or how they work together. But clearly, believers are not immune to harsh attacks. To the contrary, the more appropriate question to ask is, "What did we do right to bring on so much opposition?"

> So they shook the dust from their feet as a sign of rejection and went to the town of Iconium. And the believers were filled with joy and with the Holy Spirit. (vs. 51-52)

Paul's and Barnabas' response follows Jesus' advice when he sent the Twelve out to preach. It included this: "If a town refuses to welcome you, shake its dust from your feet as you leave to show that you have abandoned those people to their fate" (Luke 9:5).

## The Big Picture

In spite of the apostles giving ground and vacating the area, the final word is one of triumph. The believers were filled with joy and the Holy Spirit! The group of believers in Pisidian Antioch may have been sizeable, judging from that early response that seemed like the whole town came out to listen. Surely, a good number believed—Luke says it was "many." He later says, "And the word of the Lord was being spread through the whole region" (v. 49). That must mean a minimum of a few believers in a number of villages. All told, it looks like a hundred or more people had believed, perhaps several hundred.

The new believers would have to make it on their own with the apostles driven out of town. We can safely assume Paul and Barnabas had given them some good training, and some of them had been in the synagogue for years and knew the Old Testament. In all likelihood, they had also written down some of the key sayings of Jesus. Paul and Barnabas would be back again in a few months.

# 22

# TWO MORE TOWNS
## ACTS 14:1-19

## Iconium

The apostles went north:

> The same thing happened in Iconium. Paul and Barnabas went to the Jewish synagogue and preached with such power that a great number of both Jews and Greeks became believers. (Acts 14:1)

Again, a term like "a great number" in this narrative by Luke could hardly mean a few dozen. More likely it would mean over a hundred people coming to faith. But immediately, a counter narrative emerges.

> Some of the Jews, however, spurned God's message and poisoned the minds of the Gentiles against Paul and Barnabas (v. 2)

Rather than backing down, the apostles fought on, arguing and making the case.

> But the apostles stayed there a long time, preaching boldly about the grace of the Lord. And the Lord proved their message was true by giving them power to do miraculous signs

and wonders. But the people of the town were divided in their opinion about them. Some sided with the Jews, and some with the apostles. (vs. 3-4)

God got behind their preaching, adding supernatural displays of power. This went on for "a long time." The whole first journey lasted six to eight months. So this might be a month or two spent in Iconium. That's long enough to make significant progress with disciples. And if they weren't seeing continuing growth in the group, they probably wouldn't have stayed there so long.

## But Then

Then a mob of Gentiles and Jews, along with their leaders, decided to attack and stone them. When the apostles learned of it, they fled to the region of Lycaonia—to the towns of Lystra and Derbe and the surrounding area. And there they preached the good news. (vs. 5-7)

Fleeing is often a legitimate response to dangerous persecution. Jesus, for instance, prescribed fleeing when Jerusalem is surrounded by armies (Luke 21:20-21). This same mob, along with reinforcements from Pisidian Antioch, would later pursue the apostles all the way to Lystra. But before the Satanic opposition could organize, the apostles had been preaching and winning people for some time.

## Healing at Lystra

Next on the trail lay the town of Lystra. There, an amazing event ensued:

While they were at Lystra, Paul and Barnabas came upon a man with crippled feet. He had been that way from birth, so he had never walked. He was sitting and listening as Paul preached. Looking straight at him, Paul realized he had faith to be healed. So Paul called to him in a loud voice, "Stand up!" And the man jumped to his feet and started walking. (vs. 8-10)

How did Paul know this man had the faith to be healed? It must have been an intuitive knowledge given by the Holy Spirit. Apparently, people with the gift of healing know when God is going to activate their gift. This man was probably a beggar, and in such a small town, everyone would have known about him and his condition, so the miracle was once again undeniable.

We notice that Paul was preaching, perhaps street preaching? There is no mention of a synagogue in Lystra, and this was not a Jewish crowd as events would show.

> When the crowds saw what Paul had done, they raised their voice, saying in the Lycaonian language, "The gods have become like men and have come down to us." And they began calling Barnabas, Zeus, and Paul, Hermes, because he was the chief speaker. (vs. 11-12)

The Lycaonians had their own language, but also spoke Greek as a trade language. The fact that they were speaking to each other in their own language explains why it took a while for the apostles to realize what was going on. By the time they grasped what was happening, "The priest of Zeus, whose temple was just outside the city, brought oxen and garlands to the gates, and wanted to offer sacrifice with the crowds" (v. 13).

Zeus was the god of the sky. Hermes was the messenger of the gods. The idea that gods would temporarily become men or women was common in Greek mythology. They could also mate with humans, producing super men, as in the case of Hercules or Achilles.

Finally realizing they were about to be worshipped as gods, Paul and Barnabas "tore their clothing in dismay and ran out among the people, shouting, 'Friends, why are you doing this? We are merely human beings—just like you!'" (vs. 14-15).[1]

## Paul's Speech

Seeing the people had fallen quiet and were listening, Paul saw the opening and launched into a speech:

> "We have come to bring you the good news that you should turn from these worthless things and turn to the living God, who made heaven and earth, the sea, and everything in them. In the past he permitted all the nations to go their own ways, but he never left them without evidence of himself and his

---

1. This is the only verse that calls Barnabas an apostle, although he clearly does the work of an apostle in church planting.

goodness. For instance, he sends you rain and good crops and gives you food and joyful hearts." (vs. 15-17)

Here is another summary by Luke, but guided by Paul's firsthand memory from ten years before the writing. As we saw earlier, these summaries are shortened versions of the speech, and we have to imagine what the full text would have been.

## Creation

First, we see Paul contrasting what he calls "these worthless things" (the Greek gods) with "the living God, who made heaven and earth, the sea, and everything in them." This is different from his earlier preaching, where he centered on the Bible and fulfilled prophecy. Instead, he reflects on "general revelation," which involves conclusions one can reach by observing nature.

Greek gods were not the creators of heaven and earth. Their mythology had Gaia, the earth mother, emerging out of chaos. There followed mating, the gods eating each other, castration, lapping up blood, having baby gods, and finally the gods gradually growing up from childhood like over-grown humans. Their view of how we got here was a murky mess.

Paul must have compared these implausible myths with the majestic text of Genesis 1. That text answered a major question: "Where did matter come from in the first place?" According to Hebrews (a book that I believe Paul either wrote or oversaw its writing), "By faith we understand that the worlds were prepared by the word of God, so that what is seen was not made out of things which are visible" (Hebrews 11:3).

Modern science has confirmed the truthfulness of this text—that at the big bang, everything came out of nothing. Paul wouldn't have known that, but the language of Genesis 1 is clear, that God first created light. That turns out to be true. For the first moments of the universe, nothing but energy existed. Only later did it cool enough for matter to form.

Paul must have addressed origins as a way to introduce the infinite, personal God of monotheism. Like the Old Testament argued, Paul argues that idols were man-made objects, devoid of life. The true God is "the living God."

## Freedom

Paul went on to say, "In the past he permitted all the nations to go their own ways" (v. 16). Here is a striking affirmation of free will. Paul makes it clear that God has gone hands off to a significant degree. Of course, it's only because of free will that we are capable of sin. A machine without free will cannot sin. An animal, operating on instinct cannot sin. Neither could an automaton believe. To believe in God entails a choice—something only free-thinking beings can do.

We know Paul was aware of total depravity, because of passages like Romans 3. He also knew about the need for a gracious act of God to enable fallen humans to believe if they choose to. That enabling was happening in this scene through the healing and the preaching of the word, energized directly by the Holy Spirit.

It seems doubtful that he got into those issues here. It's more likely he was pointing out that just because they were born into the Greek mythological tradition doesn't mean they have to believe that polytheistic view.

## Design

Instead, he says, "He never left them without evidence of himself and his goodness. For instance, he sends you rain and good crops and gives you food and joyful hearts" (v. 17).

This looks like an argument from design. We know Paul found a design argument compelling, because he later wrote, "Since the creation of the world his invisible attributes, his eternal power and divine nature, have been clearly seen, being understood through what has been made, so that they are without excuse" (Romans 1:20).

The processes of nature and life itself work out far too well to be coincidence. The advance of science and the discovery of evolution have done nothing to blunt the force of this argument. That's because, as science has discovered the process of natural selection, it has also disclosed the intricacy of the cell, rendering abiogenesis (the conversion of nonliving molecules to a living organism) utterly implausible apart from a designer. And so we are left with special creation.

Ancient people regularly accepted rain, the crops, and food as gifts from the gods. Now we know this balanced natural cycle is more remarkable than anyone thought. We find ourselves just the right distance from just the right kind of star, with the right amount of liquid water. We have an iron core that produces an extraordinary life-saving magnetic field. That field deflects solar particles that would have stripped our atmosphere away long ago, like on Mars. Our rotation, accelerated by the Moon forming event, has now, after billions of years, slowed to an ideal 24-hour cycle. Our tilted axis causes life-expanding seasons. Truly, our earth and the ecosphere on it are stunningly improbable.[2]

## Joyful Hearts

Last comes God's gift of "joyful hearts." Is he talking about the human soul? That's what makes appreciation of nature, social relationships, music, comprehension of beauty, sense of humor, morality, creativity, and free will possible. Having a soul with its earmarks of being created in the image of God points directly away from the assumptions of polytheistic nature religions. The high order of human consciousness suggests the existence of a personal creator God who created us in his image.

## Jesus?

Luke doesn't recount Paul's explanation of the cross or the life of Jesus, but he started the talk saying, "We have come to bring you the good news..." So perhaps we may assume they included that part, unless they faced so much disorder that they couldn't finish.

> But even with these words, Paul and Barnabas could scarcely restrain the people from sacrificing to them. (v. 18)

So we can safely conclude the sermon was mostly unsuccessful. They wouldn't still be trying to sacrifice to them if they had believed his message. Even Paul failed to win his audience at times. However, they didn't give up, but persevered, eventually winning a number of people in Lystra and the surrounding villages.

# Stoned

Abruptly, we read,

---

2. See Hugh Ross, *Improbable Planet: How Earth Became Humanity's Home*, (Grand Rapids: Baker Books, 2016), for a roundup of these and other features that combine to make the earth so perfect for life.

Then some Jews arrived from Antioch and Iconium and won the crowds to their side. They stoned Paul and dragged him out of town, thinking he was dead. (v. 19)

What?! Out of nowhere comes a murderous mob. Some of them have been following him from city to city, guarding their religion from this new crackpot sect. You can tell the apostles were enjoying major success, leading to such an extreme reaction from the Jewish leadership.

The account must have jumped forward in time. By now, Lystra has a group of believers, unlike earlier: "But as the believers gathered around him" (v. 20). The language here suggests a group converging on Paul's body after the stoning. Then, "He got up and went back into the town."

Imagine these new believers and Barnabas standing around Paul's bloody body, tears probably streaming down their faces. How did God let this happen? Suddenly, the body stirs! Then, like the Terminator, he rises up, alive! Was he raised from the dead? The text suggests not. They *believed* him dead means they wrongly thought he was dead. He was no doubt unconscious. If he was really dead, there would be no reason to insert that they believed he was.

God may have put the terror of the Lord on the attackers (e.g., Genesis 35:5; or Joshua 2:9), causing them to quickly get away before the authorities caught them. Murdering people on the street of a Roman city was punishable, so they were probably in a hurry to get out of there.

Referring to this incident months later, Paul says, "From now on let no one cause trouble for me, for I bear on my body the brand-marks of Jesus" (Galatians 6:17). Stoning was a gory, painful way to die, and Paul must have been a bloody mess. Yet he recovered surprisingly quickly. It would be no problem to a God who just healed a man with lifelong paralysis to hasten the healing of his apostle. Reentering the town was probably their only choice. Where else would they go? They must have snuck him into someone's house for the night.

## The Big Picture

The outreach to Lystra was a titanic battle, including miracles, collision of worldviews, and physical violence. In the end, the apostles won. They planted a new church in the city, and we'll see them revisit this group later in Acts.

# 23

# TO DERBE AND BACK
## ACTS 14:20-28

The next day they slipped out and headed further down the road to the town of Derbe. This was a several day journey of about sixty miles. They would have camped along the way. Did someone loan Paul a horse, or a drawn cart? The text doesn't say that, but it could have happened.

They "preached the gospel to that city and made many disciples" (Acts 14:21). Here again, we see the word "many." Luke often uses the term "disciples" as a synonym for "Christians." They couldn't have raised completed disciples in this setting, because the chronology of this trip only allows them to be in Derbe for a month or two. On the other hand, they probably reached some devout Jews or God-fearing Greeks who would already be well versed in Scripture and walking with God in an Old Testament-style faith.

As fall arrived, they had to decide whether to winter over in Galatia or return to their sending church in Antioch of Syria. Ships would not be sailing during winter, and a mountain range blocked the overland route at this time of year. They decided to return quickly.

The Roman road connecting Ephesus to points east ran through Derbe,

Lystra, Iconium, and Pisidian Antioch, the same cities they had come through earlier. It's clear that each town now had a local church, and the apostles stayed with each one, probably only for a few days.

They were "strengthening the souls of the disciples, encouraging them to continue in the faith, and saying, 'Through many tribulations we must enter the kingdom of God'" (v. 22). They might have done some evangelistic work too, but the focus at this point was more on establishing and equipping the believers who would have to carry on without the guidance Paul and Barnabas could provide.

## Selecting Elders

As they journeyed through the four Galatian towns, they "appointed elders for them in every church" (v. 23). Paul and Barnabas were in Galatia for at most a few months. So, these were new local churches. They had not yet established formal leadership in the groups. But now Paul and Barnabas made that move.

Why had they waited until the return journey to appoint elders? It was because they were waiting to see whom the Holy Spirit would designate as leaders. A central assumption in the early church was that God's Spirit leads the church. Successful ministry depends on this one thing: having the Holy Spirit's power behind what you're doing.

Under a more institutional setting, leaders would be chosen by voting or by having a committee select someone. Here, in the early church, leadership emerged naturally as the Spirit empowered some to lead. The local body would sense this as God brought key people forward into greater influence in the group.

Much later, you see Paul doing the same thing through Timothy and Titus. He told Titus, "I left you on the island of Crete so you could complete our work there and appoint elders in each town as I instructed you" (Titus 1:5). Why didn't Paul select elders himself instead of leaving Titus behind? It was because it takes time to recognize who has God's hand on them for leadership. People are drawn to godly leaders. And crucially, the leaders' character also becomes evident.

The same was true with Timothy. In 1 Timothy 3 Paul told him what to look for in identifying elders. Another way to express this New Testament church assumption is that humans don't *make* leaders, they *recognize* leaders.

Throughout the biblical story, whenever leaders emerge, they are chosen by God. That goes all the way back to Abraham, Moses, the Judges, and David. In the New Testament, Jesus chose the apostles, including Paul. Since true spiritual leadership is based on God's power working through leaders, it would be pointless to take on the role of leadership without God's calling.

# Plurality

Titus and Timothy are parallel with this account in another way. Here in Acts, Paul and Barnabas, "appointed elders for them in every church." The word for elders is plural, but each "church" is singular. This is the universal practice in the New Testament. They always recognized a group of elders in each church, even in small groups.

The reason for plurality in eldership is easy to see by studying what happened to churches when this feature was replaced by singular elders, or priests, as they were later called. Instead of having a group of godly people consider and pray about what to do in the church, a single leader made the decisions. This opened a wide door for deception and caprice.

Working in a group of elders who have to agree on things is definitely a nuisance at times. But it's worth the extra patience and work for the balance and corporate wisdom it provides.

# Encouragement

We read they were "encouraging them to continue in the faith, and saying, 'Through many tribulations we must enter the kingdom of God'" (v. 22). Is that message encouraging? Yes! To be forewarned is to be forearmed. Serious believers have to fix in their minds that persecution is part and parcel of serving God.

It's not clear whether the prayer and fasting was before choosing elders, as part of that process. Or was it afterward, as part of wishing them well before God?

## Return

They returned the way they came, and this time it's clear that, "they preached the word in Perga" (v. 25). But we have no record of the outcome. They went to Attalia, a port city, and took ship back to Antioch. There, "They called the church together and reported everything God had done through them and how he had opened the door of faith to the Gentiles, too" (v. 27). What a celebration this must have been!

## The Big Picture

The first missionary journey was over. During these eight or so months, they had planted new churches in at least four (and to as many as seven) cities. At several points, Luke used language indicating significant numbers had been reached:

- In Pisidian Antioch, we read, "*many* of the Jews and of the God-fearing proselytes followed Paul and Barnabas." (13:43)
- Also, "The next Sabbath *nearly the whole city* assembled." (v. 44)
- And, "the word of the Lord was being spread *through the whole region.*" (v. 49)
- Then at Iconium, "a large number of people believed, both of Jews and of Greeks." (14:1)
- They spent a "long time" (v. 3) preaching in Iconium, and "the city was divided" (v. 4). This also sounds like a large number believed.
- We don't know how big the response was in Lystra, only that some believers were won and a church was planted.
- The brief reference to their work in Derbe includes the comment that they "made many disciples." (v. 21)

We don't know what happened at Perga, but they may have won more people there.

None of these statements take into account what happened on Cyprus, so there were probably additional believers there, including a proconsul.

In other words, the mission had been an astonishing success. Considering what Luke meant by "many" earlier in the book, it's hard to see how these notifications could refer to less than hundreds of people. But winning a lot of people to faith is never the end of the story. What happened to them after this trip?

Predictably, the enemy didn't stop working, just because Paul and Barnabas were gone. Rather, their absence signaled a new offensive against the young groups left behind. Within a short time, we'll find them in danger of falling away from the true gospel. Paul found himself wondering whether any of these groups would survive.

# 24

# THE DEADLIEST CRISIS

## ACTS 15

## Conflict in Antioch

Acts 14 ends with the comment that "they spent a long time with the disciples" at Antioch. The span of time couldn't be more than four to six months, as we will see. For Paul and Barnabas, that was a long stay compared to their recent pattern.

During this stay, two events happened that plunged the early church into a life-threatening crisis.

## Disaster in Galatia

We aren't sure which event happened first, but the two are related.

Someone from one of the newly planted churches in Galatia showed up at Antioch with bad news. Jewish "Christians" in Galatia were going from group to group contradicting what Paul and Barnabas had taught them. And the real bad news? The young churches were buying into it!

These false teachers would later be called "Judaizers." They were men who didn't understand the gospel and its implications. They were arguing

213

that believing in Jesus was a good start, but you still had to follow the law. They didn't see Jesus *replacing* the Mosaic covenant, but *supplementing* it.

We can't be certain what all they taught, but we have the book of Galatians, which Paul wrote soon after receiving word on the problem. From that book, we can infer the broad outline.

First, whatever they were teaching was sub-Christian. Paul cried out to his recent converts:

> I am amazed that you are so quickly deserting him who called you by the grace of Christ, for a different gospel; which is really no gospel; only there are some who are disturbing you and want to distort the gospel of Christ. (Galatians 1:6-7)

As far as Paul was concerned, following this teaching was nothing less than "deserting" Jesus. This new gospel was "no gospel," and that's because of a central proposition repeated over and over in the New Testament: grace plus law equals law. These are not compatible.

Grace is a free gift, while law requires obedience as a condition for blessing. Trying to affirm both is the same as saying, "something equals nothing," or, "1000 = 0." It's nonsense. The presence of law cancels out free and undeserved grace, even if it were ninety percent grace and ten percent law. In a different context, Paul explains, "But if it is by grace, it is no longer on the basis of works, otherwise grace is no longer grace" (Romans 11:6). He also said, "For Christ is the end of the law for righteousness to everyone who believes" (Romans 10:4).

Paul was furious when he heard that the hundreds of new believers recently won at so great a price were buying into this deceptive blend of law and grace. You can tell from the tone of the letter he wrote to the Galatians that he was full of anger, shock, and dismay.

> Are you so foolish? Having begun by the Spirit, are you now being perfected by the flesh? (Galatians 3:3)

> You foolish Galatians, who has bewitched you, before whose eyes Jesus Christ was publicly portrayed as crucified? (3:1)

> But now that you have come to know God, or rather to be known by God, how is it that you turn back again to the weak

and worthless elemental things, to which you desire to be enslaved all over again? You observe days and months and seasons and years [Jewish holy days]. I fear for you, that perhaps I have labored over you in vain. (4:9-11)

Tell me, you who want to be under law, do you not listen to the law? (4:21)

You have been alienated from Christ, you who are seeking to be justified by law; you have fallen from grace. (5:4)

And the list goes on. But right before Paul wrote Galatians, he got another blow.

## Men From James

Luke's account of the other event that contributed to the crisis is very short:

Some men came down from Judea and began teaching the brethren, "Unless you are circumcised according to the custom of Moses, you cannot be saved." And when Paul and Barnabas had great dissension and debate with them, the brethren determined that Paul and Barnabas and some others of them should go up to Jerusalem to the apostles and elders concerning this issue. (Acts 15:1-2)

So the Judaizers now arrived at Antioch. They were a growing party within the early church that didn't accept a break from the Mosaic Covenant. They wanted a fusion of rabbinic Judaism and following Jesus. Their doctrine was expressly legalistic: "Unless you are circumcised according to the custom of Moses, you cannot be saved." But getting circumcised was only the gateway. They intended to impose the whole Law of Moses.

In the book of Galatians, Paul gives a more detailed account of how the same incident started.

But when Cephas came to Antioch, I opposed him to his face, because he stood condemned. For prior to the coming of certain men from James, he used to eat with the Gentiles; but when they came, he began to withdraw and hold himself aloof, fearing the party of the circumcision. (Galatians 2:11-12)

So Peter showed up at Antioch. During this period, he increasingly traveled and worked in mission outreach, leaving the leadership of the Jerusalem church to James, Jesus' half-brother. It's clear that Peter had been in town for a while, probably doing some teaching and training. During this time, Peter fit in with the norm at Antioch, where Gentiles and Jewish background believers saw no distinction between each other. They ate together and had open fellowship.

Then came some "men from James." These men came from the old Hebraic core of believers in Jerusalem, where James was leading. They claimed to be speaking for James, but James later said he didn't send them and knew nothing about them (15:24). They were just using his name to seem more authoritative. Paul calls them "the party of the circumcision," which ties them clearly to the group Luke talked about in Acts 15.

These men were practicing the rabbinic teaching that Jews should not eat with Gentiles (a teaching found nowhere in the Bible). The meal must have been served in the same hall, but these new rabbis sat at their own table apart from the Gentile believers. Soon, Peter joined them. You can imagine how this felt to the Gentiles. "So, we were good enough to eat with earlier, but not anymore?" They probably didn't care about the strangers, but Peter? The most respected leader of the apostles?

## And the Rest of Them

Things got worse:

> The rest of the Jews joined him in hypocrisy, with the result that even Barnabas was carried away by their hypocrisy. (Galatians 2:13)

This is so bad! The tide of opinion was rapidly shifting as the rest of the Jewish believers joined in, separating themselves from their Gentile fellow believers. Last of all, the worst possible news: "Even Barnabas was carried away." Barnabas—one of the sweetest believers in the book of Acts—a hero of the faith in every way. This is the man of whom Luke says, "He was a good man, and full of the Holy Spirit and of faith" (11:24). This was Paul's partner during the first journey. And now he's moving over to sit with the self-righteous crew!

This point in history was a true crisis. Legalism was on the ascent. A tide of legalistic thinking had already corrupted the churches in Galatia. Jerusalem, where these men came from, had also been badly penetrated. And now, Antioch, the beating heart of Gentile outreach, was swinging over to the Judaizers.

At this dangerous moment, the barrier standing between the people of God and the fatal error of returning to rabbinic legalism had dwindled down to one man. Paul never had any doubts. He strode up to Peter's table and called out loud enough for everyone to hear:

> "If you [Peter], being a Jew, live like the Gentiles and not like the Jews, how is it that you compel the Gentiles to live like Jews?" (Galatians 2:14)

In other words, Paul looked around at the rabbis from Jerusalem and said, "You all should know that he's been sitting with the Gentiles all week before you got here...."

Peter was busted. We don't know exactly how the dialog went from there, but Luke reports, "Paul and Barnabas had great dissension and debate with them" (Acts 15:2). So Barnabas at least must have quickly realized his error. He powerfully joined into the argument on the side of radical grace.

"Great dissension" sounds like there may have been some yelling and tension. They couldn't reach a conclusion. Both sides stood their ground.

So at that point, "They determined that Paul and Barnabas and some others of them should go up to Jerusalem to the apostles and elders concerning this issue" (v. 2).

## The Big Picture

After reaching a stalemate, the early believers were taking things to the next level. The top leadership in Jerusalem, and the top leadership in Antioch were about to have it out on the critical issue of law and grace. The future of the true gospel hung in the balance.

By submitting to a council, Paul was rolling the dice that things would come out right.

# 25

# THE JERUSALEM COUNCIL

## ACTS 15

Jerusalem is 300 miles from Antioch, and they probably went by foot, so this was a trip lasting weeks. Along the way, "They were passing through both Phoenicia and Samaria, describing in detail the conversion of the Gentiles, and were bringing great joy to all the brethren" (Acts 15:3). The entire journey must have been dotted with occasional local groups of believers.

Were the Judaizers traveling along with Paul and Barnabas? That's hard to imagine. It's more likely that the leadership of Antioch was with Paul, and that the other rabbis had gone ahead earlier. They were probably already in Jerusalem gathering allies to join the fight.

Before the debate began, we read that, "When they arrived at Jerusalem, they were received by the church and the apostles and the elders, and they reported all that God had done with them" (v. 4). They were recounting the incredible story of the first journey, including everything we just read. We don't hear how the Jerusalem leaders reacted, but it must have made an impression. Who could doubt that God was with these apostles?

## The Battle Is Joined

They came to the point: "Some of the sect of the Pharisees who had believed stood up, saying, 'It is necessary to circumcise them and to direct them to observe the Law of Moses'" (v 5). So converted Pharisees led the charge. But Paul was a former Pharisee too. He knew how they thought, and that was an advantage.

What followed, Luke calls "much debate" (v. 7). The leaders must have been citing Scripture, rabbinic authorities, and arguing vigorously. Paul and others were coming right back. It seems likely they spent hours arguing.

## Peter

Then, "After there had been much debate, Peter stood up" (v. 7). Oh boy, here we go. The last time we saw Paul and Peter together, Paul was publicly rebuking Peter in front of the whole church. That must have been incredibly embarrassing for Peter. But now they were on Peter's ground. In Jerusalem, he was the man. The elders in this meeting were personally loyal to him, but barely knew Paul. Now Peter was in perfect position to dish out some serious payback.

He spoke:

> "Brethren, you know that in the early days God made a choice among you, that by my mouth the Gentiles would hear the word of the gospel and believe. And God, who knows the heart, testified to them giving them the Holy Spirit, just as He also did to us; and He made no distinction between us and them, cleansing their hearts by faith." (vs. 7-9)

All true. He's talking about the event with Cornelius and his household from Acts 10. So Peter got there first when it came to converting Gentiles (not counting the Ethiopian eunuch). The fact that none of Cornelius' household was circumcised or kosher never came into play when it came to the indwelling of the Holy Spirit.

But what about the present debate? Peter is clear:

> "Now therefore why do you put God to the test by placing upon the neck of the disciples a yoke which neither our fathers

nor we have been able to bear? But we believe that we are saved through the grace of the Lord Jesus, in the same way as they also are." (vs. 10-11)

Peter comes down strong with Paul! Here he becomes a second impressive hero in this account, and a beautiful picture of spiritual maturity. After messing up in Antioch, Peter had the humility to realize he was in the wrong, and that Paul—the one who embarrassed him—was in the right. No pride or personal hurt would be allowed to interfere with God's truth. Peter boldly joins Paul in direct opposition to the so-called "party of the circumcision."

When he charges the opponents with "placing upon the neck of the disciples a yoke which neither our fathers nor we have been able to bear" (v. 10), he echoes Paul's careful explanation of the true purpose of the law in Romans 3 and parallels. Namely, that God didn't give the law with the thought that it would be obeyed, but "so that every mouth may be closed and all the world may become accountable to God" (Romans 3:19; see also Galatians 3:23-25).

Next, Paul and Barnabas gave a further report of their mission trip. Maybe Paul also recounted his earlier years of church planting in Syria and Cilicia. "All the people kept silent, and they were listening to Barnabas and Paul as they were relating what signs and wonders God had done through them among the Gentiles" (v. 12). Would God be granting miracles like these if Paul and Barnabas were so far off theologically? Clearly not.

## James

It was time to reach a conclusion. James, Jesus' half-brother, was by now the lead elder in the Jerusalem church. That becomes clear in this account by the way he summarizes and closes the meeting. More than fifteen years had passed since that day James looked up and was shocked by a personal visit from Jesus after his resurrection.

James spoke:

"Brothers, listen to me. Simon [Peter] has told you about the time God first visited the Gentiles to take from them a people for himself. And this conversion of Gentiles is exactly what the prophets predicted. As it is written:

'Afterward I will return and restore the fallen house of David. I will rebuild its ruins and restore it, so that the rest of humanity might seek the Lord, including the Gentiles—all those I have called to be mine.

The Lord has spoken—he who made these things known so long ago.'" (vs. 13-18)

In addition to what Peter said about the Cornelius event, James points out that the prophets had already predicted this was going to happen. He first recites Amos 9:11-12. The wording is a bit different in the Greek version from which James quoted, but the meaning is the same.

The picture is that God is going to restore Israel at the end time, and other nations will be there as well: "And Israel will possess what is left of Edom and all the nations I have called to be mine" (Amos 9:12).[1] So while the main thrust of the prophecy concerns Israel, it's also clear that in this vision, God has called other nations to be his. They aren't becoming converted like Jewish proselytes; they remain with their own ethnicities.

It also seems like in verse 18, James is conflating Amos and Isaiah 45:21-22, which ends with God's grand declaration, "Turn to me and be saved, all the ends of the earth; For I am God, and there is no other."

He could have cited Genesis 12:3 where God, speaking to Abraham, said, "*all peoples on earth* will be blessed through you." As New Testament scholar John Stott said,

The inclusion of the Gentiles was not a divine after-thought, but foretold by the prophets... There was an 'agreement'

---

1. The LXX (Greek version of the OT) disagrees a bit with the MT (Hebrew text) on this passage in Amos. NASB has a footnote explaining: "9:11b-12 Greek version reads, 'and restore its former glory, / so that the rest of humanity, including the Gentiles—all those I have called to be mine—might seek me.'" Interestingly, DSS (Dead Sea text) agrees with LXX, not the Masoretic. The LXX didn't come from the DSS. Neither did the DSS come from the LXX. These are independent sources, clearly signaling some earlier Hebrew texts existed that read like the LXX and DSS. For the Masoretic Text, we have nothing older than the 900s AD. Regardless of which reading is correct, the verses still signaled that God is going to win many Gentiles to faith, and they remain Gentiles. So James' citation is spot on.

between what God had done through his apostles and what he had said through his prophets.[2]

James went on, "Therefore it is my judgment that we do not trouble those who are turning to God from among the Gentiles" (v. 19). Yes! They're coming down on the right side of the issue. But wait: "But that we write to them that they abstain from things contaminated by idols and from fornication and from what is strangled and from blood" (v. 20). What's this? It looks like he's mixing the law back in after all.

The explanation is in the next verse: "For Moses from ancient generations has in every city those who preach him, since he is read in the synagogues every Sabbath" (v. 21). What does this have to do with whether the Gentiles eat blood? It shows that James' suggestions are not based on law, but on missiology (the study of missionary methods). James is appealing to a principle in cross-cultural outreach known as contextualization.

Church planters reaching out to a different culture have to make their outreach suitable to the other culture's sensibilities. That's their context. A principle of missions is that it's on the ones reaching out to shift from their own context to the new one.

In this case, James and the other leaders don't want the Gentile churches to give up on reaching Jewish people. If they invite Jews over to one of their meetings, and the Gentiles are slurping down blood or serving non-kosher food, the Jews would be grossed out.

"Things contaminated by idols" refers to meat that had been consecrated to a Greek god. From the time of Daniel, conservative Jews had a tradition that they shouldn't eat meat offered to idols. They saw it as contaminated, but they also felt that refusing it was a statement.

Why fornication is in this list is harder to say. All the other constraints are specific to the Mosaic Covenant as interpreted by the rabbis. Fornication seems to be in a different category—objective, serious, sin. The best explanation is still missiological. Fornication or other kinds of immorality were so rampant in Greco-Roman cities that James felt the need to name it as highly offensive.

---

2. John Stott, The Message of Acts: To the ends of the earth, (Downers Grove, IL: Intervarsity Press, 1990), 194.

Notice the most important thing: Circumcision is not on the list!

## The Finding

The assembled leaders all agreed with James' formula, and they put his proposal down in a letter. Luke recounts the letter's wording and the important endorsement of Paul and Barnabas, saying they were, "men who have risked their lives for the name of our Lord Jesus Christ" (v. 26).

They also decided to send along two respected men, "Judas called Barsabbas, and Silas"[3] (v. 22, 27). These two came in case anyone suspected that Paul and Barnabas were exaggerating the agreement at the council.

After going to Antioch, Silas also joined Paul in visiting churches in Galatia to give the same message. It would be significant that a Jerusalem-based leader bear witness to what the council decided.

We know from the book of Galatians that some of the Judaizers were disparaging Paul by claiming he was not part of the Twelve, and that he had deviated from the first apostles' teaching. The Judaizers claimed that they had the true gospel from the Twelve, all of whom were there before Paul believed. (See his defense of his authenticity relative to other apostles in Galatians 1:11-12; 15-19). The truth was that the Judaizers were the ones deviating from apostolic teaching, and this letter with their signatures proved that.

## Paul and the Letter

Some interpreters wonder if Paul was unhappy with the council's letter, maybe considering it a necessary but imperfect compromise. This view comes from Paul's discussion of eating meat sacrificed to idols in 1 Corinthians 8 and 10 and Romans 14.

We don't have space to go deep into this question here. But notice that the first thing Paul and Barnabas did was read the letter to their group in Antioch, which resulted in rejoicing (vs. 30-31). Then they did the same thing in the churches in Galatia (16:4). So their behavior shows that they agreed with the letter.

---

3. Silas becomes a key player from this time on in the book of Acts. Luke calls him Silas, but Paul and Peter call him by the Romanized version of the name, "Silvanus." Some readers don't realize these are the same person.

Also, Paul's comments on eating things sacrificed to idols fully harmonizes with the decree. He allows believers to eat consecrated meat without asking questions. But if their host says the meat is consecrated to an idol, the believers should refuse to eat it (1 Corinthians 10:27-28). That fits perfectly the missiological intent of the letter. The key was what kind of statement you were making by your behavior, not that the meat was defiling or dangerous in itself. In the case where you didn't know it was offered to an idol, you weren't making a statement.

He also expressed concern over eating consecrated meat for a different reason in 1 Corinthians 8. There he discusses the case of "some, being accustomed to the idol until now" (v. 7). Paul worried about former idol worshippers who see believers eating such meat. Consecrated meat was often served in a restaurant connected to an idol temple. These former idol worshippers might conclude that ongoing involvement with idolatry is permissible alongside Jesus. This is not a missional point, but an aspect of love in the body of Christ—that believers should be willing to give up their freedoms if they cause a fellow believer to stumble.

Paul's discussion in Romans 14 was closer to the council's intent, but still different. Some in the Roman group were judging others for eating meat. These were Jews so scrupulous that they ate vegetables only, because it wasn't always clear at the market whether meat had been offered to an idol (v. 2).

This case went way beyond the scenario imagined at the council, to the point of not eating *any* meat. So Paul argues a different direction based on not judging each other (vs. 3-4). He considered this question to be a matter of conscience. But he still retains the idea of giving up meat if it will keep a brother from stumbling (v. 21). That would probably only apply when eating together with those who might stumble.

## The big picture

At the Jerusalem council, the church teetered on the edge of a fatal fall into legalism. Through the courageous stand taken by Paul, Barnabas, and Peter, the notion of retaining the Mosaic Covenant along with the New Covenant was officially laid aside. But this wasn't the end of it. Satan knows people gravitate toward legalism, and that it shreds true spirituality and any hope of evangelism. In book after book, Paul found it necessary to come back to insisting on pure grace.

Even after the supreme explanation of the relationship between the Old and New Covenants in the book of Hebrews, the church has often continued to revert to the Old Covenant. One church after another has abandoned radical grace in favor of law.

# 26

## THE SECOND JOURNEY BEGINS
### ACTS 16

### Size of the Group in Antioch

Before the apostles left on another journey, we see another indication of the size of the group in Antioch. Luke says, "They [Paul and Barnabas] and many others taught and preached the word of the Lord there" (Acts 15:35). To have many teachers and preachers suggests a very large group, possibly a thousand or more by now.

### Syria and Cilicia

> After some time Paul said to Barnabas, "Let's go back and visit each city where we previously preached the word of the Lord, to see how the new believers are doing." (v. 36)

Paul's description of the mission centered on visiting each city "where we previously preached." But looking ahead, we notice that, although Paul eventually reached Derbe and Lystra, he also "traveled throughout Syria and Cilicia, strengthening the churches there" (v. 41).

On the first journey, they never planted any churches in Syria or Cilicia. So why would Paul describe these churches as those "where we previously preached?" The answer comes when we remember that before coming to Antioch, Paul spent eight to ten years in these very provinces. That means that during the "silent years" Paul had planted plural churches in these regions.

Why is this important? Many interpreters argue that Paul had to spend twelve to fifteen years growing and deepening before getting into public ministry. That's why God set him aside in Cilicia for ten years—so he could become mature enough to begin planting churches. These interpreters argue that people shouldn't do work like this until they've had a similar period of static growth. After all, Paul says a leader "must not be a new believer, because he might become proud, and the devil would cause him to fall" (1 Timothy 3:6).

Here we see, to the contrary, that Paul began preaching within days of his conversion in Damascus: "Immediately he began to proclaim Jesus in the synagogues, saying, 'He is the Son of God'" (Acts 9:20). He went on and continued evangelistic work and church planting from then on. In fact, he never stopped. That's Paul's pattern, and we should imitate it. Paul's statement that "he should not be a new convert" refers to elders, not deacons or other Christian workers.

I began teaching and preaching when I was nineteen years old. God blessed the ministry, and scores of students came to faith. But a number of believers took offense that someone so young would assume leadership of a such a group, and they tried to use the case of Paul to argue that a young man should wait ten or more years before going into ministry.

I wondered whether they were right, but I was unsure. The argument made sense to me at the time, and I really considered quitting. Then, after studying Paul's life and chronology with friends, and getting wise counsel from older believers, I realized the argument was vacuous. Paul was a go-getter from day one! And the Lord showed me I should go on.

## John Mark

While getting ready for their next journey, Paul and Barnabas discovered they had different plans.

> Barnabas wanted to take John, called Mark, along with them also. But Paul kept insisting that they should not take him

along who had deserted them in Pamphylia and had not gone with them to the work. (vs. 37-38)

Had Mark repented? Probably. But does that mean he should be reinstated in his trusted position in the Apostolic band? Not in Paul's view. Some readers think Paul was being mean-spirited and vindictive by holding John Mark's past sin against him months after the fact.

Several reasons could have gone into Paul's thinking.

First, forgiveness and trust are two different things. Forgiveness should be freely given (Colossians 3:13). But trust must be earned. Trust results from an assessment of a person's previous and recent attitudes and behavior. Suppose you caught an employee stealing from the register in your store, but when confronted, he also repents. You might forgive him, but still not put him back on the register. There's nothing inconsistent in that. Paul may have felt that not enough time had passed to demonstrate reliability in John Mark.

Another possible reason Paul didn't want to take Mark could have been for Mark's own good. Paul may have felt that if Mark messed up badly and nothing happened as a result, it might make him more willing to mess up in the future.

A third possible reason for Paul's stand could be that he did it for the sake of the church in Antioch. He may have wanted to make more of a statement to the church that serving God is serious business and is not to be taken lightly. He may have felt that if someone "deserted" them and nothing happened as a result, it would give the church the wrong message. It would be too soft.

An important footnote to this episode is that Paul and John Mark continued to work together later. In 2 Timothy 4 Paul said, "Pick up Mark and bring him with you, for he is useful to me for service" (v. 11). That goes to show that this was not a personal rejection based on contempt.

Barnabas probably felt that John Mark should be given another chance, just out of grace. However, Barnabas and Mark were also relatives, and that sometimes skews one's view. Is it possible that Barnabas was in the wrong here by going too soft? If so, the text doesn't say that.

Then Luke says, "There occurred such a sharp disagreement that they separated from one another, and Barnabas took Mark with him and sailed away to Cyprus" (v. 39).

In fact, this decision was a judgment call that could go either way without violating Scripture. And the two apostles saw it differently. This happens periodically in ministry. The usual solution is for one party to defer to the other. But in some cases, leaders may feel that the issue is too important to defer on. In these cases, going separate ways peacefully could be a godly solution.

They weren't leaving in hostility. They were choosing to continue their ministries in different directions. This is somewhat similar to what Paul did with James, John, and Peter in Galatians 2:

> Recognizing the grace that had been given to me, James and Cephas and John, who were reputed to be pillars, gave to me and Barnabas the right hand of fellowship, so that we might go to the Gentiles and they to the circumcised. (v. 9)

This "right hand of fellowship" was an agreement and approval of each other's direction, while going to separate fields. This is really a good example of how to handle such judgment calls and different callings from God—putting the interests of the fields ahead of one's own view. Of course, it would be different if the issue was an objective, biblical teaching.

In a large community like the one I'm in, we usually have ample space to let people pursue ministries they feel called to, and God uses these to open new fields. Some of our largest ministries originally were a couple of people who wanted to do something different.

On the negative side, we too often see people storm off in bitterness because they didn't get their way on a judgment call. That's not what happened here, because the text doesn't signal anything wrong. They probably were angry at points during the argument, but anger was not what governed their actions.

## Sent Off

Barnabas took John Mark and went back to Cypress. He originally came from there and probably had contacts he could use to open more doors.

Paul chose to take Silas, and they journeyed northward overland toward

Galatia. But as we saw earlier, they also visited a number of churches in Syria and Cilicia.

## Timothy

> Paul came also to Derbe and to Lystra. And a disciple was there, named Timothy, the son of a Jewish woman who was a believer, but his father was a Greek, and he was well spoken of by the brethren who were in Lystra and Iconium. (16:1-2)

Here Paul meets Timothy, who would eventually become Paul's right-hand man. At this point he was young, possibly a teenager, because fourteen years later, Paul was still telling him not to let people look down on him because of his youth (1 Timothy 4:12). Youth here means their view of youth, not ours. Timothy must have been thirty or more when 1 Timothy was written, because synagogues didn't let rabbis teach until they were thirty.

Timothy must have been serving in both Lystra and Iconium because the text says he "was well spoken of by the brethren who were in Lystra and Iconium." Apparently, he decided to join Paul and Silas. The reason he joined them may have been because of a prophetic word. Paul reminds him years later:

> Do not neglect the spiritual gift within you, which was bestowed on you through prophetic utterance with the laying on of hands by the presbytery (elders). (1 Timothy 4:14)

He also refers to laying on of hands in 2 Timothy:

> I remind you to kindle afresh the gift of God which is in you through the laying on of my hands. (1:6)

Are these two different events? Or two ways of describing the same event? I could see them being the same event. The first one has the elders and probably Paul and Silas laying hands on. For the second reference, Paul may have been the one who actually got a prophetic word relating to this gift, so he focuses on that part.

Was it a gift of evangelism? He later says, "But you, be sober in all things, endure hardship, do the work of an evangelist, fulfill your ministry" (2 Timothy 4:5). Or was it the gift of apostleship? He behaves like an apostle (not in the capital A sense) by appointing elders in Ephesus.

# Circumcision?

Then, Paul "took him and circumcised him because of the Jews who were in those parts, for they all knew that his father was a Greek" (v. 3).

Wait, wasn't Paul the one who was just arguing that circumcision was unnecessary? Yes, and that remained his view. The reason for this circumcision was again missiology. Paul knew they would be going into synagogues, and they wanted to be able to say they were all circumcised Jews. The idea of a Jewish woman marrying a Greek would have drawn disapproval from Jews, and it would have been a distraction.

Besides, Paul later explained that he believed Jews should continue to practice cultural Judaism as long as it didn't contradict Christian doctrine (like offering blood sacrifice). He thought Jews should remain culturally Jewish, and Gentiles should remain culturally Gentile (1 Corinthians 7:18). Under Jewish custom, Timothy having a Jewish mother made him a Jew. He should have been circumcised.

# Lystra?

Why wasn't Paul more afraid of showing his face in Lystra, where he had earlier been stoned? For one thing, the mob that stoned him included people from Iconium and Pisidian Antioch. There may not have been that many from Lystra.

Also, in all likelihood, the believers in the area had gone to the Romans for legal protection. Mobs were not permitted to stone random people, especially Roman citizens like Paul. Unable to identify a specific culprit, the Romans probably warned the locals that they would be arrested and punished if any more of that happened.

# Westward

They went westward on the Roman road in the direction of Pisidian Antioch.

> Now while they were passing through the cities, they were delivering the decrees which had been decided upon by the apostles and elders who were in Jerusalem, for them to observe. (v. 4)

Here again, we see that Paul fully agreed with the decree from James and the other leaders at the Jerusalem Council.

As they went westward through Galatia to the region of Phrygia, they needed to either turn right up toward Mysia, or stay south toward Ephesus. At that point, they were "forbidden by the Holy Spirit to speak the word in Asia" (v. 6). That's curious. Ephesus was the largest city in the province of Asia, and it later became the center of an incredible spiritual eruption that spread out to thousands, including all the surrounding cities.

Then, they were planning to go into Bithynia, but again, "the Spirit of Jesus did not permit them" (v. 7). But again, Bithynia was later evangelized according to 1 Peter 1:1.

Why would God tell them not to go there? We don't know. Silas was a prophet (15:32), so he may have received a word. But we do know that later God sent them to Ephesus after all.

From those facts alone, we can infer that God knows things we don't know about any ministry field. Perhaps there were factors in Ephesus that weren't ready for a movement. Or it could have been that God wanted to prioritize outreach to Macedonia (where Philippi and Thessalonica were) and Achaia (where Athens and Corinth were).

We can also infer that a divine leading at one point in time might be temporary, like in this case. Later, for whatever reasons, he sent them in a different direction. That could happen to us today.

One of the most annoying and damaging aspects of organized religion is its reluctance to change. Churches still sing music from the 1700s and wear robes from medieval times. We've seen that in Acts, when God could hardly get the original Jewish Christian community to change over to accepting Gentiles as they are.

Here in this account is an example of what God wants. This band was light on their feet and ready to follow the Spirit's direction wherever and whenever he led.

We know that after they ended up on the coast at Troas, it was through a vision—a dream? "A vision appeared to Paul in the night: a man of Macedonia was standing and appealing to him, and saying, 'Come over to Macedonia and help us'" (v. 9).

Many Christian workers have never had anything this direct from God. I have only had a handful. I think for most of us, it's quite rare. Other believers claim they have running conversations with God covering every detail of life. "God just told me..." and then he said, "Don't do this, you should do that instead..."

I don't know what to think about those claims, but I will observe that even for the Apostle Paul, it was rare enough to record in his history. If this was a daily or hourly event, I doubt we would be reading about it.

God does speak, and through the subtle promptings of the Spirit he engages in ongoing fellowship with his people. But communication with words and syntax like this is rare. These communications usually accompany something important, like in this story in Acts.

## The Big Picture

God often doesn't explain the reason for a given leading. You could imagine Paul arguing, "What's wrong with Ephesus? It's a big city, and they don't know the gospel..." But part of following God is not always knowing where you're going or why.

It's not that the leading is nonsensical or irrational. It's just that you don't know all the details. Abraham showed his faith when he struck out with his family, "not knowing where he was going" (Hebrews 11:8). God gave him a direction to go, but didn't describe the destination.

At other times, leadings from God make perfect sense and he supplies the reasons, as we saw earlier in 1 Corinthians 16:8-9. There Paul argued that a wide door for effective service and the presence of many adversaries were ample reasons for him to stay on in Ephesus.

At this point in history, God had in mind seeing the gospel break into Europe. Their next stop was in the European city of Philippi.

# 27

# PHILIPPI

## ACTS 16:10-40

Suddenly, we have the first "we" passage. The author has joined the band!

> When he had seen the vision, immediately we sought to go into Macedonia, concluding that God had called us to preach the gospel to them. So putting out to sea from Troas, we ran a straight course to Samothrace, and on the day following to Neapolis; and from there to Philippi, which is a leading city of the district of Macedonia, a Roman colony; and we were staying in this city for some days. (Acts 16:10-12)

In this account, we immediately notice a shift in narrative to include far more detail. Before Troas, he just referred to going through "cities." Now he names three cities on successive days of sailing. The ministry in Philippi also has more detail and is lengthier than any other city they visited. This pattern continues into every other "we" passage. The author was actually there, seeing and reporting the succession of events in detail.

This is an outstanding mark of authenticity. The shift is quite noticeable and consistent whenever the author joins the band. You'll see fine details like what hour it was, which islands they passed, on which side of the ship, the direction of the winds, and dozens of other fine details not really necessary for the story. It's simply the difference between a second-hand and an eyewitness account.

Luke may have lived in Troas. Or, a case could be made that he lived in Philippi, because this "we" passage stops in Philippi. And the second "we" passage (20:5–15) begins when Paul revisits Philippi during the third journey. Or, Luke may have moved to Philippi to serve in the church there.

# Philippi

Luke points out that Philippi was a "leading city" and a "Roman colony." Roman colonies were towns taken over by immigrating Romans, often from the military. After serving twenty years, Roman soldiers were given the choice of moving to one of the provinces where he would be given a farm or other land stead to live on. The Romans considered this good policy because it helped to Romanize the provinces, and the land cost the government nothing. They just seized it.

Retired Roman soldiers were relatively wealthy for their day, and often related to centrally located towns. Such towns tended to be wealthy and proud of their Roman origins. The city reported directly to the emperor rather than to the provincial administration. Paul's band decided to take a stand there.

# Lydia

> And on the Sabbath day we went outside the gate to a riverside, where we were supposing that there would be a place of prayer; and we sat down and began speaking to the women who had assembled. (v. 13)

The mysterious description here is the result of rabbinic rules we can access in the *Mishnah*. The band had discovered that Philippi had no synagogue. The probable reason was that there were too few Jews in Philippi to make a quorum. The rabbis taught that a minimum of ten men were needed to establish a synagogue.[1] Women didn't count.

They went to the next most likely location for a gathering—outside the

---

1. *Mishnah*, Sanhedrin 1:6.

city gate. This location suggests their separation or distinctiveness from the Gentiles. There were some women, and possibly a few men.

God supplied the open door to Philippi using just what they needed—a strong woman:

> A woman named Lydia, from the city of Thyatira, a seller of purple fabrics, a worshiper of God, was listening; and the Lord opened her heart to respond to the things spoken by Paul. And when she and her household had been baptized, she urged us, saying, "If you have judged me to be faithful to the Lord, come into my house and stay." And she prevailed upon us. (vs. 14-15)

So here we have a single woman far from her hometown of Thyatira (known to produce rare purple dye from a certain root growing there) in the province of Asia. She's doing successful business selling costly purple fabrics to the wealthy Romans in Philippi. We can tell she was successful because she leads a household, apparently including servants or employees.

She is described as "a worshipper of God," which means she was a Gentile follower of Jewish Bible teaching. She was probably not a full proselyte, because they are usually identified as such.

Lydia was an assertive woman. No husband is in the picture, so she was probably either a widow or a divorcee. For a woman to establish a successful business in a foreign town during this patriarchal time was an unusual feat requiring drive and skill. She talked Paul and his band into staying at her house, apparently in the face of some reluctance. Luke says, "She prevailed upon us."

She also led the rest of her household to faith and baptism. Now they had a group of people won over and a headquarters in a sizeable house—it must have been good-sized if she lived there with her multiple household members, and could invite another four men to move in. Lydia was the first convert in Europe and the first house church no doubt met at her house.

Later, in the book of Revelation, we learn there was a local body in Thyatira (Revelation 1:11; 18-29). Surprisingly, Lydia isn't mentioned in Paul's letter to the Philippians, so it's quite possible that she had returned home and may have had a hand in planting the church there. Paul and his band never went to Thyatira.

## Hello, Satan

Everywhere Paul and his band go, satanic opposition shows up on cue. Philippi was no exception.

> It happened that as we were going to the place of prayer, a slave-girl having a spirit of divination met us, who was bringing her masters much profit by fortune-telling. Following after Paul and us, she kept crying out, saying, "These men are bond-servants of the Most High God, who are proclaiming to you the way of salvation." She continued doing this for many days. (vs. 16-18)

How strange that a demonic spirit would choose to cry out this message! It's counter-intuitive, but there must have been something twisted in what she was saying or how she was saying it. We read that "Paul was greatly annoyed" (v. 18). She may have been crying out in an inappropriate way. At the very least, she was blowing their cover. They hardly needed a demon possessed girl announcing their presence and mission to the city.

Satan's tactic here is infiltration and counterfeit. He moves someone under his control into the church and then has them bellow and shriek out a version of the gospel in the most tasteless and annoying way.

Pseudo-evangelists on our campus at Ohio State stand in the central green screaming and crying out accusations and insults at passersby. They make a disgraceful picture which is mistakenly taken to be a fair representation of Christians by the thousands of secular students. Those students want nothing to do with such an ugly way.

Paul spoke a word of authority: "He turned and said to the spirit, 'I command you in the name of Jesus Christ to come out of her!' And it came out at that very moment" (v. 18). This was the authority Jesus said believers have: "Behold, I have given you authority to tread on serpents and scorpions, and over all the power of the enemy" (Luke 10:19).

Strangely, this is the only detailed case of exorcism in the New Testament after Jesus' life. Luke mentions that exorcisms occurred in a couple of other places in Acts, but nothing more—none of them are recounted. Then, in all the Epistles, so full of advice and instruction for ministry, we never hear a word about exorcism or any instructions on how to do it.

This is surprising after the flurry of demonic possession during Jesus' life. Possibly the demons knew something important was happening with Jesus, and swarmed into that area.

At the very least, the lack of instruction on exorcism suggests that it's not a key area for ministry. Instead, we are given extensive information on combating Satan's far more typical forms of attack: temptation, persecution, infiltration, deception, and accusation.

## Counter Punch

> But when her masters saw that their hope of profit was gone, they seized Paul and Silas and dragged them into the market place before the authorities, and when they had brought them to the chief magistrates, they said, "These men are throwing our city into confusion, being Jews, and are proclaiming customs which it is not lawful for us to accept or to observe, being Romans." (vs. 19-21)

Instead of rejoicing that this young girl had been delivered from the power of Satan, her owners were furious. Their only interest was in how they could exploit the girl for profit.

Notice the racial twist the complainers introduced, "being Jews" versus "being Romans." They were playing to the endemic anti-Semitism in the city. The reaction was potent. Within minutes,

> The crowd rose up together against them, and the chief magistrates tore their robes off them and proceeded to order them to be beaten with rods. When they had struck them with many blows, they threw them into prison, commanding the jailer to guard them securely; and he, having received such a command, threw them into the inner prison and fastened their feet in the stocks. (vs. 22-24)

This was a vicious beating, especially when Luke mentions "many blows." It's not unlikely that they suffered cracked ribs, deep contusions, and torn skin from this beating with rods.

Only Paul and Silas were taken. Luke and Timothy either were somewhere else, or not identified as part of the group.

## Suffering in Faith

The head jailor was ordered to lock them securely, so he put them in the inner cell and locked their ankles in the stocks. That would have made their pain worse as they stiffened up and were unable to change position.

In their throbbing pain and agony, what went through their minds? They looked up to God. "What's the meaning? You allowed this to happen in front of the whole city that we've been praying for and reaching out to." Of course, they couldn't know the answer. But they could safely assume God had his reasons. Under godly reflection, the shock of the attack abated. Faith began to flow in... all that Paul later taught about rejoicing in momentary light affliction came to mind... they began to pray and sing praises!

What astonishment the jailor and other prisoners must have felt! What's wrong with these guys? We read that "the prisoners were listening to them."

Then God moved.

> Suddenly there came a great earthquake, so that the foundations of the prison house were shaken; and immediately all the doors were opened and everyone's chains were unfastened. (v. 26)

Even the other prisoners looked down and their chains were loosed. Apparently, nobody fled. The other prisoners must have made the connection that these guys spoke for God.

The jailor had his sword out and was going to commit suicide, because under Roman law, a jailor who lost his prisoner was subject to the death penalty. And they weren't too sympathetic about special conditions like visiting angels or earthquakes. "But Paul cried out with a loud voice, saying, 'Do not harm yourself, for we are all here!'" (v. 28).

Then,

> The jailor called for lights and rushed in, and trembling with

fear he fell down before Paul and Silas, and after he brought
them out, he said, "Sirs, what must I do to be saved?" (vs. 29-30)

Falling down before them could have been an expression of awe, or an
acknowledgement that they were in charge. Then follows the question,
"What must I do to be saved?" Why would he ask that? Clearly, they had
been talking about it. They weren't just having a time of worship; they
had been preaching to the inmates and the jailor.

Their answer to his question was quite simple and clear: "Believe in the
Lord Jesus, and you will be saved." Anything someone adds to this simple statement, like "and be baptized," or "and commit yourself to the
Lordship of Christ," or "and promise you'll stop that sin," would make
this statement propositionally *false*. Under such additions, believing in
the Lord Jesus is *not* enough to be saved.

Notice that under a grammatical-historical reading, verses like this gov-
ern other verses like Acts 2:38, where Peter says. "Repent, and each of
you be baptized." The only way to harmonize these two texts is to see
the lowest common denominator as good enough: salvation by faith. Of
course, faith plus baptism would also save.

Paul adds the thought, "you and your household" (v. 31). Ancient households tended to think together, making corporate decisions based on
consensus. But Paul isn't making a blanket promise here, that all families of those who believe will also believe. That often happens, but Paul
himself warns believers, "For how do you know, O wife, whether you
will save your husband? Or how do you know, O husband, whether you
will save your wife?" (1 Corinthians 7:16). Rather, this was probably a
prophetic word, applying only to this case.

They went to the jailor's house, where he cleaned their wounds and fed
them. The other prisoners? They must have been locked up again. Or, if
there were only a couple of them, maybe they went along to the jailor's
house?

During the possibly several hours they were at the jailor's house, he must
have assembled his household (which would include extended family,
employees, and servants) to hear the gospel. Paul must have given them
his Greco-Roman sermon, and they were persuaded and moved. They
all believed and were baptized. They had the recent earthquake to consider as well.

They were back in prison before dawn. Then came the word from the city magistrates who sent their officers saying Paul and Silas were free to leave.

> But Paul said to the officers: "They beat us publicly without a trial, even though we are Roman citizens, and threw us into prison. And now do they want to get rid of us quietly? No! Let them come themselves and escort us out." (v. 37)

The two officers looked at each other, startled. This was real bad news! Beating and imprisoning Roman citizens without a trial was a serious offense. They had assumed Paul and Silas were just wandering Jews. Nobody said anything about Roman citizenship. Of course, neither did anyone ask. The mob that attacked them was mindless and full of racist fury.

Paul insisted, "But let them come themselves and bring us out" (v. 37). Paul is not just making the magistrates grovel; he has a plan to extract concessions.

As a Roman colony, Philippi had a large measure of autonomy, but not to the extent of messing up Roman citizens without a trial. The government had two magistrates and two officers. The officers carried out the decisions of the magistrates. Here, they go back to report the bad news. We read, "They were afraid when they heard that they were Romans" (v. 38).

So the magistrates came down to the prison and "appealed" or "pleaded" with Paul and Silas. They were trying to make peace and play down what happened.

We have every reason to think Paul used this situation to compel these leaders to adopt a new, fairer position toward Christians in the city. They had ongoing opponents in the city (Philippians 1:28-30), but it wasn't enough to keep them from growing into a model local church.

Finally, "When Paul and Silas left the prison, they returned to Lydia's home. There they met with the believers and encouraged them once more" (v. 40). They probably exhorted them along the same lines he wrote to them later: "For you have been given not only the privilege of trusting in Christ but also the privilege of suffering for him" (Philippians 1:29).

They may have stayed at Lydia's house for a few days. That would allow time for healing their wounds as they were nursed and their bandages changed. Without that, it's hard to imagine them making the ninety-mile hike to Thessalonica.

## The Big Picture

In the years to come, the Philippian body grew and flourished. They became the main funding group for Paul's subsequent journeys and imprisonments, constantly sending funds to wherever he was.

They began immediately. Paul wrote to them more than a decade later,

> As you know, you Philippians were the only ones who gave me financial help when I first brought you the good news and then traveled on from Macedonia. No other church did this. (Philippians 4:15)

He wrote this letter from prison in Rome, and it turns out the Philippians had sent a messenger all the way to Rome with another bountiful gift. That gift enabled him to rent a house, continue to teach, receive guests, and write four irreplaceable letters: Ephesians, Colossians, Philippians, and Philemon.

In the long term, the Philippian outreach was one of the most successful we know of. And Paul and Silas paid a bitter price in the course of the ministry. Who knows fully how much they impacted the course of spiritual history? But it's important to see that they snuck out of town, probably feeling like things had gone poorly.

# 28

# THESSALONICA
## ACTS 17:1-9

Paul, Timothy, and Silas left Luke in Philippi and began journeying west, further into Macedonia. Luke says they "passed through" Apollonia and Amphipolis. For some reason, it doesn't sound like they stopped at either town to preach. They were smaller towns, and Paul may have decided that it was more strategic to focus on major cities like Philippi and Thessalonica.

Thessalonica was the biggest city in Macedonia then, and still today. It lay at the junction of important Roman roads, from Italy to the east, and from the Aegean to the Danube. In 42 BC, Rome declared Thessalonica a free city because it sided with Augustus and Mark Antony (the winners) in the second civil war. Like Philippi, they had a high degree of autonomy and could issue their own coins.

## To the Synagogue

Paul's team launched another outreach:

> They came to Thessalonica, where there was a Jewish synagogue. As was Paul's custom, he went to the synagogue, and

for three Sabbaths reasoned with them from the Scriptures. He explained the prophecies and proved that the Messiah must suffer and rise from the dead. He said, "This Jesus I'm telling you about is the Messiah." (Acts 17:1-3)

You can see clearly that Paul's custom in preaching was not just to declare the gospel, but also to persuade using confirming evidence. "Reasoning with them," "explaining," and "proving" are all words associated with persuasion.

In this setting, he had a room full of Jews, but also "many" God-fearing Greeks. These Greeks would have a significant knowledge of Old Testament Scripture. So when Paul took them to prophetic texts showing that the Messiah must die and rise from the dead—again, an aspect of the Messiah they had never been taught before—they found it convincing. They already respected the authority of Scripture.

The same arguments work today, even in our biblically illiterate culture. We just need to add some steps before reaching the conclusion—e.g., dating of the texts, how we know, dating of the fulfillment, and how we know that. Even those with no knowledge of the Bible when confronted with this set of facts are amazed. It's not a long step to realizing God is behind it. Our ministry has seen thousands come to faith, and we put emphasis on fulfilled prophecy, just like Paul did.

"Proving" is too strong, although for those who accept the divine inspiration of Old Testament prophecy, the case for Jesus becomes so strong that it verges on proof. Better is the NASB translation that they were "giving evidence." The word here means to "set before" like a lawyer in a trial, setting evidence before the judge and jury.

These public lectures in the synagogue were not monologues. Questioners could stand and come forward to make points about the passage in view. A copy of the text would lie on the table in the middle where men could point to key phrases using a stylus, or a little stick pointer. They wouldn't touch the expensive text.

The people were listening. "And some of them [Jews] were persuaded and joined Paul and Silas, along with a large number of the God-fearing Greeks and a number of the leading women" (v. 4). Here again, we see a significant group being persuaded. Paul would later write, "We persuade men" (2 Corinthians 5:11).

Contrary to those preachers today who believe that rational argument is a waste of time, and that only appeals to the heart lead to conversion, Paul believed in persuasion, and he regularly rolled out the highly persuasive evidence for Jesus.

His persuasion was quite effective here in Thessalonica. When you notice Luke's mention of the numbers in this passage, you see "some" Jews, a "large number" of God-fearing Gentiles, and "quite a few" (NLT) prominent women.[1] In this book, those terms add up to more than just dozens of new believers. Probably more than a hundred people believed. This sounds like substantially more than at Philippi. And these were only the people won from the synagogue. More came later.

When we read 1 Thessalonians, he refers to how everyone kept hearing how they "turned away from idols to serve the living and true God" (1 Thessalonians 1:9). That makes it sound like most of them were reached while worshiping idols. So these are in addition to the God-fearing Greeks, who would have already forsaken idols. These are still others—apparently even a larger number—reached as idol worshippers. That means the total group must have been two hundred or more. Maybe much more.

The statement that those from the synagogue who were persuaded "joined Paul and Silas" indicates what common sense would suggest— Paul and Silas had one or more meeting places for gatherings in between Sabbaths. To "join" them was to show up at one of these other venues. We know later that Paul lectured "daily" at Ephesus, and he probably did that here, too. Silas and Timothy probably also taught. Each day, people would bring out more friends, and the group grew.

They might have met outdoors, just because indoor spaces that could handle a crowd like this would be hard to get. It was late spring or early summer by now, so the weather would permit. However, since some "eminent women" believed, they might have owned large houses with substantial courtyards.

The crowd of new believers was large enough to cause jealousy from the synagogue leadership. Satan had his opening. Although too late to prevent the conversion of numerous people, he could keep Paul's outreach from going further.

---

1. The literal Greek here says "not a few" meaning in our idiom, "quite a few."

He incited the jealous leaders:

> So they gathered some troublemakers from the marketplace to form a mob and start a riot. They attacked the home of Jason, searching for Paul and Silas so they could drag them out to the crowd. Not finding them there, they dragged out Jason and some of the other believers instead and took them before the city council. (vs. 5-6)

We don't know who Jason was, but he had other believers at his house, so he might have been hosting meetings. A Jason shows up in Romans 16:21 with Paul in Corinth. But Jason (the Greek form of Joshua) was a common name.

This city council was dangerous. They had the authority to beat, imprison, or kill. The accusers launched their charge:

> "These men who have upset the world have come here also; and Jason has welcomed them, and they all act contrary to the decrees of Caesar, saying that there is another king, Jesus." (vs. 6-7)

What a wonderful description of a handful of Christ-followers! They had upset the world! The expression has the sense of "turned the world upside down" (ESV). The dynamic power of the gospel proclaimed in faith was exerting its polarizing effect, seen so often with Jesus. He warned, "Do you suppose that I came to grant peace on earth? I tell you, no, but rather division" (Luke 12:51). And we often see, "A division occurred in the crowd because of Him" (John 7:43).

Their reference to Jesus as "another king" matches the charge against Jesus at his trial. But he answered Pilate that "My kingdom is not of this world." This was a popular line of attack against the believers—that they were a revolutionary force, rejecting Roman authority.

> And when they had received a pledge from Jason and the others, they released them. The brethren immediately sent Paul and Silas away by night to Berea. (vs. 9-10)

They put up a "bond" or "pledge," which probably was a sum of money they either put on deposit or signed for. This money would be forfeited if there were any more trouble. The believers must have concluded that they were fortunate to get away without any violence or imprisonment.

They quietly snuck Paul and Silas out of town in the dark. Luke doesn't mention Timothy, who may have stayed behind to continue training.

## Aftermath

Satan was too late to prevent a robust outbreak of gospel outreach. Only weeks later, Paul wrote the book of 1 Thessalonians from the city of Corinth, and sent it back with Silas and Timothy, who had caught up by then.[2] In the letter he comments on the spread of the word from Thessalonica outward—apparently people were so excited about meeting Jesus that they were going out to friends and family in other cities to pass the word.

Paul wrote:

> You became an example to all the believers in Macedonia and in Achaia. As a result, you have become an example to all the believers in Greece—throughout both Macedonia and Achaia. And now the word of the Lord is ringing out from you to people everywhere, even beyond Macedonia and Achaia, for wherever we go we find people telling us about your faith in God, so that we have no need to say anything. (1 Thessalonians 1:8)

This was a stunning victory, and was clearly accompanied by added persecution. He talks about how they "received the word in much tribulation" (v. 6). How they "also endured the same sufferings at the hands of your own countrymen" (2:14). He said he was trying to "keep you from being shaken by the troubles you were going through. But you know that we are destined for such troubles" (3:3).

In the same book we hear the enigmatic statement, "We wanted very much to come to you, and I, Paul, tried again and again, but Satan prevented us" (2:18). Was it the bond they posted? Did Satan attack his health? Or did things get so wild in Corinth he dared not leave? We can only speculate. But we're not just guessing when we say Satan constantly comes against and tries to block the plans of God's servants.

---

2. It's difficult to follow Silas' and Timothy's movements in this period. According to Acts 18:5, both Silas and Timothy returned to Corinth from the journey to Macedonia. But 1 Thessalonians only refers to Timothy visiting. They may have both gone north together, but Timothy focused on Thessalonica while Silas focused on Philippi and/or Berea.

## The Big Picture

This battle joined in the largest city in Macedonia looked highly successful for the Jesus followers at first. But the counterattack drove Paul and Silas out of town. Because of constraints in the chronology of this part of Paul's life, we can determine that the whole thing probably only lasted a month or two.

False teachers appeared in Thessalonica before long, apparently showing letters they falsely claimed were from Paul (2 Thessalonians 2:2). In typical fashion, the evil one struck early with physical threats, but quickly moved to his more insidious covert attack on truth. None of it worked. The Thessalonian body continued to expand and reach more people.

# 29

# BEREA AND ATHENS
## ACTS 17:10-34

## Berea

Forty-five miles west of Thessalonica lay Berea. They had a Jewish community and a synagogue, so as usual, Paul and Silas went there to declare the gospel:

> And the people of Berea were more open-minded than those in Thessalonica, and they listened eagerly to Paul's message. They searched the Scriptures day after day to see if Paul and Silas were teaching the truth. As a result, many Jews believed, as did many of the prominent Greek women and men. (Acts 17:11-12)

Once again, we are left to imagine what the word "many" means. Berea was a smaller city, so if it's relative to the population, maybe it's less than a hundred. On the other hand, it's both many Jews and many Greeks. So it's over a hundred.

Their response was "eager" and "open-minded," but not fanatical or impulsive. Instead, they searched the Scriptures carefully to determine whether this new message was true. The term here translated "day after day" really means "daily" (NASB), so their study displaced other activities. Anyone who does that will soon learn that the evidence for Jesus in the Old Testament is strong. That's all God needed to bring spiritual new life to this group.

## Counterattack

Winning "prominent Greek women and men" would be an advantage because of the protection they usually afford. But not this time. Word somehow got back to Thessalonica that Paul and Silas were preaching in Berea. They sent a posse there and were able to rouse another public riot.

The believers were able to keep Paul out of reach from the mob and got him to the Aegean Sea. Luke doesn't say how they traveled, but there was a coastal road that ran down to Achaia and Athens. Otherwise, Paul could have taken a trading ship. The journey was long—over three hundred miles, so a ship would make sense.

Paul didn't have to travel alone. "Those who escorted Paul brought him as far as Athens" (v. 15). Then, his escorts left, but with instructions for Silas and Timothy (who by now was in Berea) to meet him in Athens. He had decided to target the intellectual ground zero for Greek philosophy, and he was all alone.

## Athens

Athens' time of supremacy lay almost five hundred years in the past, before the Peloponnesian War and later the conquest by Philip of Macedonia. Then finally it was conquered again by Rome in 146 BC. But it was still honored as the seat of an advanced culture. The spectacular Parthenon was visible from anywhere in the city.

Did Paul's escorts from Berea have contacts or family in Athens where he could stay? Perhaps. But he is pictured as being completely alone in this famous city.

He spent a lot of his time studying their religions. We read: "Now while Paul was waiting for them at Athens, his spirit was being provoked within him as he was observing the city full of idols" (v. 16).

Athens was loaded with temples and shrines according to contemporary sources. Ancient geographer Strabo said temples and shrines were so numerous in Athens that, "I am unable to point them all out one by one;

for Attica is the possession of the gods, who seized it as a sanctuary for themselves."[1]

Greek temples, like most ancient temples, were seen as the homes of the gods. They were places where people could feed the gods and keep them comfortable. They were not places to gather and worship or hear preaching like a church today. They did have ceremonies on key holy days, and people were constantly burning sacrifices.

Paul would later say, "For as I walked around and looked carefully at your objects of worship..." (v. 23). Paul wasn't afraid of heathen temples. He went in and examined them carefully, probably learning the mythology their adherents believed. By the time he encountered an open door to preach to the Athenians, he had already devised a strategy, and had found a key opening named "The Unknown God."

As usual, "he reasoned in the synagogue" (v. 17). We don't hear much about results there. But once again, we see him practicing a reasoned approach to preaching the gospel based on predictions and typology in the Old Testament.

## In the Market

He was also out talking to people, probably Gentiles, in the marketplace. That's where the pushback came:

> A group of Epicurean and Stoic philosophers began to debate with him. Some of them asked, "What is this babbler trying to say?" Others remarked, "He seems to be a proclaimer of strange deities,"—because he was preaching Jesus and the resurrection. And they took him and brought him to the Areopagus, saying, "Come and tell us about this new teaching that you are presenting. You are bringing some strange ideas to our ears, and we would like to know what they mean." (vs. 18-20)

Epicurean and Stoic philosophies were the main competing worldviews popular in Athens. Epicureans didn't deny that the gods existed, but they saw them as completely uninvolved in human affairs. Stoics saw god as the "World Soul," basically pantheism. Neither group was close to Paul's theism.

---

1. Strabo, *The Geography of Strabo*, Book IX, 1:16.

# Before the Areopagus

Mars Hill served as the meeting place for the Areopagus Court, the highest court in Greece for civil, criminal, and religious matters. By this time, Roman law and courts had taken over most functions. But this was the highest council in the city made up of philosophers and other intellectuals. They could punish or banish teachers of unacceptable doctrines.

# Paul's Talk

Once again, we have a summary of Paul's speech. Luke wasn't there to hear him, but he was sitting, pen in hand, taking down Paul's recounting of a speech he would have easily remembered in detail. Naturally, we have to read between the lines to detect the full speech.

### To an Unknown God[2]

> Paul stood in the midst of the Areopagus and said, "Men of Athens, I observe that you are very religious in all respects. For while I was passing through and examining the objects of your worship, I also found an altar with this inscription, 'To An Unknown God.' Therefore what you worship in ignorance, this I proclaim to you." (vs. 22-23)

In a brilliant opening, Paul laid the groundwork for what followed. The Greeks can hardly claim they have it all figured out if they have an altar admitting there is a god they know nothing about. Paul's opening is good news: "I know who he is!"

It's a great example of worldview contextualization. In this approach, the cross-cultural worker finds common ground in some aspect of the audience's thinking. Using that point of agreement, the communicator moves on to gospel related material. The hearers will be more likely to consider what's being said because the dialog began favorably.

### What God? Who's God?

> "The God who made the world and all things in it, since he is Lord of heaven and earth, does not dwell in temples made with

---

2. Second century geographer, Pausanias, in his description of Athens refers to "altars of the gods named Unknown." Pausanias, *Description of Greece*, Book 1.1.4.

hands; nor is he served by human hands, as though he needed anything, since he himself gives to all people life and breath and all things; and he made from one man every nation of mankind to live on all the face of the earth, having determined their appointed times and the boundaries of their habitation." (vs. 24-26)

Francis Schaeffer argued that "There is no word so contentless as the word 'god.' The true God must be identified and carefully described."[3] That was true in the first century as well. Paul begins his discussion about God by answering the key questions: "Who's God?" "What God?" This should also be the beginning point for us today. Unless we define the triune, infinite, personal God of the Bible; creator of all things, we may be talking right past each other in postmodern dialog.

Paul declared that the true God created "the world and all things in it." This was not true of the Greco-Roman gods. Rather, they were themselves created, according to their own mythology.

When Paul declares that the true God "does not dwell in temples made with hands; nor is he served by human hands, as though he needed anything" (vs. 24-25), he is contrasting the transcendence and infinitude of the God of the Bible to the limitations of their nature gods. Their gods were like overgrown humans: often deceived, in need of rest and food, sinful and in need of human servants.

## Creation through One Man

He explicitly declares that "He made from one man every nation" (v. 26). That flatly contradicts what theistic evolutionists argue. They either deny that the story of the creation of Adam ever happened, or that if there was an Adam, he was part of a community of at least thousands of Homo sapiens. Paul shows that he believes Genesis 2 and 3 are real history.

Did Paul bring up God's creation of humans through a single man because he was explaining why we all have a fallen nature? That would make sense. In moving toward the gospel message that "the free gift of God is eternal life in Christ Jesus" (Romans 6:23b), people must first hear that "the wages of sin is death" (Romans 6:23a). What's the point of the cross if one doesn't understand the consequences of sin?

---

3. Francis Scheaffer, *The God Who Is There*, (Hodder & Stoughton, 1969), 146.

This would be especially important with an ancient Greek audience. Their religion was essentially amoral. They had no consistent ethical system, and under different conditions, almost anything could be justified. More importantly, the gods were also amoral. So not even in theory was there a moral law like that in the Bible.

## God's Plan of Rescue

He points out that God "determined their [the nations] appointed times and the boundaries of their habitation" (v. 26). This points to God's supremacy over all humans, but also probably signals a discussion of his role in human history. That, in turn, would refer to his plan of rescue for humans.

It definitely refutes the henotheistic notion that different peoples have different gods who favor that nation or district. Athena was the main goddess and namesake of Athens, and Paul was standing only feet away from the Parthenon's immense 38-foot gold covered statue of Athena with her sacred snake next to her. The infinite God he was representing was nothing like her.

Paul went on, saying that the purpose of all this was "that they would seek God, if perhaps they might grope for him and find him, though he is not far from each one of us" (v. 27). This squares with Paul's later point in Romans that people are without excuse if they refuse to acknowledge the Creator when looking at his awesome creation.

His hearers intuitively knew that if a god existed, he must be more than what Greek mythology advanced. The existence of thousands of God-fearing Greeks attending synagogues during this period signals the widespread disappointment Greek thinkers felt in their often comical mythology. They were looking, seeking, and they were sensing that biblical monotheism had the answers.

## Greek Authors Agree

Paul next used their own literature to make his point:

> "For in him we live and move and exist, as even some of your own poets have said, 'For we also are his children.' Being then the children of God, we ought not to think that the Divine

Nature is like gold or silver or stone, an image formed by the art and thought of man." (vs. 28-29)

If their own poets proclaim God is our father, how could he be an object fashioned from silver or stone? It's a good observation of one of the many internal contradictions inherent in idol worship. It's similar to Isaiah's very funny illustration of a man using half a log he cut from the forest to cook his dinner, and then using the other half to fashion a god, which he bows down to in worship (Isaiah 44:14-15).

Paul knew Scripture, but he also read and learned pagan mythology and poetry. He was able to quote it from memory here, thus gaining credibility with his hearers and helping to make a point. Of course, he wasn't suggesting that Epimenides or Aratus (both of whom he quotes) are inspired. Rather, he's playing off the fact that even unbelieving authors sometimes say things that are true.

It's a good example we should follow today when communicating with non-believers. These statements by non-believing authors were common ground. Christians should be sharp and knowledgeable about Scripture, but also well-versed in secular knowledge and culture. That's what Paul called "being all things to all men, so that I may by all means save some" (1 Corinthians 9:22).

## The New Standard

"Therefore having overlooked the times of ignorance, God is now declaring to men that all people everywhere should repent, because he has fixed a day in which he will judge the world in righteousness through a man whom he has appointed, having furnished proof to all men by raising him from the dead." (vs. 30-31)

In what sense did God overlook the ignorance of peoples the world over? One possibility would be that he hasn't sent a world flood or similar temporal judgment that would destroy non-believers.

But it's also clear that the standard for saving faith must be different for those in ignorance than for those (like his audience) who had by now heard the gospel. Paul later implied this in the book of Romans when he said those without the Word are "without excuse" (Romans 1:20). If they are without excuse, they must be capable of doing something that God accepts, because otherwise they would have an excuse—that responding to God was impossible. This is also suggested here when Paul talks about the nations, "that they would seek God, if perhaps they might grope for him and find him" (v. 27).

God doesn't tell us what such people can do, probably because we don't need to know. But he does warn of what is not good enough, and that is "worshiping the creation rather than the Creator" (Romans 1:25).

He also says they suppress the truth when they intuitively sense that an infinite, personal God must exist (Romans 1:18-19). When people make idols and worship them, they know inwardly that someone higher exists, but they suppress that truth in favor of a safer and more tangible "god."

We do encounter people throughout the Old Testament, outside the Jewish people, who know God, like Balaam or Job. Modern missionaries also occasionally encounter native people who already believe in the infinite personal God, although this is quite rare.[4]

Paul's point here in Athens is that things have changed. God is sending out his people to spread the word to all the peoples on earth, and as a result, they are now becoming responsible to the gospel. And Paul, unlike so many preachers today, bores right into the central point: "He has fixed a day in which he will judge the world in righteousness" (v. 31).

## The Resurrection

The stamp of authenticity for the gospel is the resurrection of Jesus. But most Greek thinkers at this time had been influenced by Plato and others to adopt a form of dualism. Plato divided the world into the ideal, which included everything spiritual, and matter, which was tainted and

---

4. John Wesley referred to what he called "prevenient grace," which means preceding grace or enabling grace. Under this view, God loves "the world" (John 3:16), not just believers, and he actively reaches out to them, enabling them to overcome their sinful natures and believe. This doctrine is backed up by verses like John 16:8-11, where Jesus said the Spirit would "convict the world concerning sin, because they do not believe in Me" and Romans 1:19 where Paul says "That which is known about God is evident within them; for God made it evident to them." Free will theologians argue that receiving such enabling grace or conviction makes it possible to believe, but not necessary. Calvinists argue that God's grace is irresistible.

An important caveat to this doctrine is that apparently very few take advantage of such enabling grace, as shown by the fact that most people in unreached areas worship and serve the creature rather than the creator. However, when missionaries come into isolated populations we may see millions believe. So the idea of enabling grace only brings people to a threshold where they are accountable. More persuasion and the power of the gospel will reach many more. That further means that missions to unreached populations are necessary and important.

without value. This is why Greek thinkers had so much trouble with the idea of resurrection. The idea that God would value humans' physical bodies and even make them everlasting was repugnant to these dualists. That's why we read:

> Now when they heard of the resurrection of the dead, some began to sneer, but others said, "We shall hear you again concerning this." So Paul went out of their midst. (vs. 32-33)

Greek dualism would become a recurrent problem in the early church, as is evident in books like 1 Corinthians, Colossians, 1 and 2 Timothy and 1 John.

## Fruit Borne

Not everyone was sneering.

> But some men joined him and believed, among whom also were Dionysius the Areopagite and a woman named Damaris and others with them. (v. 34)

So Dionysius was probably an upper class debater and thinker because he belonged to the council. He and Damaris make two, and the minimum of others must be three or more, to be called "some." That means at least five and maybe more believed.

I would consider that an excellent result for one talk, especially coming from an unfamiliar culture. Unlike reaching out to God-revering Gentiles (which would be near-neighbor outreach) these people were hearing, not only of the gospel, but of the Bible itself, for the first time.

Some readers claim this result was weak, and that as a result, Paul abandoned this contextualized, apologetic approach in favor of a simple proclamation approach. We will consider that view in the next chapter.

## The Big Picture

We read nothing more about Paul's time in Athens. That doesn't mean nothing else happened, but it is strange that the church in Athens never comes up in the rest of the New Testament. On the other hand, neither does the church in Derbe come up again, even though a large number there believed. Arguments from silence are often mistaken.

It's probably safe to say that any church planted in Athens was small, and didn't have the kind of impact we see from groups like Corinth, Thessalonica, or Philippi.

Paul was still by himself and according to 1 Thessalonians, feeling bad. "When we could endure it no longer, we thought it best to be left behind at Athens alone," he says. And again, "when I could endure it no longer" (1 Thessalonians 3:1, 5). He must have been terribly lonely, and as he explains, agonized by anxiety about the hundreds of new believers he had left behind. How were they doing?

# 30

# CORINTH

## ACTS 18:1-17

## Why Corinth?

Corinth was a major city, lying at the southern end of the tiny isthmus connecting the Peloponnesus to Achaia. The isthmus is only four miles wide at one place. Today, a sea-level canal bisects it, built in the late 1800s. In antiquity, several emperors considered digging the canal, but it was either too expensive or the emperors died before work got far.

Instead of a canal, they built a road called the Diolkos. It was a limestone road about five miles long, built in very ancient times, about 600 BC. Ships could have their cargo taken over by cart, and the ship itself would be canted, slid up a stone and wood ramp onto a wheeled platform or sledge, and dragged over by oxen or slaves. The crossing took about four days to complete, plus time waiting in line to get started.

Most ships were much smaller then, and their weight was manageable. And sailing the four-hundred-mile route around the Peloponnesus was dangerous.

As a result, lots of sailors stopped off at Corinth. They had money and usually had been at sea for some time. They were ready to party.

Ancient authors talk about the raw, loose lifestyle in Corinth, even developing a word "to Corinthianize," meaning to engage in debauchery. The city was full of occult, shamanistic healers, mystery religions, and fertility cults that included ritual prostitution.

The huge temple to Aphrodite (goddess of love) was said to have a thousand temple prostitutes. Young girls given into this fate by their parents had no say in their own future. If they got pregnant, they were summarily aborted, and usually didn't live too long. This cruel practice is typical of manmade religion.

So Corinth was a hardcore center of sensuality and sin, but it was not resistant to the gospel. Many came to faith here. Back then, and still today, people who live by a code of pleasure-seeking eventually look up and cry out, "Is this all?"

Going back to Paul's story, we read, "After these things he left Athens and went to Corinth." Why did Paul move from Athens to Corinth? For one thing, Corinth was a far larger city. Archeologists have excavated the site, and found clear evidence that Corinth was one of the largest cities in the Roman Empire—probably second only to Rome. Estimates for this period range up to a quarter million souls. Paul probably discerned that this was fertile ground for the gospel, and its position astride major trade routes made it likely that the word would spread.

## Change of Philosophy?

Some commentators argue that Paul failed at Athens, and as a result changed his philosophy of ministry when going to Corinth.[1] They get this view from Paul's first letter to the Corinthians, where he reminisced about his arrival there (right after Athens).

> And when I came to you, brethren, I did not come with superiority of speech or of wisdom, proclaiming to you the testimony of God. For I determined to know nothing among you except Jesus Christ, and Him crucified. I was with you in weakness and in fear and in much trembling, and my message and my preaching were not in persuasive words of wisdom, but in demonstration of the Spirit and of power, so that your faith

---

1. For instance, Richard Longenecker, *"The response to Paul's address,"* The Expositor's Bible *Commentary* Vol. 9.

would not rest on the wisdom of men, but on the power of God. (1 Corinthians 2:1-5)

This passage, along with the view that Paul failed at Athens, has become ground zero for an anti-intellectual and anti-contextualizing approach to preaching the gospel.

The argument runs that Paul realized that his efforts on Mars Hill, to defend the gospel intellectually, and his citing of Greek poets or philosophers, had failed, as seen from the low number of conversions. Therefore, in Corinth, he turned to simply declaring the gospel without any effort to defend it. This proclamation approach assumes that when chosen people hear the gospel, the Spirit will touch their hearts, and they will believe.

Paul also dismissed human knowledge and wisdom in general, according to this view.

We argued earlier to the contrary, that the number of those won from the speech in Athens was actually quite gratifying for a single talk to a culturally distant audience. Paul never says he viewed the effort as a failure. He apparently didn't spend much time in Athens, but that was probably because Athens was in decline, while Corinth was a surging metropolis. Paul gravitated toward large, influential cities.

More importantly, when Paul says, "I determined to know nothing among you except Jesus Christ, and him crucified," he isn't referring to defending the truthfulness of the gospel. Neither when he says, "My message and my preaching were not in persuasive words of wisdom, but in demonstration of the Spirit and of power." Rather, his discussion in this section of 1 Corinthians is about how God's wisdom dwarfs and shames the wisdom of man.

Paul was rejecting the Corinthians' admiration of Greek formal rhetoric, with its frequent verbal flourishes and their pride in their own eloquence. Greek was a second language for Paul, because Tarsus would have been an Aramaic speaking city (as was Jerusalem). He observes that the Corinthians were saying that his "personal presence is unimpressive and his speech contemptible" (2 Corinthians 10:10).

So Paul wasn't able to speak in the fancy manner they admired, but he also had no interest in doing so. Such speech flatters self and draws attention away from God and toward the speaker. It can result in a human following of charismatic leaders. Paul was very critical of the Corinthians' pride in their intellectual prowess. And this is what he is speaking against in this passage.

Paul was unwilling to play the game of showy speeches. But we have no reason to believe he abandoned the approach that had borne so much fruit in all the cities we've studied so far. Everywhere he went, he reasoned, gave evidence, and persuaded. Neither had he abandoned apologetics in favor of a mystical approach. Right in his letter to the Corinthians, he lays out an evidential apologetic for the resurrection, backed by eyewitness testimony (1 Corinthians 15:1-8). He also later says to these same Corinthians, "Knowing the fear of the Lord, we persuade men" (2 Corinthians 5:11).

## Aquila and Priscilla

After an unknown time of loneliness, we read:

> He found a Jew named Aquila, a native of Pontus, having recently come from Italy with his wife Priscilla, because Claudius had commanded all the Jews to leave Rome. He came to them, and because he was of the same trade, he stayed with them and they were working, for by trade they were tent-makers. (Acts 18:2-3)

What a relief this must have been to Paul! This couple goes on in the book of Acts to become major players in the spread of the gospel. Luke doesn't say whether they were already believers when Paul met them, but they probably were, because Paul never calls them his converts, unlike others he led to Christ. People from the city of Rome were among those who earlier believed on the day of Pentecost and took the gospel back home.

As Luke's narrative continues, he begins referring to the couple as Priscilla and Aquila, with her name first. In Greek, putting words in the first position meant more than it does in English. Word order signified importance, suggesting that Priscilla was the big bat. She led the way in their ongoing ministry and was probably the more gifted spouse.

# Claudius and the Jews

This short paragraph contains another striking evidence that Acts is authentic, firsthand history. Luke says Aquila and Priscilla left Rome because "Claudius had commanded all the Jews to leave Rome." It so happens that one of our key Roman historians for this period, Suetonius, refers to this very event: "Since the Jews constantly made disturbances at the instigation of Chrestus, he [Claudius] expelled them from Rome."[2] In the view of most scholars, Chrestus is probably a misspelling of Christus, that is, Christ. If true, that would make this one of the earliest mentions of Jesus in secular history.

At this early period Claudius probably didn't know exactly who Jesus was. Even decades after this event, another Roman historian, Tacitus, has to explain to his readers who Jesus was. They didn't know. Tacitus also knows him as "Christus" rather than as Jesus.[3]

If the Jews in Rome were anything like the Jews in several other cities we've seen, it's not hard to imagine "disturbances" being the result of people preaching the Christian gospel.

The expulsion happened in the 9th year of Claudius' reign. His reign began in AD 41, so that puts this event in late AD 49 or 50. That winter is exactly when Paul arrived in Corinth, and Aquila had "recently" arrived there from Rome.

This is an outstanding example of correlation with other histories on a fine detail in Luke's text. There's no way an author in the first century would be able to date these events together, and Suetonius hadn't even written his book yet. He was an early second-century author.

# Tent Making

Luke says Paul went to Aquila and Priscilla, "for by trade they were tent-makers" (v. 3). Cilicia, where Paul grew up, was well-known for making tents out of a felt-like cloth made from a certain goat's hair. In ancient times, there were few inns and no motels. People traveled with sturdy tents on a pack animal that they could pitch each night. Paul

---

2. Gaius Suetonius, *The Twelve Caesars: Life of Claudius*, 21:4.
3. Cornelius Tacitus, *Annals*, Book 15, 44.

probably learned tent making when he was young, before he moved to Jerusalem to begin study with Gamaliel.

Paul and his new friends were able to support themselves by selling their tents at the same time they worked on spreading the gospel. Today, "tent-making" has become a term for missionaries and other Christian workers who support themselves financially through a secular career rather than charitable gifts.

Paul wasn't just making tents. As usual, "He was reasoning in the synagogue every Sabbath and trying to persuade Jews and Greeks" (v. 4). This again confirms that he had not rejected reasoning and persuading in favor of simple proclamation. This probably went on for weeks or months.

## Timothy and Silas

Then came a joyous event:

> But when Silas and Timothy came down from Macedonia, Paul began devoting himself completely to the word, solemnly testifying to the Jews that Jesus was the Christ. (v. 5)

These two had last seen Paul in Berea months earlier. The journey from Berea to Corinth would have taken a month on foot. But they had first journeyed in the opposite direction, to Thessalonica and Philippi, making their journey even longer. They might have sailed from Philippi. Then, after a significant time, they began their journey south, probably toward Athens—the last place Paul was known to be. Believers in Athens probably told them Paul had moved on to Corinth, fifty miles further south and west.

These two brought something important—a sack of money. Most of it came from Philippi. In Thessalonica, someone had accused Paul of being on the take for money. He responded by refusing thereafter to take anyone's money in that city (2 Thessalonians 3:8). That may have changed later; we don't know. Maybe with Timothy and Silas, things were different. But we do know that Philippi gave him financial support several times during this period, as we saw earlier (Philippians 4:13-16).

Paul was not against financial support for his ministry, even though he took the same extreme stand in Corinth, not allowing anyone from that city to give him any support (1 Corinthians 9:1-13). He never says why he did this, except that it was a good example, and that he would not allow critics to charge him with being in it for the money.

This accusation must have come up in Thessalonica and Corinth. We know of no other city where he took this stand. In cities where their attitude was good, he gratefully accepted support, as in this case. Even in cities with a bad attitude, he was insistent that he had the right to be paid, even though he refused to accept it.

This is why he stopped making tents and gave himself over completely to preaching and teaching. By now he probably had a significant group started.

## The Thessalonian Correspondence

This is also when Paul wrote 1 Thessalonians and sent it back north with one or more of his guys; we don't know who, but probably Timothy and Silas.

The letter carriers came back two or more months later with bad news. False teachers had arrived, sporting a letter they claimed was from Paul. It was a forgery, claiming that "the day of the Lord has come" (2 Thessalonians 2:2).

The day of the Lord is an expression often used in the Old Testament to refer to various times of divine judgment. In this context, it refers to the great tribulation Jesus predicted prior to his second coming (e.g., Matthew 24:15; 21).

Paul responded by writing 2 Thessalonians. In chapter 2, he refers to material from Daniel and Jesus' Olivet discourse. But he also has material we haven't seen from any other source, such as a "restrainer" who holds back the "man of lawlessness" (the character in Daniel 9:27). He also talks about a "deluding influence" that will create confusion and deception at the end of history.

Where did Paul get this new information? We don't know, but it could have come from his amazing revelation about twelve years earlier that included "inexpressible words, which a man is not permitted to speak" (2 Corinthians 12:2-4).

His response also reveals how important Paul thought it was to study and learn predictive prophecy. Even though his stay at Thessalonica was short—probably less than two months—he had instructed them fully on the end times. "Do you not remember that while I was still with you, I was telling you these things?" (2 Thessalonians 2:5).

So, after writing the second letter to the Thessalonians, he sent either Silas and Timothy, or both, back up to Macedonia yet again.

## Growth in Corinth

The gospel began to drive a wedge between people in Corinth:

> But when they [synagogue members or leaders] resisted and blasphemed, he shook out his garments and said to them, "Your blood be on your own heads! I am clean. From now on I will go to the Gentiles." Then he left there and went to the house of a man named Titius Justus, a worshiper of God, whose house was next to the synagogue. Crispus, the leader of the synagogue, believed in the Lord with all his household, and many of the Corinthians when they heard were believing and being baptized. (vs. 6-8)

We've seen this divisive aspect of the gospel before. But in this case, Paul and the other believers took a particularly bold stand by holding their meetings directly next door to the synagogue! People would have to walk right by Titius' house on their way to synagogue. Titius' was "a worshiper of God," meaning he was a believing Gentile.

To have Crispus, the leader of the synagogue, join them with his household was a big win. Households at this time could include dozens of people, because it was the extended family and their servants and employees who lived with them.

## A Vision

One would think Paul must have been thrilled as he saw the Corinthian body grow and flourish. But in fact, when we read on, we learn that he had an unexpected feeling: Paul was scared.

> And the Lord said to Paul in the night by a vision, "Do not be afraid any longer, but go on speaking and do not be silent; for I

am with you, and no man will attack you in order to harm you, for I have many people in this city." (vs. 9-10)

On one level, it feels good to see that even a spiritual giant like Paul sometimes felt fear. We know from what follows that he had virulent enemies in town who were plotting to get him. That's always scary. But the Evil One can also whisper threats that cause an inordinate level of fear. Soft reassurance from Jesus feels wonderful at such times.

Notice that this is not Jesus appearing in his glorified state, like in Isaiah 6 or Revelation 1. How he appears probably depends on what the situation calls for.

Jesus also said, "I have many people in this city." This is significant because it's a statement he could probably make about many cities, even today. Those engaged in spreading the gospel know they have to count on God hooking them up with these people who he knows will be responsive. That leads to the evangelistic prayer ministry of the church,

Paul took Jesus at his word, and we read that "he settled there a year and six months, teaching the word of God among them" (v. 11). That's much longer than he stayed in any city during the first or second journey.

## Response in Corinth

When we put together the notifications of size for the Corinthian church, we saw Jesus said there would be "many." The fact that Paul stayed so long also suggests that it was not a small group. Earlier, we saw that "Paul began devoting himself completely to the word" (v. 5). That would probably not happen unless the group was of significant size. Finally in verse 8 we read, "many of the Corinthians when they heard were believing and being baptized." So this group was another big one—probably not less than hundreds.

## Before Gallio

Their success was also enough to arouse a new level of persecution. "But when Gallio became governor of Achaia, some Jews rose up together against Paul and brought him before the governor for judgment" (v. 12).

Rome didn't practice religious freedom like we have. Certain religions were permitted, usually because they had a long history in a given area.

These included Judaism. But new religions lacked this status of being called a *religio licita*. The Romans were mainly interested in money and power, and they knew that new religious movements could be revolutionary and could cause disturbances.

At the same time, they were inconsistent in how they responded to new groups. Whether they were fierce or lenient probably depended on how many complaints they got.

First century Christians insisted that they were teaching true Judaism as revealed in the Old Testament and correctly completed by Jesus, the promised Messiah. Those rejecting the Christian gospel were adamant that Christianity was not Judaism, but a dangerous cult.

But when the Jews' case came to trial, things didn't go like they hoped.

They began their complaint, "This man persuades men to worship God contrary to the law" (v. 13). Their spokesman was apparently the leader of the synagogue, named Sosthenes. His opening was pathetic. This is exactly the kind of question the Romans couldn't care less about.

Before Paul could say anything,

> Gallio turned to Paul's accusers and said, "Listen, you Jews, if this were a case involving some wrongdoing or a serious crime, I would have a reason to accept your case. But since it is merely a question of words and names and your Jewish law, take care of it yourselves. I refuse to judge such matters." And he drove them away from the judgment seat. (vs. 14-16)

As the Jewish delegation cried out to clarify, soldiers used their spears sideways to push them away. It's a total disgrace to the Jews.

They took their frustration out on Sosthenes: "And they all took hold of Sosthenes, the leader of the synagogue, and began beating him in front of the judgment seat. But Gallio was not concerned about any of these things" (v. 17). The scene ends with this hilarious anecdote.

But the story isn't over. Years later, Paul wrote this group a letter we know as 1 Corinthians. Look how he starts the letter:

> Paul, called as an apostle of Jesus Christ by the will of God, and Sosthenes our brother, To the church of God which is at Corinth (1 Corinthians 1:1-2)

Wait. Sosthenes? No way! But Paul didn't feel any need to explain who Sosthenes was. He seems to assume they already know him. Sosthenes isn't a very common name... It's him! They already won the earlier leader of the synagogue, Crispus (v. 8).

It's easy to imagine Paul in the courtroom after everyone had been driven out and the noise faded away. He goes up to Sosthenes, laying on the floor, badly beaten. "Brother," Paul says, "You need some new friends...."

Well, we don't know, but it's not too far-fetched. Sosthenes wouldn't have felt much like going back to hang out with his synagogue members. And a worker like Paul would have been watching for any opening.

The result of this almost-trial was like a legal precedent. From this point on, there's no way the synagogue would try that again.

## The Delphi Inscription

It turns out we know Gallio from secular history. His full name was L. Junius Gallio Annaeanus. Both Tacitus and Dio Cassius mention him multiple times.[4] He was the brother of famous Roman philosopher Seneca.

The emperor Claudius wrote an inscription referring to Gallio as proconsul of Achaia, and it's dated. The date given is the 26th "imperial acclamation" of emperor Claudius. An imperial acclamation was an honorary appellation voted to emperors once or twice per year by the senate. The 26th and 27th imperial acclamation of Claudius occurred in AD 52.

The inscription also mentioned another act of acclaim called the 12th Tribunician Power. By comparing these, we can determine that the Delphi Inscription was written between Jan. 25, AD 52, and Jan. 25 AD 53. The better reading for Acts 18:12, when Gallio became proconsul, indicates he had recently arrived. This puts Paul's trial before Gallio in the early summer of AD 52.

This remarkable correlation puts a firm stake in the ground that locks down Paul's chronology. From there we can go backward with the units of time given in Acts and Galatians all the way back to Paul's conversion in AD 34. It also dates events looking forward from this point in time.

---

4. For example, Cornelius Tacitus, *Annals*, Book 16.17.

The whole saga fits perfectly and results in a high degree of confidence in Acts as history.[5]

Whenever the winding thread of secular history crosses paths with the thread of a biblical narrative like Acts at precisely the right point, it's no coincidence. Neither is it in any way possible that Luke knew of the inscription—he was never anywhere near where the inscription was found. And even though the topic of the Delphi Inscription is trivial, its witness to the correct date for Gallio's encounter sheds credibility and trust to Luke's entire book.

## The Big Picture

Paul stayed several more months in Corinth. By the time he left, the Corinthian church was sizeable. He later refers to the "church [singular] of God which is at Corinth," but he also refers to "the churches [plural]" (1 Corinthians 1:2; 14:34). This shows that multiple house churches had been planted, maybe quite a few.

Strangely, however, in Paul's correspondence with them, he never mentions their elders or deacons. Neither does Luke in the book of Acts. Some commentators wonder if the group was so unruly and lacking in mature leadership that they put off naming elders until later. But it's nothing more than an argument from silence.

---

5. To study this chronology in more detail see my essay on it. https://dwellcc.org/learning/essays/chronological-study-pauls-ministry. Or for a more technical scholarly and detailed coverage see Jack Finegan's section in, *Handbook of Biblical Chronology: Principles of Time Reckoning in the Ancient World and Problems of Chronology in the Bible*, (Peabody, MA: Hendrickson Publishers, 1998). It's not clear whether the whole 18 months Paul was in Corinth happened before the Gallio episode, or if the aborted trial was sometime during those months, but the way Luke tells it makes it sound like it was toward the end of the period.

# 31

# THE JOURNEY HOME
## ACTS 18:18-28

As late summer came, the sailing season was nearing an end. So Paul along with Aquilla and Priscilla, and maybe others, crossed over the isthmus to Cenchrea, the port city for Corinth on the Aegean Sea.

Before taking ship home, he cut his hair off "according to Jewish custom, marking the end of a vow" (Acts 18:18). This is recognizable as a temporary Nazirite vow. In the Old Testament some Nazirites were for life, like Samuel and Sampson. But people could also make temporary vows. Vows were deals people made with God, usually involving a prayer they wanted answered.

We don't have extensive information on how these vows worked, or how they relate to New Testament theology. Paul may have made this vow years earlier. During the intertestamental period, these vows apparently all became temporary.

Paul had his hair cut here at Cenchrea, and then brought it to Jerusalem where it was burned on the altar. It wasn't a blood sacrifice, which would clearly be out of line, because Jesus' work is finished. But Paul apparently felt Jews could keep non-atoning festivals and rituals.

Later in the book of Romans Paul introduces Phoebe, "who is deacon in the church at Cenchrea" (Romans 16:1). We have no record of how a church was planted there, but it could have come from this visit by Paul, or someone from Corinth could have come over.

# Ephesus

> Next, Paul "set sail for Syria, taking Priscilla and Aquila with him. They stopped first at the port of Ephesus, where Paul left the others behind. While he was there, he went to the synagogue to reason with the Jews. They asked him to stay longer, but he declined. As he left, however, he said, "I will come back later, God willing." Then he set sail from Ephesus. (vs. 19-21)

Ephesus was in the province of Asia where the Holy Spirit had earlier forbidden them to preach (Acts 16:6). Now, for some reason, things had changed. When Paul went in and lectured in the synagogue, they must have responded favorably, because they wanted him to stay and keep teaching.

He refused to stay, because he seemed to have made up his mind that he needed to make it to Jerusalem. But though he wouldn't stay with them, he did something else: He left them two powerful workers—Priscilla and Aquilla (v. 26). By the time Paul returned to Ephesus months later, a thriving local body was already growing under their leadership. Conditions would be ripe for a major spiritual explosion.

Paul took ship again, but whereas his original ship was headed to Syria (v. 18), this one was bound to Caesarea, which was in Judea, not far from Jerusalem. He may have stayed long enough in Ephesus that his original ship sailed. Or, he may have switched to this ship because it was headed closer to his ultimate goal—Jerusalem.

When he had landed at Caesarea, he went up and greeted the church, and then went down to Antioch (v. 22). When it says he "went up" it means he went up to Jerusalem. The confusing language makes it sound like Jerusalem is north of Antioch, because from there "he went down to Antioch." That's because as we saw earlier, you always go up to Jerusalem and down from Jerusalem because of its mountain top location. Antioch is actually north of Jerusalem.

We don't have any other information about this visit to the church at Jerusalem, but he probably completed his vow and reported on the progress made during the second journey. He must have seen evidence of ongoing poverty in the Jerusalem church, because he soon set about promoting a big relief project for poor believers in Judea.

Much of the poverty in this group probably went back to Paul's own persecution described in Acts 8. That attack destroyed businesses and property, and was so severe that people fled Jerusalem. No wonder Paul was so zealous to help these people financially.

## Apollos

Sometime between Paul's visit to Ephesus and his return there during the third journey, Luke records a story that Paul must have learned about later:

> A Jew named Apollos, an eloquent speaker who knew the Scriptures well, had arrived in Ephesus from Alexandria in Egypt. He had been taught the way of the Lord, and he taught others about Jesus with an enthusiastic spirit and with accuracy. However, he knew only about John's baptism. When Priscilla and Aquila heard him preaching boldly in the synagogue, they took him aside and explained the way of God even more accurately. (vs. 24-26)

The first thing we notice is that Apollos was eloquent and learned in the Scriptures. The more literal translation is that Apollos was "mighty in the Scriptures" (NASB). Also, he came from Alexandria in Northern Egypt, which was a Jewish center of learning. The philosopher Philo was one famous thinker from that city. Their huge library, even though partially burned, was world-renowned.

Apollos was proclaiming Jesus, but also the baptism of repentance advanced by John the Baptist. It's possible that he was exposed to Jesus between the time Jesus began his ministry and when he died. That would have left him with only half the story. Jesus certainly did identify with John the Baptist's ministry. Or, Apollos may have received second-hand instruction from someone who didn't understand the gospel correctly.

In any case, you can see the wide influence John the Baptist had even far outside Judea. Apollos lived in Alexandria in northern Africa. Yet he had been impacted by John.

The beautiful part of this encounter is the interaction between Priscilla, Aquila, and Apollos. Priscilla and Aquila listened to Apollos preach, and correctly discerned that he was missing key material about Jesus and the cross. Instead of rising to set him straight in front everyone, they patiently waited until after the meeting. Then they sought out a private meeting with him.

That was wise, and a good example to follow when possible. In some situations, the danger of an error is such that it's not possible to discuss it later. We saw an example of that with Paul and Peter at Antioch when the men from James arrived. Paul opposed Peter publicly.

The second good example comes from Apollos. He was a scholar, and these strangers were saying his understanding was deficient. He could have given them a hard time, but he didn't. They probably had a lengthy discussion, including study of the word concerning Jesus. They might have shown him whatever they had in writing about Jesus.

When they came out of this meeting, Apollos knew the rest of the story, and he wasn't too proud to teach the new material. Within a short time, he was a powerful voice for Jesus:

> Apollos had been thinking about going to Achaia, and the brothers and sisters in Ephesus encouraged him to go. They wrote to the believers in Achaia, asking them to welcome him. When he arrived there, he proved to be of great benefit to those who, by God's grace, had believed. He refuted the Jews with powerful arguments in public debate. Using the Scriptures, he explained to them that Jesus was the Messiah (vs. 27-28).

When Luke says "Achaia," he's primarily referring to Corinth. We know Apollos taught there and that his powerful preaching unfortunately resulted in the fleshly-minded Corinthians forming a faction in his name (1 Corinthians 1:12; 3:3-6).

When Paul made it to Antioch, the second journey was over. When it says he "stayed some time there" (v. 23), it refers to winter. His next journey would take him back over the mountains in eastern Turkey, so he wouldn't have started before the weather warmed.

# 32

## THE THIRD JOURNEY BEGINS

### ACTS 18:23-19:41

## Back to Galatia and Phrygia

It's spring, AD 53. Luke only mentions Paul traveling "through Galatia and Phrygia, visiting and strengthening all the disciples" (Acts 18:23). But this was actually months of hard work, traveling, patiently counseling believers, and equipping them with deeper knowledge of the word. This was the third time he had cycled through Derbe, Lystra, and Pisidian Antioch. There were also other groups out in the countryside as we saw earlier. Everyone wanted to hear Paul speak.

Was he traveling alone? Luke mentions no co-traveler. If so, that would be a break with his normal practice of always traveling with a team. Maybe he didn't feel the need because he was traveling toward his target—Ephesus. There, he knew Priscilla, Aquilla, and others were waiting.

A more likely scenario: Later in the narrative, Timothy and Erastus suddenly appear in Ephesus, and it's not clear how or when they got there. They were probably traveling with Paul and Luke just didn't mention them.

This journey to Ephesus was almost 1000 miles one-way! So the journey was already several months long.

## Ephesus

Ephesus began as a Greek colony more than 1000 years BC. It grew and became the biggest city in Anatolia. But by Paul's day, it was declining, because excessive deforestation and over-grazing were causing erosion, which was silting up the port for Ephesus at the mouth of the Meander River.

Although several efforts were made to dredge the port at Miletus, it never solved the problem for long. As a result, Ephesus was losing its importance as a center of trade. Yet in Paul's day, the city was still large, and had a strong tourist trade centered on their famous temple to Artemis.

## Twelve Men

After Apollos left for Corinth:

> Paul passed through the upper country and came to Ephesus, and found some disciples. He said to them, "Did you receive the Holy Spirit when you believed?"
>
> And they said to him, "No, we have not even heard whether there is a Holy Spirit."
>
> And he said, "Into what then were you baptized?"
>
> And they said, "Into John's baptism."
>
> Paul said, "John baptized with the baptism of repentance, telling the people to believe in him who was coming after him, that is, in Jesus." When they heard this, they were baptized in the name of the Lord Jesus. And when Paul had laid his hands upon them, the Holy Spirit came on them, and they began speaking with tongues and prophesying. There were in all about twelve men. (19:1-7)

This encounter is quite strange. Where do you find twelve men who are apparently together? They describe themselves as disciples of John the Baptist, but he had been dead for decades by now. It could have been a *scholae* or mini-school led by a disciple of John the Baptist. John definitely practiced disciple making even before Jesus did (e.g., Matthew 9:14; 11:2).

It sounds like Paul encountered them on his way into town rather than as part of the local church in Ephesus. They were probably young men, because in that culture people got married early. These guys sound like they lived together.

We see no evidence that these men were Christians. They were "disciples," but disciples of John the Baptist, not Jesus. Of course, John regularly promised that one was coming after him who was greater. That probably explains why these men were so easily persuaded to believe in Jesus. But John died before Jesus went to the cross, so if one of his followers left Judea to go back home, he probably wouldn't know that part. That must be what happened. The leader or founder of this group was working with only half the story.

Paul's question—had they received the Holy Spirit?—immediately unveiled where they were in their faith. Paul knew that anyone without the Holy Spirit cannot be a Christian: "If anyone does not have the Spirit of Christ, he does not belong to Him" (Romans 8:9). So when they shrugged their shoulders in ignorance, he launched into an explanation of the gospel. It didn't take long before they excitedly comprehended what God had so recently accomplished.

# Strange Baptism

Paul began to baptize them one by one or maybe in small groups. Then, after the water baptism, he laid his hands on them, and only then did the Holy Spirit enter them. They could tell because "they spoke in other tongues and prophesied" (v. 6).

These men clearly believed and were baptized, but only when Paul laid his hands on them did they receive the Spirit. That's why this story has become important in the debate over Pentecostalism. Pentecostals point to this gap of time between the twelve men coming to faith and the baptism of the Spirit. They argue that it proves that Christians first are regenerated and only later receive the baptism of the Spirit.

But it doesn't really show that.

First, this story doesn't fit the Pentecostal scenario. They argue that people believe and are immediately indwelled by the Spirit. Then, later, they receive the baptism of the Spirit. You can see that is not what happened here. At the time Paul laid hands on them, they had received *neither the baptism nor the indwelling* of the Spirit. They said they had never even heard of the Spirit (v. 2).

So this sequence doesn't match either the Pentecostal or the typical traditional picture. It's a unique event not seen elsewhere, but somewhat similar to the delay in the coming of the Spirit we saw in Acts 8.

The best guess is that God caused a short delay (probably only minutes) in the coming of the Spirit so that it would happen exactly when Paul's hands touched each man. That was an unmistakable statement that Paul had apostolic authority. They should listen to him from now on.

You can easily see God's hand in this episode, and we can only imagine where it went from there. No doubt these men began serving God under their new standing in Christ. Without question, Paul immediately had some quality, young disciples to work with.

## Battle Joined

Once again, Paul strode into the synagogue and began "reasoning and persuading them about the kingdom of God" (v. 8). This confirms what we saw in chapter 18, that Paul never discarded the notion of reasoning with people or persuading them. And he continued to rely on sound arguments and persuasion to the end (see 24:25; 26:28; and 28:23).

Before too long, Paul's welcome ran out:

> But some became stubborn, rejecting his message and publicly speaking against the Way. So Paul left the synagogue and took the believers with him. Then he held daily discussions at the lecture hall of Tyrannus. This went on for the next two years, so that people throughout the province of Asia—both Jews and Greeks—heard the word of the Lord. (vs. 9-10)

This was far longer than Paul stayed in any previous city. By the time we add all the time notifications, it adds up to over three years. The reason is in the last statement. It's obviously hyperbole, but must relate to something. This is clearly Luke's effort to describe an explosive outbreak of gospel power.

# Miraculous Healing

As more people believed, God got behind the revival with an extraordinary outbreak of miracles:

> God was performing extraordinary miracles by the hands of Paul, so that handkerchiefs or aprons were even carried from his body to the sick, and the diseases left them and the evil spirits went out. (vs. 11-12)

Based on this story, TV faith healers sometimes sell "prayer cloths" that they have been praying over for weeks. "Just $45 and we'll send it right out." But God doesn't charge for his miracles, and nobody is seeing anything like this today. Even then, Luke says, "God was performing extraordinary miracles by the hands of Paul" (v. 11). Not just miracles—extraordinary miracles. This was truly rare even on the front line of first century mission.

It was an unprecedented case of God transferring his spiritual power, speeding the spread of the gospel. "Where did that cloth come from?" "Come with me and I'll show you."

# The Sons of Sceva

Watching the dynamic spiritual activity in the city, some exorcists for hire tried facing a demon possessed man, saying, "I adjure you by Jesus whom Paul preaches" (v. 13). The funny reply, "I know Jesus, and I know Paul, but who are you?" was followed by a thorough beating. Why did they come out naked? Remember people wore robes at this time, not tailored clothes like today.

# Renunciation

Ephesus was a hotbed of occult practices. Luke recounts how:

> Many also of those who had believed kept coming, confessing and disclosing their practices. And many of those who practiced magic brought their books together and began burning them in the sight of everyone; and they counted up the price of them and found it fifty thousand pieces of silver. (vs. 18-19)

This event was a prayer meeting for renouncing previous occult practices. They may have sought for healing, predictions, spells, or curses from occult practitioners. That's dangerous. These practices can result in ongoing spiritual subjection that can interfere with your spiritual life.

That's why they did this renunciation. Gathering all their books, and no doubt idols, charms, effigies, magic poultices, and medicine bundles, they cast them into a big fire. The example put forward here includes publicly confessing what links might exist between believers and their former occult lives. Then they destroyed the paraphernalia. You renounce in prayer any known or unknown covenant you might be under—in the name of Jesus. That's how believers can sever any lingering link with the occult.

Another important observation comes from the cost of the books. They counted up the cost as people cast the books into the fire and it added up to the staggering sum of 50,000 pieces of silver. This probably refers to Greek drachmas—each coin equivalent to a day's wage!

Books were much more expensive then, as each had to be copied by hand, and writing materials were also expensive. Still, this was a huge pile of books, and that implies that the crowd that produced it was also huge.

## Lost Letter

Somewhere during this two year ministry Paul wrote a lost letter to the Corinthians. He refers to the letter in 1 Corinthians 5:9-11, revealing that they were misinterpreting what he said. He wanted them to remove sexually immoral people from the church, but they apparently thought he meant not to associate with *any* immoral or idol-worshipping people period. That would clearly be wrong, as it would deprive the world of the witness they needed most.

They must have written him back, because he also refers to their letter, "Now concerning the things about which you wrote" (1 Corinthians 7:1). He also got a negative report from a group he calls "Chloe's people" (1 Corinthians 1:11) to the effect that the Corinthians were fighting and competing with each other (1 Corinthians 1:10-11; 3:3).

## Side Trip to Achaia and Macedonia

Paul felt the Spirit leading him to take up an offering for the poor in Judea and at the same time visit the groups he had earlier planted:

> Now after these things were finished, Paul purposed in the Spirit to go to Jerusalem after he had passed through Macedonia and Achaia, saying, "After I have been there, I must also see Rome." (v. 21)

He sent Timothy and Erastus ahead before him, which was different than his previous practice. He probably sent them to get started on the collection. We don't know who Erastus was, but later he comes up in 2 Timothy 4:20 in a way that shows Timothy knew him, and that he had an interest in Corinth.

Before Paul could join them, a riot broke out.

## Riot in Ephesus

Luke explains:

> About that time, serious trouble developed in Ephesus concerning the Way. It began with Demetrius, a silversmith who had a large business manufacturing silver shrines of the Greek goddess Artemis. He kept many craftsmen busy. He called them together, along with others employed in similar trades, and addressed them as follows:

> "Gentlemen, you know that our wealth comes from this business. But as you have seen and heard, this man Paul has persuaded many people that handmade gods aren't really gods at all. And he's done this not only here in Ephesus but throughout the entire province! Not only is there danger that this trade of ours fall into disrepute, but also that the temple of the great goddess Artemis be regarded as worthless and that she whom all of Asia and the world worship will even be dethroned from her magnificence." (vs. 23-27)

Notice that this passage indicates amazing growth for the church at Ephesus. For Demetrius to argue plausibly that the followers of Jesus were becoming so numerous that it threatened the ongoing worship of

Artemis says a lot. This temple was considered one of the seven ancient wonders of the world.

The original temple burned down, then was rebuilt in 356 BC. The new temple was nearly *four times the size of the Parthenon in Athens!* If you've ever seen the Parthenon, you can appreciate how immense it was. People would travel from all over the empire to see this amazing temple, and usually buy souvenirs like Demetrius' model shrines.[1] It was sacked and destroyed by the Goths in AD 263.

After Demetrius gave his plea:

> Their anger boiled, and they began shouting, "Great is Artemis of the Ephesians!" Soon the whole city was filled with confusion. Everyone rushed to the amphitheater, dragging along Gaius and Aristarchus, who were Paul's traveling companions from Macedonia. Paul wanted to go in, too, but the believers wouldn't let him. Some of the officials of the province, friends of Paul, also sent a message to him, begging him not to risk his life by entering the amphitheater. (vs. 28-31)

Paul was well advised to stay well away from this mob. They probably would have torn him to pieces. It's interesting to see that he has friends among the "Asiarchs," noble and wealthy leaders in the province. Luke probably saw this detail as showing that Paul was well-connected with the nobility and the Roman establishment. That might be good to point out at his trial in Rome. By now the crowd was irrational and even hysterical:

> Inside, the people were all shouting, some one thing and some another. Everything was in confusion. In fact, most of them didn't even know why they were there. (v. 32)

Then, a surprising development—Jews in the crowd push Alexander forward to explain what was going on. Were they Christian Jews? Was he a believer? It seems like he was, but it didn't matter. He never got to speak:

> But when the crowd realized he was a Jew, they started shouting again and kept it up for about two hours: "Great is Artemis of the Ephesians! Great is Artemis of the Ephesians!" (v. 34)

---

1. "Artemis of Ephesus was not the fair and chaste huntress of Greek mythology but a Near-Eastern mother-goddess of fertility." Richard Longenecker, *Acts,* "At Ephesus." The image that fell from the sky, probably was a meteorite.

You can see the anti-Semitism in this otherwise comical story. But the danger was real.

Finally, the mayor got them to quiet down. He pointed out that Artemis was in no danger, and that, "we are in danger of being charged with rioting by the Roman government," because they had no legitimate reason for the commotion (v. 40). He said if they had a complaint, they should handle it through the courts. Then, the riot abruptly broke up. People must have felt pretty awkward, walking home in silence.

You can see how this story would be important in Paul's defense in Rome. The charges that he was a trouble-maker and guilty of sedition were utterly refuted in this account. Yes, there was a riot (which the Romans hated), and Rome may have already received a report about this disturbance. But any reader can see that it was the idol craftsmen and the rest of the town that caused the riot. Paul was nowhere near. His prosecutors would be siding with the mob instead of the level-headed mayor, who had it right.

Scholars suggest that this riot is what Paul referred to in 1 Corinthians 15:32 where he says he "fought wild beasts in Ephesus." Was he speaking metaphorically of this rowdy crowd? That's a stretch, considering that he wasn't even in the amphitheater.

Or is it possible that he literally fought wild beasts as a prisoner? It's hard to believe Luke wouldn't mention that, unless he thought it would be a negative reference to Paul's legality. We know of cases where gladiators and condemned prisoners gained their freedom by winning their contest, or by being ransomed for money—something the large group in Ephesus could easily have done.

Or was Paul attacked by literal wild predators while journeying near Ephesus? A pack of wild dogs?

It's probably better to simply say we don't know. The quip must have interested the Corinthians, because they apparently asked for more information about his trial in Asia, which Paul gave them in 2 Corinthians 1:8–11.

## The Big Picture

Luke is done talking about the Ephesian outreach. His coverage was brief, considering this lasted over three years. Although it's easy to miss, the outcome of this ministry was dazzling in terms of its size and success. Let's gather the brief notifications we have of the size of this outreach.

Luke explained how Paul had to leave the synagogue and move to the schoolroom of Tyrannus for daily preaching and teaching. Then he adds, "This went on for the next two years, so that people throughout the province of Asia—both Jews and Greeks—heard the word of the Lord." And he wasn't kidding.

When we open the book of Revelation, we see letters to seven churches in chapters 2 and 3. All but one share one thing in common: They lie in a circle around Ephesus. But Paul never visited any of these towns according to what we have in Acts. These churches must have been planted by believers coming out of Ephesus.

Also Colossae is the city Paul wrote in the book of Colossians. He confirms that he had never been there, saying, "You learned it [the gospel] from Epaphras," and "I want you to know how great a struggle I have on your behalf and for those who are at Laodicea, and for all those who have not personally seen my face" (Colossians 1:7; 2:1). This verse confirms that Laodicea had never met him either.

Miletus, the port city for Ephesus, isn't explicitly said to have a local church, but it does seem implied in chapter 20 when Paul visits there. So Asia wasn't just hearing the gospel, they were believing it. All this church planting activity is part of the Ephesian awakening. In addition, notice the language Luke uses:

- After the story of the seven sons of Sceva we read, "The story of what happened spread quickly all through Ephesus, to Jews and Greeks alike. A solemn fear descended on the city, and the name of the Lord Jesus was greatly honored" (v. 17). He makes it sound like much of the city was believing.

- Next, we saw that the price for the pile of occult books cost 50,000 drachmas (v. 19). Only a very large group could have amassed such a fortune in books. If we say a day's wage today is $150 (about $40,000 per year) and we multiply that day's wage by 50,000, we get $7,500,000. Of course, we are wealthier than they were, but they counted days of work the same way we do.

- After that event, Luke says, "So the message about the Lord spread widely and had a powerful effect" (v. 20).

- Finally, probably the strongest piece of evidence comes from Demetrius' speech before the riot in Ephesus. He said, "This man Paul has persuaded many people that handmade gods aren't really gods at all." Duh. But notice his term "many." Then he adds, "And he's done this not only here in Ephesus but throughout the entire province!" (v. 26).

Then he argues, "I'm also concerned that the temple of the great goddess Artemis will lose its influence and that Artemis—this magnificent goddess worshiped throughout the province of Asia and all around the world—will be robbed of her great prestige!" (v. 27).

That Demetrius could make this argument and that the other craftsmen agreed is incredible. There were so many followers of Jesus in Ephesus and surrounding area that these men seriously thought that nobody would be left to buy their images.

The Roman province of Asia was on fire with God's word by the end of these three years (plus the previous work done by Priscilla and Aquilla). The number of those won to faith couldn't be less than thousands.

Judging from the book of Colossians (written almost ten years later), the word continued to grow and expand after these years (Colossians 1:6). This was the most successful local awakening in Paul's entire career. Only the original group in Jerusalem might have been bigger.

# 33

# OTHER JOURNEYS
## ACTS 20

## Corinth?

Having sent Timothy and Erastus ahead, Paul now set out on a journey back to Macedonia and Corinth. He must have visited Corinth sometime after his first visit in chapter 18, and before this trip, no doubt by ship. In 2 Corinthians 1:23 Paul wrote, "But I call God as witness to my soul, that to spare you I did not come again to Corinth." And he adds in 2:1, "But I determined this for my own sake, that I would not come to you in sorrow again."

When was he there in sorrow the first time? We see no hint of that in his time there during the second journey. There must have been another visit, and it must have become contentious and sorrowful. This is confirmed in 2 Corinthians 12:14: "Here for this third time I am ready to come to you." It was probably a short visit. Otherwise, Luke probably would have mentioned it.

He had earlier sent word that he was coming to visit a third time, but because of conditions in Corinth, and the negative earlier visit, he decided not to come. Instead of visiting again, he wrote the letter of

1 Corinthians. It's a severe book at multiple points, loaded with sharp rebuke. So it fits the description of his "severe letter" in 2 Corinthians 7.

He sent Titus with the letter to Corinth and waited behind for him to return with word on how things went. Paul describes his agonizing wait to see whether the Corinthians were going to respond favorably to his letter of rebuke or reject what he said. "For out of much affliction and anguish of heart I wrote to you with many tears" (2 Corinthians 2:4).

Paul waited at first in Troas for Titus' return. "Now when I came to Troas for the gospel of Christ and when a door was opened for me in the Lord, I had no rest for my spirit, not finding Titus my brother; but taking my leave of them, I went on to Macedonia" (2 Corinthians 2:12-13). Paul must have been incredibly upset to pass up on a wide door in favor of pressing his search for Titus.

He finally found Titus in Macedonia:

> For even when we came into Macedonia our flesh had no rest, but we were afflicted on every side: conflicts without, fears within.
>
> But God, who comforts the depressed, comforted us by the coming of Titus; and not only by his coming, but also by the comfort with which he was comforted in you (Corinthians), as he reported to us your longing, your mourning, your zeal for me; so that I rejoiced even more.
>
> For though I caused you sorrow by my letter, I do not regret it; though I did regret it—for I see that that letter caused you sorrow, though only for a while—I now rejoice, not that you were made sorrowful, but that you were made sorrowful to the point of repentance; for you were made sorrowful according to the will of God, so that you might not suffer loss in anything through us. (2 Corinthians 7:5-9)

The Corinthians had responded with heartfelt repentance. Now Paul knew it was safe to go there in person without expecting a big, ugly fight. He sent this letter, 2 Corinthians, ahead, again announcing his third visit, while he took care of things in Macedonia (including the big collection for Judea).

# Illyricum?

Paul told the Roman church, not long after this, that he had preached as far away as Illyricum (Romans 15:19). This province is even further from Ephesus than Macedonia, reaching to the top of Italy. Later, he comments that Titus was returning to Dalmatia, which is in Illyricum (2 Timothy 4:10). So, although Luke doesn't go into it, Paul must have reached out to Illyricum, probably during this trip.

# The Collection

Paul and his team were also organizing the big multi-church collection for the poor believers in Judea. Paul described to the Corinthians how well the campaign was going in Macedonia and urged the Corinthians to complete what they had earlier promised (2 Corinthians 8:1-5; 9:5). This passage alone establishes the legitimacy of taking pledges during ministry fundraising campaigns.

When Paul finally reached Corinth, "he spent three months" there (20:3). During these months he wrote the all-important letter of Romans (see Romans 16:23 and 2 Timothy 4:20 on Erastus). At that point he discovered a plot against his life just as he was getting ready to set sail. So the assassins were probably waiting in Cenchrea, the eastern port city, planning to grab him as he approached the ship. To foil the plan, he headed north overland.

# The Posse

As the third journey drew toward its conclusion, they assembled a sizeable crew of men to guard the large batch of cash in silver and gold (paper money didn't exist), as they journeyed toward Jerusalem.

> And he was accompanied by Sopater of Berea, the son of Pyrrhus, and by Aristarchus and Secundus of the Thessalonians, and Gaius of Derbe, and Timothy, and Tychicus and Trophimus of Asia. (Acts 20:4)

Notice that the different men come from different churches. That's because each local church contributed a man as a security guard. They probably carried swords. With Paul, there are eight men here, and they would add others as they moved, including our author, Luke.

The group went ahead of Paul to Troas, for unknown reasons. Possibly it was because they were Gentiles, and Paul was celebrating Passover and the Feast of Unleavened Bread at Philippi. Luke says he "sailed from Philippi after the days of Unleavened Bread" (v. 6). Did he see Passover as a Jewish thing, where they didn't belong? That doesn't match up well with his doctrine that Jews and Greeks were one in Christ (Galatians 3:28).

Or were they sent ahead to scout the city and make sure they weren't going to have trouble? Arranging rooming for a dozen men would take some time. When Paul sailed behind them he was also accompanied by Luke—the second "we" passage begins here. Once again, we see the sudden upsurge in detail, signaling that Luke was there in person.

> We sailed from Philippi after the days of Unleavened Bread, and came to them at Troas within five days; and there we stayed seven days. (v. 6)

Time of year, time to sail, time spent there, all carefully articulated.

## Eutychus

Now in Troas on the east coast of the Aegean Sea, Paul met with the local body of believers and taught them. They were in an upper room, and Luke includes the minute detail that the room was "lit by many flickering lamps" (v. 8). The effect probably struck Luke at the time, but this is the kind of detail that would only come from someone who was there. It doesn't advance the story.

Paul lectured and preached until midnight, at which point a young man named Eutychus fell asleep while sitting on the window sill, and fell out from three stories up! Luke says he fell "to his death" (v. 9).

But as the believers scrambled down and out to the street, "Paul ran to him, bent over him, and took him into his arms. 'Don't worry,' he said, 'he's alive!'" (v. 10). Was he raised from the dead? That's doubtful. How would Luke know he had died? Maybe they all thought he was dead but he wasn't? That's what Paul's words seem to suggest. He doesn't call on him to rise, but seems to discover that he wasn't dead.

Luke ends the story saying, "The young man was taken home alive and well, and everyone was greatly relieved" (v. 12).

The most surprising part of the story is verse 11:

Then they all went back upstairs, shared in the Lord's Supper, and ate together. Paul continued talking to them until dawn, and then he left.

I've been in gatherings like this, with people so excited and eager to learn that they would talk all night if possible. It's a mark of a people getting vision and sensing God working in their midst.

# Sailing South

For some reason, Paul sent Luke and the others by ship, while he walked down the coastal road to Assos. Did he send the money with them, on the theory that a ship was more secure than trails sometimes attacked by bandits? He apparently stayed a bit longer in Troas, so he might have had more unfinished business there.

You can immediately tell we're reading one of Luke's "we" passages, because every detail is included:

> Paul went by land to Assos, where he had arranged for us to join him, while we traveled by ship. He joined us there, and we sailed together to Mitylene. The next day we sailed past the island of Kios. The following day we crossed to the island of Samos, and a day later we arrived at Miletus. (vs. 13-15)

He explains that, "Paul had decided to sail on past Ephesus, for he didn't want to spend any more time in the province of Asia. He was hurrying to get to Jerusalem, if possible, in time for the Festival of Pentecost" (v. 16). But while he didn't want to get bogged down in Ephesus, he did want to talk to their elders. So he sent them a message and had them come down to the port town of Miletus for a leadership meeting.

# Meeting with the Ephesian Elders

When they arrived, Paul addressed them in a talk that Luke recounts with significant detail and in this case, Luke was actually sitting there and listening. It's an important example of how Paul worked with fellow leaders. All of his other speeches and defenses were before nonbelievers. Here is our only example of how he reasoned with believers, and specifically, leaders. We can observe ten distinct lessons from the encounter.

## Plurality

We can't tell how many elders came, but it was a group. So once again we see Paul's expectation that multiple elders in an area work together as a team, rather than setting up a single leader, like they did later in the second century.

## Close Modeling

Paul wasn't boasting, he was modeling. When modeling, you have to make sure those following your model perceive the right things. That means reminding them what you did and why.

Paul reminds the elders that he was with them in close relationship so that they could see for themselves what his character was like. He said he was "serving the Lord with all humility and with tears and with trials which came upon me through the plots of the Jews" (v. 19). He wasn't distant or hard to access, but close up and personal.

This is an essential feature if a leader hopes to be a model that people follow. They have to see you as a real person and one who they understand well. That results in people identifying with you and naturally wanting to follow your example.

## Whole Counsel of God

He reminded them, "how I did not shrink from declaring to you anything that was profitable, and teaching you publicly and from house to house" (v. 20).

Some biblical themes, like the love of God, are popular and easily received by most audiences. Others, like God's judgment, may incite rage. But a man of God like Paul has already made up his mind that he's going to teach it all—the whole counsel of God—not just what he estimates will please his listeners.

He also talks about speaking in "public," which would refer first to the synagogue, and then to the schoolroom of Tyrannus. But he also reveals that he was teaching "from house to house." These are the house churches that characterized the early church from one end to the other. Only much later did Christians begin constructing church buildings.

Our earlier analysis showed that more than a thousand people were involved in the fellowship in Ephesus. Given the size of ancient homes, which were mostly far smaller than ours in modern America, the number of house churches must have numbered a hundred or more.[1]

## The Gospel

Paul said he was "solemnly testifying to both Jews and Greeks of repentance toward God and faith in our Lord Jesus Christ" (v. 21). Here is a better way to understand "repentance." It's not repenting from your sins, like NLT interpolates. It's repentance toward God. When I repent, I stop going my own autonomous way apart from God, and I turn toward him to follow.

Of course, Paul was always adamant on faith apart from works.

## Bound by the Spirit

Next he said:

> "And now, behold, bound by the Spirit, I am on my way to Jerusalem, not knowing what will happen to me there, except that the Holy Spirit solemnly testifies to me in every city, saying that bonds and afflictions await me." (vs. 22-23)

This statement comes up later in Acts as we follow Paul's journey toward an ominous visit to Jerusalem. Everywhere he goes, people plead with him not to go. Even prophets warn him he will be bound if he goes. Was Paul being self-willed here, and refusing to submit?

The expression here could be translated either "bound in spirit" (meaning bound in his own spirit), or "bound by the Spirit" (meaning bound by the Holy Spirit). These two ways of reading it result from the way verbs in this case can be either instrumental (by the Spirit) or locative (in the spirit). It doesn't really matter, because Paul's theology sees one's spirit as united with God (1 Corinthians 6:17).

Although the picture remains ambiguous for some time, in the end it becomes clear that Paul was truly following the will of the Spirit the whole way.

---

1. Some "simple church" advocates hold that each small group should have one elder in it. I don't see any evidence for that, and it seems like it would quickly result in too many elders to have fruitful deliberations. When an eldership includes too many elders, it takes forever to make decisions, and it's frustrating.

## Finishing the Course

> "But I do not consider my life of any account as dear to myself, so that I may finish my course and the ministry which I received from the Lord Jesus, to testify solemnly of the gospel of the grace of God. And now, behold, I know that all of you, among whom I went about preaching the kingdom, will no longer see my face." (vs. 24-25)

Paul believed that God gives his servants a specific ministry that is like a cross-country racecourse. When running a race, you can't take a shortcut to cut off a loop in the course. If you did that you would be disqualified. Also, there's no prize for going part way on your course. It's essential that workers finish their course. (See these points argued in 1 Corinthians 9:24-27; 2 Timothy 2:5; 4:5-8; and Ephesians 2:10).

Paul says this last statement, about not seeing them again, not as necessarily from God. He had reached this conclusion, but was it a word of prophecy? Or was he just saying what he thinks is most likely? Later evidence suggests he actually made it back to Ephesus eventually, but we can't be sure.

## Why They Are Leaders

> "Be on guard for yourselves and for all the flock, among which the Holy Spirit has made you overseers, to shepherd the church of God which he purchased with his own blood." (v. 28)

Paul is clear on his theology of leadership. Leaders are made by the Holy Spirit. We saw this earlier in the first journey. Paul's view is the organic model of the church, where leadership arises naturally in a community through service. The people recognize leaders, rather than having them qualified by degrees or a committee hiring them.

He also reminds them that they are leading sheep that belong to Jesus. He paid a high price to rescue each one, and leaders are never to hold their own people in contempt.

## Counterattack

> "I know that after my departure savage wolves will come in among you, not sparing the flock; and from among your own

selves men will arise, speaking perverse things, to draw away the disciples after them. Therefore be on the alert, remembering that night and day for a period of three years I did not cease to admonish each one with tears." (vs. 29-31)

It's discouraging to think that the attack is going to come from inside the people of God, but unfortunately, that is often the case. If the enemy can infiltrate players into the leadership, he is in perfect position to take things any direction he wants. This also works with disgruntled ex-leaders who circulate in the city claiming they know all the negatives in the group.

Paul later wrote the books of 1 and 2 Timothy while Timothy was helping lead in Ephesus. By studying those books you can see that the enemy was already busily sowing false doctrine in the church (1 Timothy 1:3-7; 19-20; 4:1-5).

Paul even says, "You are aware of the fact that all who are in Asia turned away from me" (2 Timothy 1:15). That makes it sound like most leaders in the area including Ephesus no longer followed Paul's leadership. Or, some think it refers to Asian leaders who were in Rome when Paul was in prison there. For sure however, Jesus charged the Ephesian church with losing their first love (Revelation 2:4). So no matter how glorious and amazing a local body begins, they have no guarantee they will stay that way.

## The Protective Power of the Word

"And now I commend you to God and to the word of his grace, which is able to build you up and to give you the inheritance among all those who are set apart." (v. 32)

Paul clearly believed that teaching members in the body how to handle God's word was the best way to protect the church. But the word can easily be misused. He qualifies himself by adding that it's the word interpreted under grace. The word interpreted under legalism is just as dangerous as any other false teaching.

## Giving, Not Taking

Paul went on:

> "I have coveted no one's silver or gold or clothes. You your-
> selves know that these hands ministered to my own needs and
> to the men who were with me. In everything I showed you that
> by working hard in this manner you must help the weak and
> remember the words of the Lord Jesus, that he himself said, 'It
> is more blessed to give than to receive.'" (vs. 33-35)

They all knew it was true. They would have remembered how Paul
continued working on tent making, even well after it was no longer necessary. What an impression it would have made when people saw this
world-class scholar struggling with his leather and felt sewing.

We noted earlier that his quote from Jesus here is not found in our gospel
books, although the concept certainly is. It shows that he had access to
some early source for Jesus' sayings.

### The Parting

The meeting was over.

> When he had said these things, he knelt down and prayed with
> them all. And they began to weep aloud and embraced Paul,
> and repeatedly kissed him, grieving especially over the word
> which he had spoken, that they would not see his face again.
> And they were accompanying him to the ship. (vs. 36-38)

This incredible scene of naked emotional love is something known to
walking believers. The deep attachment Paul had built into his friendships with these leaders was palpable, humble, and God-centered. We
don't know if they ever saw him again, but if they did, it was after the
period covered by Acts.

## The Big Picture

As the elders ambled back up to Ephesus, Paul, Luke, and probably several others got ready to board ship. It took great bravery to face the future
in Jerusalem, knowing that more trials awaited them.

Bringing the large gift from the Greco-Roman churches to the believers
in Judea would make an eloquent statement about the solidarity and unity of the Jewish and Greek branches of the body of Christ. Would it have
the desired effect? Would it finally relieve and repair some of the damage

done to these believers under Paul's earlier persecution and more since? Would it lead the Jerusalem body to finally and completely accept the Gentile wing of the church?

Paul knew he had critics in Jerusalem—Jewish Christians who resented hiss offering the gospel to Gentiles without any conditions from Jewish law. He calls them "those who are disobedient in Judea" (Romans 15:31). Not to mention the non-Christian Jews who viewed him as the worst kind of traitor.

# 34

# TO JERUSALEM
## ACTS 21

As Paul and his companions boarded another ship, Luke continues his "we" passage with full detail of each part of the trip.

> When we had... set sail, we ran a straight course to Cos and the next day to Rhodes and from there to Patara; and having found a ship crossing over to Phoenicia, we went aboard and set sail. When we came in sight of Cyprus, leaving it on the left, we kept sailing to Syria and landed at Tyre; for there the ship was to unload its cargo. (Acts 21:1-3)

They had to transship once, and instead of sailing to Caesarea near Jerusalem, They ended up more than two hundred miles north at Tyre. As so often before, a local body of believers was already in place. This one was another artifact of the persecution Paul launched earlier:

> So then those who were scattered because of the persecution that occurred in connection with Stephen made their way to Phoenicia and Cyprus and Antioch, speaking the word to no one except to Jews alone. (Acts 11:19)

Tyre is in Phoenicia.

Luke goes on, "After looking up the disciples, we stayed there seven days; and they kept telling Paul through the Spirit not to set foot in Jerusalem" (v. 4). If they were speaking "through the Spirit" saying not to go, how do we reconcile that with Paul saying he was "bound in Spirit to go?" (20:22-23).

One possibility is that the expression "through the Spirit" means mediated through speaking in tongues. Paul uses similar language for speaking or praying in tongues in 1 Corinthians 14:15 in context.

If so, he might have doubted that these speakers were inspired by God.

Another possibility is that the Spirit told them Paul would be bound, but they added the part about how he shouldn't go there. That would match a later even in this chapter.

It seems clear that Luke is telling this whole ominous story of the journey to Jerusalem from the perspective that Paul was doing his duty.

Whatever the explanation is, one thing is very clear throughout the journey: Paul and his team always sought out the people of God wherever they went. They knew that they needed fellowship and community.

Once again, "After kneeling down on the beach and praying, we said farewell to one another" (v. 5).

## Still Finding Other Groups

They took another ship south toward Caesarea, stopping at a town called Ptolemais, "and after greeting the brethren, we stayed with them for a day" (v. 7). How fun this must have been to meet new believers and hear their stories at every stop. At the height of the Jesus movement in the late 60s and early 70s we often had this experience.

After a lengthy time of camping and backpacking our group of guys were expressing how we were missing fellowship. We drove through a small town in Northern Idaho, stopping to cruise through the parking lots of several restaurants. We were looking for a car with a bumper sticker having something to do with Jesus. We found one at McDonalds and strode inside. There was a long-haired guy talking to a couple of others. To one side was a Bible. Walking up, we asked if they were believers, and they were. We shared how we were missing time with the body of Christ. They said we were in luck because they were on their way to a Bible study.

The group was about twenty student aged and young married people. When they heard we had just attended a month-long Bible Institute, they insisted we teach the word. In the end I got the honors, and we had a delightful time thinking through the Samaritan woman in John 4. Later, the long-haired brother took us out to a house he was house sitting and we wound up sharing and praying together until the early hours. It's impossible to explain to a non-believer what unity in the Spirit is. A fantastic night! Things like that were happening all over the country. Unfortunately, this was before cell phones, so we lost track of them.

## Philip the Evangelist

Then, "We went on to Caesarea and stayed at the home of Philip the Evangelist, one of the seven men who had been chosen to distribute food" (v. 8). This is the same Philip the Evangelist who we saw winning over the city of Samaria and the Ethiopian eunuch in chapter 8. Now twenty or more years later, he has a family, including four daughters with the gift of prophecy (v. 9).

This several day layover is probably where Luke got his detailed information on the conversion of Samaria and the Ethiopian eunuch—directly from the man who was there.[1]

## Agabus

Then another prophet showed up:

> Several days later a man named Agabus, who also had the gift of prophecy, arrived from Judea. He came over, took Paul's belt, and bound his own feet and hands with it. Then he said, "The Holy Spirit declares, 'So shall the owner of this belt be bound by the Jewish leaders in Jerusalem and turned over to the Gentiles.'" When we heard this, we and the local believers all begged Paul not to go on to Jerusalem. (vs. 10-12)

This is the same Agabus that predicted a famine in Judea in chapter 12. That was about 12 years earlier. Notice his prophecy didn't say not to go to Jerusalem. It only said he would be bound.

---

1. According to early church historian, Eusebius, who in turn got it from the much earlier writer, Papias, Philip and his prophetess daughters later moved to Heiropolis in Asia. There, they gave Papias info on early happenings in Judea. Eusebius, *Ecclesiastical History* 3.39.

Luke says "we" begged him, so even Luke was pleading with Paul not to go to Jerusalem.

Later in Acts, we will see that Jesus confirmed that Paul was still in God's will. His arrest and imprisonment would result in him going to Rome, just as God intended.

As they pleaded, Paul cried out,

> "Why all this weeping? You are breaking my heart! I am ready not only to be jailed at Jerusalem but even to die for the sake of the Lord Jesus." When it was clear that we couldn't persuade him, we gave up and said, "The Lord's will be done." (vs. 13-14).

Paul's crew went on toward Jerusalem.

## The Big Picture

This section of our story causes ominous feeling about Paul's future. Somehow, he was certain that he needed to go to Jerusalem regardless of the danger. His courage is impressive considering the hostility he knew awaited him. The big financial gift would hopefully go a long way to healing any remaining animas among the believers. But what about his sworn enemies?

# 35

# JERUSALEM AGAIN
## ACTS 21:15-40

Paul had last been to Jerusalem in AD 49, now about 7 years in the past. After the sixty-five-mile journey uphill, they arrived.

> The next day Paul went with us to meet with James, and all the elders of the Jerusalem church were present. After greeting them, Paul gave a detailed account of the things God had accomplished among the Gentiles through his ministry. After hearing this, they praised God. (Acts 21:18-20)

So the reception was warm and affirming of their work in Gentile lands. But,

> Then they said, "You know, dear brother, how many thousands of Jews have also believed, and they all follow the Law of Moses very seriously. But the Jewish believers here in Jerusalem have been told that you are teaching all the Jews who live among the Gentiles to turn their backs on the laws of Moses. They've heard that you teach them not to circumcise their children or follow other Jewish customs." (vs. 20-21)

Their description of the Christian Jews' attitude toward the law sounds suspect. The phrase, "follow the law of Moses very seriously," should read, "they are all zealous for the law" (NASB). Is that a good description of liberated believers in the gospel? Or was the party that lost in the Jerusalem council (converted Pharisees) still unrepentant and influential?

In any case, this rumor was false. We know what Paul actually taught from his books. In 1 Corinthians 7 (written years before this day) he argued,

> Was any man called when he was already circumcised? He is not to become uncircumcised. Has anyone been called in uncircumcision? He is not to be circumcised. (v. 18)

Of course, it was impossible to become uncircumcised. He means they should not forsake their Jewish culture. Paul taught that becoming a believer in Jesus didn't nullify one's Jewishness, but completed it. We have already seen that Paul continued to celebrate Jewish festivals and personally circumcised Timothy, though for other reasons. But he also taught that the uncircumcised Gentiles need not follow Jewish custom.

Paul's opponents were probably deliberately exaggerating what he taught as a straw man attack. At the same time, these believers were also interested in winning non-Christian Jews in the city. They probably felt that a public show of loyalty to Jewish custom might lead to a reduction in hostility.

They advanced a plan:

> "What should we do? They will certainly hear that you have come. Here's what we want you to do. We have four men here who have completed their vow. Go with them to the temple and join them in the purification ceremony, paying for them to have their heads ritually shaved. Then everyone will know that the rumors are all false and that you yourself observe the Jewish laws." (vs. 22-24)

And for the Gentile believers? "They should do what we already told them in a letter" (v. 25). So James is explicit that the issue is Jews being urged to abandon their culture, not Gentiles.

If James and the other leaders were intending to appease the hardline opposition, it was a mistake. The result would be to water down the gospel and remove the offense of the cross (1 Corinthians 1:22-23). It would also show they were naive about the opponents—that all they needed was a little show of loyalty to Judaism. This same group of Christians in Jerusalem gradually lost their cutting edge, and the law-livers began winning believers back into ritual Judaism. This becomes evident in the book of Hebrews.

If they were only demonstrating the compatibility between the gospel and Jewish custom, that could be justified.

## Vows

Vows were practiced in the Old Testament. Vows are linked to swearing. Many Christians are surprised to learn that God prescribed swearing oaths (Exodus 13:19; Leviticus 5:2; 19:12; Numbers 5:21; Deuteronomy 10:20). Jesus made oaths obsolete when he said not to swear (Matthew 5:37). James says the same thing in his book (James 5:12).

So why these first century Jewish followers of Jesus were making oaths is unclear. A number of questions arise.

First off, what kind of vow was it? In the Old Testament, the only vow involving cutting one's hair was the Nazarite vow described in Numbers 6. A significant problem with that is that verse 11 says, "The priest shall offer one [animal] for a sin offering and the other for a burnt offering, and make atonement for him concerning his sin."

Such a blood sacrifice would clearly be wrong, because as Hebrews explains, the work of atonement was finished with Jesus. It's wrong and actually insulting to go back to animal sacrifice, because it suggests that Jesus' work on the cross wasn't good enough.

In this case, it's clear that Paul is not undertaking the oath, because 30 days was the minimum length of time for this oath. But by paying for and participating with the young men, he was still endorsing it.

The seven days of purification came from the fact that Paul had been out of the country and needed to undergo seven days of purification before he could participate in other temple rituals. This purification only involved sprinkling with water.

We noticed earlier that Paul made his own oath and cut his hair in Cenchrea. That's not explained either. It is possible that carrying out these oaths was improper, and a mistake on Paul's part. The biblical text

records what people do, often without moral commentary. We are supposed to use our own discernment to recognize wrongdoing.

According to one view, Paul conceded here wrongfully, but with more
reflection, later realized believers needed to completely break with temple ritual—a view he explained in the book of Hebrews.

We read,

> So Paul went to the temple the next day with the other men.
> They had already started the purification ritual, so he publicly
> announced the date when their vows would end and sacrifices
> would be offered for each of them. (v. 26)

So it sounds like at least the other four were preparing to offer sacrifice.
It would be one thing if it was a thank offering. But according to the
Nazarite vow, these were for atonement. I cannot see any way that this
action was justified. And it didn't work.

## Reaction

In any case, it seems clear from the language that they never offered
them:

> The seven days were almost ended when some Jews from the
> province of Asia saw Paul in the temple and roused a mob
> against him. They grabbed him, yelling, "Men of Israel, help
> us! This is the man who preaches against our people every-
> where against our people and the law and this place; and
> besides he has even brought Greeks into the temple and has
> defiled this holy place." (vs. 27-28)

Jews from Asia? That's incredible! Asia is where Ephesus is, a thousand
miles away. And enemies from there just happen to be in the temple and
recognize Paul? What bad luck! But there's no luck here. Satan knows
how to bring enemies of the people of God into contact at the critical
moment. Or was it God engineering a situation that would prevent Paul
from making a big mistake and ultimately carry him to Rome? Or both?
God is well able to cause Satan's schemes to backfire onto him.

Luke explains that the Jews thought Paul had brought a Gentile into
the temple. That was wrong, and they probably knew it. If he had let
a Gentile in with him, where is Trophimus now? He has mysteriously

disappeared. Paul would never be foolish enough to bring a Gentile into the temple, especially right when he's trying to show he's orthodox.

> Then all the city was provoked, and the people rushed together, and taking hold of Paul they dragged him out of the temple, and immediately the doors were shut. While they were seeking to kill him, a report came up to the commander of the Roman cohort that all Jerusalem was in confusion. At once he took along some soldiers and centurions and ran down to them; and when they saw the commander and the soldiers, they stopped beating Paul. (vs. 30-32)

The Romans wouldn't tolerate riots in their cities. This kind of disturbance is exactly what they were there to prevent. Experience had shown that keeping the *pax Romana* (the peace of Rome) was the best way to prevent unexpected uprisings. The Roman cohort was stationed right adjacent to the temple mount in the so-called Antonio Fortress. They would have arrived within minutes. During the interval the crowd was pounding on Paul and trying to tear him to pieces.

When the Roman formation pushed into the crowd, fully armored and carrying spears and shields, people let them through. The Romans secured Paul, chained him, and "began asking who he was and what he had done" (v. 33). But "some were shouting one thing and some another" (v. 34). The commander was baffled. They began taking him to the fortress.

> When they got to the stairs, he [Paul] was carried by the soldiers because of the violence of the mob; for the multitude of the people kept following them, shouting, "Kill him, kill him!" (vs. 35-36).

They have to carry him over their heads, as the crowd tries to reach through the soldiers to land a punch on him.

Just as they were about to go inside, Paul asked the commander, "May I have a word with you?"

"Do you know Greek?" the commander asked, surprised. He went on to ask if Paul was the Egyptian revolutionary in recent history.[1]  Paul said

---

1. Flavianus Josephus, *Wars of the Jews* II, 261–63. Josephus, who tends to exaggerate, put the number of followers of this false prophet at 30,000. The commander's 4000 is probably more accurate. He led his followers to the Mount of Olives in preparation for the messianic overthrow of Jerusalem.

no, and this results in an interesting contrast—the false prophet who was violent political, and Paul who was neither.

Paul pleaded for a chance to speak to the people, and the commander agreed.

## First Defense

> Paul, standing on the stairs, motioned to the people with his hand; and when there was a great hush, he spoke to them in the Hebrew dialect (i.e. Aramaic). (v. 40)

The hush must have been dramatic—most of them probably didn't know who Paul was, and wanted to hear. The fact that he spoke in Aramaic seems to have surprised them. They must have been assuming he was Hellenistic.

They continued to listen as Paul recounted his growing up in Jerusalem and his education under Gamaliel—a name that would be familiar to many. "I persecuted this Way to the death, binding and putting both men and women into prisons" (22:4). He went on to describe his fateful trip to Damascus and encounter with Jesus on the road. The crowd remained silent. Some of them must have felt amazed—was it true? Why would he make this up? Some of them might have remembered: "Yeah, this is the guy we sent to Damascus..."

> "'Saul, Saul, why are you persecuting me?' And I answered, 'Who are you, Lord?' And he said to me, 'I am Jesus the Nazarene, whom you are persecuting.'"(vs. 7-8)

He literally didn't know who it was? Paul went on to describe being led into Damascus by the hand since he was blinded. Then his healing by Ananias, who went on to say, "Now why do you delay? Get up and be baptized, and wash away your sins, calling on his name" (v. 16). Paul probably elaborated a bit more here, explaining the gospel. There's little chance that he wouldn't have taken advantage of this opportunity to give it.

Then he disclosed something we hadn't heard before:

> "It happened when I returned to Jerusalem and was praying in

---

They were crushed by Felix and his Roman force, but some got away.

the temple, that I fell into a trance, and I saw him saying to me, 'Make haste, and get out of Jerusalem quickly, because they will not accept your testimony about me.'" (vs. 17-18)

It sounds like he argued with the Lord, citing his murder of Stephen and heavy persecution of the others. But Jesus answered, "Go! For I will send you far away to the Gentiles" (v. 21).

That was it. At the word "Gentiles," pandemonium broke out—they had heard enough!

> The crowd listened until Paul said that word. Then they all began to shout, "Away with such a fellow! He isn't fit to live!" They yelled, threw off their coats, and tossed handfuls of dust into the air. (vs. 22-23)

This is absolute hysteria! The Romans formed ranks around Paul and hustled him away, into the fortress.

## Cross Examination

The commander still had no idea what was going on, partly because of the language barrier. He probably only got small quips from the Aramaic. As the story progresses, he becomes increasingly confused. At this point, he decides to clear the matter up with some good old-fashioned torture.

> The commander brought Paul inside and ordered him lashed with whips to make him confess his crime. He wanted to find out why the crowd had become so furious. (v. 24)

But as they were tying him to the whipping post, Paul calmly asks the officer in charge, "Is it legal for you to whip a Roman citizen who hasn't even been tried?" (v. 25).

That stopped everything. The officer scurried out to the commander and said, "What are you doing? This man is a Roman citizen!" (v. 26).

> So the commander went over and asked Paul, "Tell me, are you a Roman citizen?"
>
> "Yes, I certainly am," Paul replied.
>
> "I am, too," the commander muttered, "and it cost me plenty!"
>
> Paul answered, "But I am a citizen by birth!" (vs. 27-28)

Roman citizenship was the ticket to privilege at this time. You could buy citizenship as the commander said, and it cost a fortune. It not only gave advantage to the buyer, but his descendants automatically became Romans as well.

The nuance only hinted at here is that those born as natural citizens were considered more authentic. Paul was definitely flashing his credentials.

The commander was frightened when he realized he had unlawfully bound a Roman citizen. He had him untied and decided to go a different direction. He would summon the priests and the Sanhedrin and have Paul questioned there. The commander still had no idea what was going on: "He wanted to find out what the trouble was all about" (v. 30).

There's a good chance the commander had Paul over for dinner and drinks as well, to pacify him and keep him from making trouble.

# 36

## BEFORE THE SANHEDRIN

### ACTS 23

## Under Judgment by His Enemies

The following day the Romans took Paul to the high counsel; the Sanhedrin. This must have been quite ominous in Paul's mind. This was the group he "betrayed" when he abandoned his commission from them to capture more Christians, and instead became a leading proponent.

Although more than twenty years had passed, they would have kept the memory alive. It's hard to see anyone being fair with Paul in this crew.

The meeting didn't start out well:

> Gazing intently at the high council, Paul began: "Brothers, I have always lived before God with a clear conscience!"

> Instantly Ananias the high priest commanded those close to Paul to slap him on the mouth. But Paul said to him, "God will slap you, you corrupt hypocrite! What kind of judge are you to break the law yourself by ordering me struck like that?"

> Those standing near Paul said to him, "Do you dare to insult God's high priest?"

"I'm sorry, brothers. I didn't realize he was the high priest," Paul replied, "for the Scriptures say, 'You must not speak evil of any of your rulers.'" (Acts 23:1-5)

We aren't told the reason for the slap, but Paul may have spoken out of order in some way. Maybe they expected him to wait until called on?[1]

The point is how graphically we see the bristling, crackling hostility. Paul knew he was facing torture and death. He must have remembered Stephen standing in the same setting, and that didn't go well. Trying to be reasonable with this crowd was pointless.

## The Pharisee Ploy

Looking around, he noticed a rough balance between his old club, the Pharisees, and the cynical, money loving Sadducees, and he hit on a plan. He shouted, "Brothers, I am a Pharisee, as were my ancestors! And I am on trial because my hope is in the resurrection of the dead! (v. 6)."

Paul was playing the Pharisees. He knew that wasn't why he was on trial. The effect was immediate:

> This divided the council—the Pharisees against the Sadducees—for the Sadducees say there is no resurrection or angels or spirits, but the Pharisees believe in all of these. So there was a great uproar..." (vs. 7-9).

They began jumping up, shouting, and gesticulating. In moments, the council had been reduced to a brawl. The commander must have been utterly dumbfounded! He decided he needed to get his prisoner out of there before they tore him apart. The soldiers moved in again, shoving outraged members aside until they had Paul secure in their midst, and escorted him out.

Although a Roman would not normally be allowed to be in the room during a meeting of the council, in this case the commander had called for the meeting and may have refused to let his prisoner out of his sight given the fanaticism the crowd had earlier displayed. They probably had to admit him if they wanted to get at Paul.

The commander, later identified as Lysias, still had no idea what was

---

1. Ananias the son of Nedebaeus reigned as high priest from AD 48 to 58 or 59. Josephus says he paid large bribes to both Romans and Jews (cf. Antiq. XX, 205–7 [ix.2], 213 [ix.4]).

going on. The council had revealed nothing. Lysias' confusion about the meaning of Jewish and Christian conflict becomes more and more humorous as the story goes on. From his Greco-Roman mindset, he simply could not comprehend why people were so upset about religion.

## A Night Visit

Paul must have felt the walls closing in on him as he was taken back to prison. How was he ever going to get out of this? Then:

> On the night immediately following, the Lord stood at his side and said, "Take courage; for as you have solemnly witnessed to my cause at Jerusalem, so you must witness at Rome also." (v. 11)

Once again, the fear building in Paul was probably ruinous. Jesus stepped in with assurance. Nothing is wrong. This is all unfolding as planned. And here's where it's headed... What a relief! I wonder if Paul shed tears of joy to be visited again by Jesus? I think I would. Again, Jesus isn't on a flashing throne. He appears simply as a man standing next to Paul. Did he put his arm around Paul?

From this point on in the story, Paul knows what the future holds, at least in the longer term. Whatever happens in the near term, he's not going to die; he's going to Rome. Once Jesus said this, there was zero chance that it wouldn't happen. Paul's courage must have risen in orders of magnitude.

## Murder Plan

> The next morning a group of Jews got together and bound themselves with an oath not to eat or drink until they had killed Paul. There were more than forty of them in the conspiracy. (vs. 12-13)

What incredible hate! How can modern readers comprehend this?

First, you start with the ancient Jewish view of truth—that it's real and objective. They viewed Paul as a false teacher who threatened Judaism at its core. And under the law of Moses, false teaching was one of a handful of crimes that deserved capital punishment.

Of course this was not an orderly court that could convict someone. They were under Roman occupation, and they knew the Romans would never execute Paul for what he believed. They just didn't care about that. These Jews decided to take matters into their own hands.

Another principle comes from the book of Proverbs:

> Let a man meet a bear robbed of her cubs,
> Rather than a fool in his folly. (17:12)

These people had heard and maybe seen the miracles God was performing through followers of Jesus. They knew by now which Old Testament prophecies exactly matched the life and death of Jesus. They knew about the sightings of Jesus resurrected and that the tomb must have been empty. Otherwise why wouldn't the leaders just exhume the body?

But instead of refuting what the believers taught, they just wanted them dead. We saw this same phenomenon in the rage-killing of Stephen.

Their plan was simple. They went to the leaders and said,

> "So you and the high council should ask the commander to bring Paul back to the council again. Pretend you want to examine his case more fully. We will kill him on the way." (v. 15)

## Murder Thwarted

The leaders apparently had no resistance to the plan. "But Paul's nephew—his sister's son—heard of their plan and went to the fortress and told Paul" (v. 16). So Paul had a sister living in Jerusalem? She must have been considerably younger than he to have a young son, described as a "lad," meaning a boy. We don't know how he knew about the plot, but probably the conspirators were shooting off their mouths like many criminals, boasting about what they were going to do.

Paul had him report the story to the commander, who warned the boy to tell no one that he had reported the plan.

Lysias, the commander, decides to handle the situation Roman style:

> Then the commander called two of his officers and ordered, "Get 200 soldiers ready to leave for Caesarea at nine o'clock tonight. Also take 200 spearmen and 70 mounted troops.

> Provide horses for Paul to ride, and get him safely to Governor Felix." (vs. 23-24)

A force of 470 armed soldiers was overwhelming, and that's exactly what he intended. He wasn't taking any chances.

He also sent a letter to Governor Felix explaining the situation. Often referred to as governor, Felix's technical title was procurator of the province of Judea.

> "From Claudius Lysias, to his Excellency, Governor Felix: Greetings!
>
> This man was seized by some Jews, and they were about to kill him when I arrived with the troops. When I learned that he was a Roman citizen, I removed him to safety. Then I took him to their high council to try to learn the basis of the accusations against him. I soon discovered the charge was something regarding their religious law—certainly nothing worthy of imprisonment or death. But when I was informed of a plot to kill him, I immediately sent him on to you. I have told his accusers to bring their charges before you." (vs. 26-30)

Lysias is quite self-serving in this account. He makes no mention of his illegally binding a Roman. And the claim, "When I learned that he was a Roman citizen, I removed him to safety," is a plain lie. As we already saw, he didn't know Paul was a citizen until later, and that's not why he arrested him. There is some truth in saying he removed him for safety.

The armed force left at dark and marched with Paul part of the way, then let the mounted group ride the rest of the way.

How did Luke get to see the contents of this letter? It has a very realistic feel. The most likely explanation would be that Lysias showed it to Paul. They seem to be on improving terms, and Lysias wouldn't want Paul contradicting his story. So he probably showed him the letter and called on him to agree. Or, it could easily be that when they got to Caesarea Felix had the letter read or read it himself aloud in Paul's presence.

## In Caesarea

Felix told Paul he would hear his case as soon as his accusers arrived, and put him up in "Herod's praetorium." That refers to the apartment, or some say, the palace that Herod would occupy when in town. This was far from a normal dungeon. It shows the deference shown to a Roman citizen.

It could also suggest that Felix was inclined to accept Lysias' opinion that, "There was no charge against him that deserved death or imprisonment" (v. 29). Luke welcomed this additional case of a respected Roman declaring that Paul was innocent.

# 37

# BEFORE KINGS AND RULERS
## ACTS 24-26

Jesus had told Paul that he would speak before kings and rulers. He had already spoken to Sergius Paulus. Now he would speak before Felix. You can tell Luke is still present, because he gives the number of days and the name of the prosecutor.

> After five days the high priest Ananias came down with some elders, with an attorney named Tertullus, and they brought charges to the governor against Paul. (Acts 24:1)

Tertullus is a Roman name. Apparently, after the disgraceful disorder in Paul's first hearing, the leadership realized they needed to do things the Roman way. They hired this sharp lawyer to state their case. After buttering Felix up liberally, Tertullus laid his charge:

> We have found this man to be a troublemaker who is constantly stirring up riots among the Jews all over the world. He is a ringleader of the cult known as the Nazarenes. Furthermore, he was trying to desecrate the temple when we arrested him." (vs. 5-6)[1]

---

1. Later manuscripts add almost two verses here, but they contribute nothing to the story.

In this short statement we can discern three serious charges against Paul.

1.  He stirs up riots throughout the empire. That would likely be a capital offense if he is convicted. Romans liked to make examples of any who disrupted the *pax Romana*.

2.  He is a ringleader of the cult of the Nazarenes. This reference is historically accurate. We have rabbinic writings from this period frequently referring to Christians as "Nazarenes" because Jesus came from Nazareth.[2] This charge would probably not draw any sentence from the Romans. It was a religious complaint. He may have supplied additional information about why Nazarenes were bad.

3.  He defiled the temple. This could result in death as well. The Jews had placed a sign in the temple courts between the court of the Gentiles and the Holy Place that said:

    "Gentiles are not permitted beyond this point. If you enter, you will have only yourself to blame for your ensuing death."

The Romans had permitted the sign and agreed that it could be enforced, even on a Roman.

## Paul's Defense

Felix motioned for Paul to speak, and he stood up:

Paul said, "I know, sir, that you have been a judge of Jewish affairs for many years, so I gladly present my defense before you. You can quickly discover that I arrived in Jerusalem no more than twelve days ago to worship at the temple. My accusers never found me arguing with anyone in the temple, nor stirring up a riot in any synagogue or on the streets of the city. These men cannot prove the things they accuse me of doing." (vs. 10-13)

He raises strong points. First, he only arrived in Jerusalem twelve days ago, so how could he foment a revolution against Rome?

---

2. The Christians called themselves "the way." The term Christian is hardly ever used—just one time in 1 Peter 4:16. Nazareth was a low prestige town in the more backward part of the province, so there was a back handed smack down in the name. It also made it sound like the Way just came from a group of yokels up north, when the movement really came out of Jerusalem.

Second, he came to worship, not to agitate. He points out nobody ever saw him arguing or agitating anyone.

He went on:

> "But I admit that I follow the Way, which they call a cult. I worship the God of our ancestors, and I firmly believe the Jewish law and everything written in the prophets. I have the same hope in God that these men have, that he will raise both the righteous and the unrighteous. Because of this, I always try to maintain a clear conscience before God and all people." (vs. 14-16)

So they were calling legitimate groups cults even back then!

Here Paul explained that "the Way" was nothing new, and came directly from the Old Testament Scriptures. The correct name of his religion was Judaism, properly understood.

Then,

> My accusers saw me in the temple as I was completing a purification ceremony. There was no crowd around me and no rioting. But some Jews from the province of Asia were there—and they ought to be here to bring charges if they have anything against me!" (vs. 18-19)

These points could be fatal to the third charge. Yes, he was in the temple, no, he had no Gentile with him—are they seriously suggesting that he had a Gentile in the temple and they let the Gentile get away, but captured Paul? It's ridiculous.

Also, where are the witnesses? Under Roman law, someone on trial had the right to face his accusers. The accusers were the men from Asia, and they had probably already returned there.

# Imprisonment

> At that point Felix, who was quite familiar with the Way, adjourned the hearing and said, "Wait until Lysias, the garrison commander, arrives. Then I will decide the case." (v. 22)

Felix would not keep his word here. He probably could see how incendiary the whole issue was for the Jews and just as clearly that Paul was innocent. He probably didn't want to acquit Paul and have to face a firestorm in his province.

So the prosecutors went back to Jerusalem and Felix set Paul up with a nice arrangement in Herod's palace.

> He ordered an officer to keep Paul in custody but to give him some freedom and allow his friends to visit him and take care of his needs. (v. 23)

So Paul would have freedom within the palace, but maybe not to go outside. Or, perhaps he was even free to wander the grounds of the fortress inside the walls. We see him later saying he is in chains, but that might only be when he went outside the palace.

The most important point is that he could have friends come to visit and to provide for him. One of these friends was Luke. This "prison" is the setting for the writing of Luke and probably most of Acts. Paul could oversee and help with the writing. They could interview eye-witnesses either there in the palace or Luke could go up to Jerusalem or other coastal cities.

## Strange Hearing

Felix must have been struck by Paul's story and discussed the trial with his Jewish wife, Drusilla. She must have said she was interested in hearing from him, so they set up a private hearing. They were "well aware of the Way" so they may have heard the gospel presented from someone earlier. Was Drusilla a secret believer? Or just curious? They sent for Paul.

> They listened as he told them about faith in Christ Jesus. As he reasoned with them about righteousness and self-control and the coming day of judgment, Felix became frightened. "Go away for now," he replied. "When it is more convenient, I'll call for you again." (vs. 24-25)

This statement that Felix became frightened means to quiver in fear. What was he afraid of? People who often share the gospel are well acquainted with this phenomenon. It's when someone is listening to the word and suddenly awareness comes, a sense of knowing, with the thought that "I get the feeling this might all be true!"

This awesome impression lands when the Holy Spirit bears witness to the truthfulness of the gospel. The hearer wonders, "Am I going to live the rest of my life being dishonest with myself? Or am I going to face a complete turn-around that changes everything?"

This is what Jesus was talking about when he said, "And he [the Holy Spirit], when he comes, will convict the world concerning sin and righteousness and judgment" (John 16:8). To hear from God can be frightening, especially when you don't know him. With bulging eyeballs, the person suddenly knows he or she is dealing with God.

Such an experience results in polarization. To some, it's a wonderful experience that draws them toward faith. Others realize this doesn't fit in with their plans at all, and therefore it drives them away from God. Paul described it as an aroma of Christ, which is "to the one an aroma from death to death, to the other an aroma from life to life" (2 Corinthians 2:16). In Felix's case, the aroma was from death to death. He interrupted Paul, closed his ears, and sent Paul back to his house.

Luke also suggests that from this point Felix became cynical and tried to use Paul to his own advantage:

> He also hoped that Paul would bribe him, so he sent for him quite often and talked with him. (v. 26)

This is the Felix we know from secular history. Corrupt and violent, Tacitus says that he was "a master of cruelty and lust who exercised the powers of a king with the spirit of a slave."[3] Paul had mentioned earlier a financial gift he brought to Jerusalem, and Felix knew followers of Jesus were numerous, so they could have bribed him.

> After two years went by in this way, Felix was succeeded by Porcius Festus. And because Felix wanted to gain favor with the Jewish people, he left Paul in prison. (v. 27)

These two years would have been so much harder to take if Jesus hadn't appeared to Paul that night in Jerusalem. Paul's awareness that history was unfolding according to God's plan led him often to refer to himself as a "prisoner of Christ Jesus" (Ephesians 3:1). In his mind, his earthly jailers were irrelevant—it was Jesus himself who had put Paul in prison.

Under such a God-centered mentality, he and Luke were able to avoid

---

3. Cornelius Tacitus, *Histories*, 5.9. He also confirms that Felix married Drusilla.

sitting around feeling sorry for themselves. Instead, they embarked on a project that would end up being almost a third of the New Testament—the books of Luke and Acts.

## Festus

As soon as the new governor, Festus, arrived and went up to Jerusalem, the priests and council members pounced. Two years of waiting had done nothing to dampen their zeal to get Paul. This was their chance to revive Paul's case and nail him. Or better yet, some were still ready to ambush Paul and kill him. "They requested Festus, as a favor to them, to have Paul transferred to Jerusalem, for they were preparing an ambush to kill him along the way" (25:3).

Festus refused. He told them to bring their case back to Caesarea and he would hold court again.

When court was convened and they brought Paul in,

> The Jews who had come down from Jerusalem stood around him. They brought many serious charges against him, but they could not prove them" (v. 7).

This must have been quite intimidating. Usually, the accused and the prosecution faced each other and the court. The gathering around Paul amounted to "getting up in his face," where he could feel their rage. Paul, of course, denied violating any Jewish or Roman laws, as Luke's readers already know. But then:

> Festus, wishing to do the Jews a favor, said to Paul, "Are you willing to go up to Jerusalem and stand trial before me there on these charges?" (v. 9)

Festus, as a new governor, probably didn't fully realize what he was dealing with in this case. He had no way to know about the Jerusalem Jews' murderous zeal against Paul.

Paul was adamant:

> "No! This is the official Roman court, so I ought to be tried right here. You know very well I am not guilty of harming the Jews. If I have done something worthy of death, I don't refuse

to die. But if I am innocent, no one has a right to turn me over to these men to kill me. I appeal to Caesar!" (vs. 10-11)

Here Paul asserted another right he had as a Roman citizen: the *provocatio ad Caesarem*, the "appeal to Caesar." Citizens could make this appeal under Roman law, and they would have to be transferred to the court in Rome if they were under a serious charge, like Paul was. It may seem strange that Paul would appeal to Nero, a persecutor and killer of Christians, but that was later. At this point in time, about AD 60, he would have had no reason to believe that Nero was anti-Christian.

Festus could have acquitted Paul, nullifying the appeal, but he could see that the Jews would have gone berserk if he did that. He had no motive for freeing Paul. In fact, this was a very convenient way for him to get out of the dilemma facing him. Festus conferred with his advisers and then shrugged his shoulders. "Very well! You have appealed to Caesar, and to Caesar you will go!" (v. 12). The Jewish accusers may have been frustrated, but as Festus pointed out, there was nothing he could do.

## Agrippa

A few days later King Agrippa arrived with his sister, Bernice, to pay their respects to Festus. (v. 13)

Agrippa was a great grandson of Herod the Great. It was his father who killed James son of Zebedee and arrested Peter intending to kill him as well (Acts 12). The Romans had given this Herod a small kingdom in central Judea and southern Galilee.

Luke tells how Festus discussed Paul's case with Agrippa. He was musing about what to write to the emperor when he sent Paul there. He didn't know how to describe the scene before him.

We don't know how Luke learned about this conversation between Festus and King Agrippa, but that doesn't mean he made it up. It could have occurred in public at a lunch or dinner, for instance. Others might have listened in.

At the same time, Paul had a tendency to win people anywhere he went, including wealthy and influential people. For example, later in Rome he won people from Caesar's own household (Philippians 4:22)! He apparently won some of the Asiarchs (19:31). He may have either made friends with someone or even won over someone who would have dined with the nobles.

Fortunately the conversation was captured, because it again illustrates the hilarious inability of secular Romans to comprehend what following Jesus was. As he explains Paul's case to Agrippa, Festus says,

> "But the accusations made against him weren't any of the crimes I expected. Instead, it was something about their religion and a dead man named Jesus, who Paul insists is alive." (vs. 18-19)

Everything he's heard and seen has sailed over his head.

You can see how this kind of confusion about what was bothering the Jews fits in with Luke's desire to demonstrate Paul's innocence under Roman law. Festus would have been seeking Agrippa's advice because he had more understanding of Jews and Judaism. When Agrippa said he wanted to hear Paul, Festus was glad to set up a hearing for the following day.

The following scene set in an "auditorium," (v. 23) so it was apparently a public hearing. Luke's source could have been himself and of course, Paul, who was also there.

"What shall I write to the Emperor?" Festus mused, as he called on Paul to speak (v. 26).

This is Paul's fifth defense since being arrested in Jerusalem. He covers mostly material we have already heard, including his own testimony.

He says of his days of persecution: "I caused many believers there to be sent to prison. And I cast my vote against them when they were condemned to death" (26:10). So the scope of his persecution was "many" sent to prison, and a number put to death—the language here is plural, so Stephen was not the only one he killed.

He also adds that "Many times I had them punished in the synagogues to get them to curse Jesus" (v. 11). This is no doubt referring to torture. We saw earlier that whippings could be administered in synagogues. Paul is describing beating people until they denied Christ.

When describing his encounter with Jesus on the road to Damascus, Paul adds a line we haven't seen before. Jesus said to Paul, "It is hard for you to kick against the goads" (v. 14). "Kicking against the goads" was a common idiom in both Greek and Latin literature. It refers to a wooden member hanging to the rear of horses or oxen pulling a cart. If the animal tried to take off running, its rear legs would strike the knobs on the goad. The animal quickly realizes that's not a good idea.

So Paul was under pressure in his own mind as he heard valid testimonies from people he was torturing and imprisoning. He apparently was sensing that they were telling the truth, but he was too proud to give in. He was actually injuring himself by kicking the goads. The more their testimonies made him wonder, the more fanatical his attacks became. We see the same thing today.

Another detail added only in this telling was Jesus saying that he was going to send Paul to the Gentiles,

> "Yes, I am sending you to the Gentiles, to open their eyes so that they may turn from darkness to light and from the dominion of Satan to God, that they may receive forgiveness of sins and an inheritance among those who have been set apart by faith in me." (vs. 17-18)

This is a unique description of Paul's mission, and by extension, our mission as well. Jesus sees the heart of the matter as turning people from the dominion of Satan to the dominion of God. So these are two kingdoms, one chopping away at the other. Then comes the thought that they will receive forgiveness from sin and an inheritance, referring to their place in heaven.

Paul went on to teach prophecies about the suffering servant of the Lord, just as he was so used to doing during his journeys. "I teach nothing except what the prophets and Moses said would happen" (v. 22). Since it was a public hearing, he launched into the gospel. "The Messiah would suffer and be the first to rise from the dead, and in this way announce God's light to Jews and Gentiles alike" (v. 23).

## Blow Up

Suddenly at this point, "Festus shouted, "Paul, you are insane. Too much study has made you crazy!" (v. 24). Notice that Festus pops his cork at the same place the people in the temple did—when he mentioned Gentiles.

Once the proposition was that this doesn't just have to do with the Jews, he lost it.

Unperturbed, Paul went on:

> "I am not insane, Most Excellent Festus. What I am saying is the sober truth. And King Agrippa knows about these things. I speak boldly, for I am sure these events are all familiar to him, for they were not done in a corner! King Agrippa, do you believe the prophets? I know you do!" (vs. 25-27)

But Agrippa wasn't going to get trapped.

> Agrippa interrupted him. "Do you think you can persuade me to become a Christian so quickly?"

> Paul replied, "Whether quickly or not, I pray to God that both you and everyone here in this audience might become the same as I am, except for these chains." (vs. 28-29)

## The Big Picture

They all got up and left and Paul went back to his prison. But someone was listening to the rulers' conversation on their way out—perhaps Paul himself?—and heard them:

> They talked it over and agreed, "This man hasn't done anything to deserve death or imprisonment." (v. 31)

So Luke's point for Theophilus, perhaps Paul's future Roman defender, stands once again: Roman officials saw Paul as innocent under Roman law.

At the same time, after two years in prison, it must have been a struggle for Paul to accept his condition in faith. He knew Jesus hadn't lost control of the situation because of his visit to Paul two years earlier. But for a man of action, like Paul, sitting around reading and writing must have driven him stir crazy. But God didn't need Paul traveling around at this time. He wanted the vast knowledge Paul and Luke had to be written down. They were serving millions of people they couldn't see, because they were still in the future.

# 38

## JOURNEY TO ROME
### ACTS 27

Luke has been with Paul on and off throughout the imprisonment. He hasn't used the "we" voice, mainly because the narrative has all been about "they." It doesn't mean he wasn't present for much of this time. But as they take ship, it's clear he is going to join with Paul for the journey to Rome. Another "we" passage begins.

Once again, Luke's highly detailed recounting begins. We're even given the home port of the ship they're on (Adramyttium on the northwest coast of the province of Asia).

Amazingly the captain, named Julius, allowed Paul go ashore to visit friends! (Acts 27:3). Afterward, Julius transshipped his prisoners to a huge grain ship from Egypt, headed for Rome.

As they headed west against contrary winds, they sailed south of Cypress instead of the usual north side. When they made it into a harbor called Fair Havens it was already October—way too late to be sailing in the Mediterranean. Paul warned the crew that trying to sail further could be fatal, but they wouldn't listen. They wanted to make it to a better port for wintering.

## Storm at Sea

As they took off under mild winds, things looked good. But suddenly the winds shifted to the northeast. A gale force nor'easter blew in, driving their ship away from shore.

They continue to fight this storm for the next two weeks, drifting help-lessly most of that time. As hope was running out, Paul came forward and announced that he had been visited by an angel who told him that the ship would be wrecked, but nobody would die.

Luke describes them throwing cargo and even ship's gear overboard to lighten the ship. They were probably taking water, because they passed ropes under the hull to support the hull.

The night before the shipwreck Luke describes Paul gathering the whole crew and complement of prisoners together and persuading them to eat—all 276 of them (vs. 33-38).

## Shipwreck!

Eventually, they approached land not knowing where they were. Some of the crew tried to escape using the rescue dinghy, but Paul saw them and reported the desertion to the captain. He had soldiers cut the ropes to the rescue boat, and it fell away.

Finally, they tried to sail the ship into a small bay and run aground, but as they were headed in, the ship grounded on a sandbar, way too far out. The ship began to break up in the pounding surf (vs. 39-40).

The Roman jailers were about to kill their prisoners so they wouldn't escape—the normal practice in this situation. But again, Paul's incredible persuasive ability won the captain over and he blocked the executions, in part because he didn't want to see Paul killed. Instead, they sent those who could swim ashore, and the rest grabbed large planks and beams from the breaking ship and rode those ashore. Everyone lived, as Paul had predicted (vs. 42-44).

Commenting on Luke's account of this voyage, Richard Longenecker says:

> Luke's account of Paul's voyage to Rome stands out as one of the most vivid pieces of descriptive writing in the whole Bible. Its

details regarding first-century seamanship are so precise and its portrayal of conditions on the eastern Mediterranean so accurate that even the most skeptical have conceded that it probably rests on a journal of some such voyage as Luke describes.[1]

---

1. Richard Longenecker, *Acts*, "The Journey to Rome."

# 39

# ON MALTA

## ACTS 28:1-15

The crew and passengers spent the rest of the winter on the island on which they crashed, which turned out to be Malta. They had drifted a thousand miles and yet hit a peanut sized island in the middle of the Mediterranean Sea.

When they got ashore, drenched in icy late November water, they also had to withstand a steady rain. The locals came out and welcomed them with an ocean-side fire. The passengers joined in, including Paul, who was busily gathering an armful of sticks. Casting the bundle on the fire, a poisonous viper slithered out and bit onto his hand!

That's just a bad day! First the soldiers are lining up to kill you, then your ship disintegrates and you have to struggle ashore in icy water, it's raining, and now a viper is pumping venom into your hand!

The locals saw the strike and waited for Paul to swell up and die. They interpreted the attack in animistic fashion: This was punishment for an earlier murder Paul committed. But as time went on, Paul showed no symptoms. At that, the locals changed their analysis: Paul must be a god!

Gods masquerading as humans happened occasionally in Greco Roman mythology.

Luke's point is that God was protecting Paul. As we saw earlier, Paul had not yet testified in Rome, and no viper could interfere with the plan.

# Publius

A wealthy landowner named Publius was "the leading man of the island," a title for the Roman governor. He hosted the passengers generously for three days. During that time, Publius' father became sick with recurring dysentery. Paul came and prayed over him. When he laid his hands on him, he was healed.

The healing led to a significant ministry on the island.

> The rest of the people on the island who had diseases were coming to him and getting cured. They also honored us with many marks of respect; and when we were setting sail, they supplied us with all we needed. (Acts 28:9-10)

You can tell from the language that Paul and his crew had built warm friendships with the people, and we don't need to hear that the gospel was part of it—that's obvious. This was another church plant. The financial help they gave would have helped Paul get started in his private home prison instead of the public prison.

Paul must have been given considerable freedom as a prisoner. It's already clear that he has made friends with Julius, the ship's captain, who would have remained in command. During the wreck, he was acting as a leader—really the true leader of the whole ship.

# To Rome

Another big grain ship was wintering on Malta, and they agreed to take the castaways on board for the trip to Rome. Luke is one of them, as his detailed "we" passage continues. He even explains the ship's figurehead, based on the Twin Brothers (Castor and Pollux, sons of Zeus).

They sailed to Syracuse on the east coast of Sicily, then a hundred miles north to Rhegium. From there, they waited for a south wind, and when it came, they sailed 180 more miles north to Puteoli, modern Pozzuoli, just northwest of Naples.

Amazingly, Paul and Luke were permitted to go ashore (probably with a guard) and they somehow found another group of believers! We know there was a community of Jews there,[1] so some of them may have been at Pentecost. Or, believers from Rome maybe have ventured out to plant this group. It fits the picture we've seen through much of Acts, where groups of believers were springing up everywhere they went. This one is extraordinary at more than 2000 miles from Jerusalem.

In verse 14 Luke says, "And so we came to Rome," probably referring to the outskirts of the administrative district of Rome.

They were traveling overland to Rome on the Via Appia and were met by believers from Rome at two places.

Paul had been in Puteoli for seven days, which is plenty of time to send one of his guys (not Luke) ahead to Rome to announce his coming. We know from Romans 16 that Paul was friends with a number of leaders in Rome and probably had sent some of them there. They must have organized the welcoming committee.

Some of the Roman believers must have left earlier than the others, because they made it to the Market of Appius, over forty miles from Rome. Others arrived, probably the next day, at Three Taverns, around thirty miles out. Then, they all walked to Rome together.

Julius the ship captain was probably a believer by now. He must have been amazed at his first real experience of assembled fellowship. How many Roman soldiers were walking with this procession?

Paul was thrilled and comforted by this reunion with the body of Christ.

## The Big Picture

When he finally reached Rome, Paul was immediately able to arrange for a private house and guard. Julius probably helped him with the red tape. But he also had believers working ahead of time to make a place ready. By the time they had been there only three days he was ready to meet

---

1. Flavius Josephus, *Wars*. 2, 104.

with the Jews of Rome. We know from the book of Romans that Paul was longing with all his heart to win over many in this group.

# 40

# MEETING WITH THE JEWS

## ACTS 28:16-31

As always with Paul, his first order of business was to go to the Jews. For Paul it was always, "to the Jew first and also to the Greek" (Romans 1:16). It had to do with Paul's understanding of the Abrahamic covenant, but he probably also had good missiological reasons.

Jews didn't feel like they needed spiritual instruction from the Gentiles. The Gentiles were foolish idol worshippers. That's why if a situation developed where Christians were mostly or all Gentile, it would be very difficult to win Jews. But if the Jews felt like Jesus was their own Messiah, there would be no problem if some Gentiles joined in. So Paul knew that failure to win over Jews early would be a one-way door.

So Paul knew this meeting was critically important.

He had invited "the leading men of the Jews," which would include older community leaders and rabbis. This way, they could consider his case carefully without the pressure of their congregations listening in. This was the best setting for Paul to convey his bountiful load of Scripture and his own amazing story.

He began by explaining why he was in chains:

"Brethren, though I had done nothing against our people or the customs of our fathers, yet I was delivered as a prisoner from Jerusalem into the hands of the Romans. And when they had examined me, they were willing to release me because there was no ground for putting me to death. But when the Jews objected, I was forced to appeal to Caesar, not that I had any accusation against my nation. I asked you to come here today so we could get acquainted and so I could explain to you that I am bound with this chain because I believe that the hope of Israel—the Messiah—has already come." (vs. 17-20)

In that last statement, it's clear that he made some kind of case for Jesus. He must have explained the gospel. They replied,

"We have neither received letters from Judea concerning you, nor have any of the brethren come here and reported or spoken anything bad about you. But we desire to hear from you what your views are; for concerning this sect, it is known to us that it is spoken against everywhere." (vs. 21-22)

Fortunately, they hadn't heard anything about Paul, because it would have been negative. "This sect" referred to the Way—following Jesus. That's all we have on the first meeting. We're not sure what else they heard from Paul. They set up another date.

## The Second Meeting

Luke recounts the second meeting:

When they had set a day for Paul, they came to him at his lodging in large numbers; and he was explaining to them by solemnly testifying about the kingdom of God and trying to persuade them concerning Jesus, from both the Law of Moses and from the Prophets, from morning until evening. (v. 23)

This was an epic meeting! Paul was giving them everything he had to give. "From morning until evening" could refer to ten or more hours. They surely heard Paul's personal story, but also "From both the Law of Moses and from the Prophets."

The obvious question must have arisen: "If Jesus is king Messiah, why are we still living in a world of sin?" To that, Paul would have rolled out the astonishing claim that there are two comings of the Messiah. Yes, that would be hard for them to choke down. But he had abundant Scripture that pointed to that conclusion. Most of them, maybe all of them were hearing this proposition for the first time.

This is the same presentation Paul had been giving during his journeys with so much fruit borne. And fruit was being borne here: "Some were persuaded by the things spoken, but others would not believe" (v. 24). So this is similar to previous scenes, where the gospel brought polarization. The key to Paul was "some were being persuaded." He must have been excited to once again see fellow Jews believe.

But,

> Others would not believe. Paul warned them, "The Holy Spirit was right when he said to your ancestors through Isaiah the prophet, 'Go and say to this people: When you hear what I say, you will not understand. When you see what I do, you will not comprehend. For the hearts of these people are hardened...'" (vs. 24-27)

It was a warning reminiscent of one from Jesus himself (Matthew 13:10-17). If you say no to God, the danger is that the next time you say no, it's easier. And so on. This is how one's heart gets hardened. Saying no to God is always perilous.

The fact that Luke finishes his account this way suggests that the resistant Jews were not a small minority. His final statement, "Therefore let it be known to you that this salvation of God has been sent to the Gentiles; they will also listen" (v. 28) clearly signals that Paul didn't see enough response to hesitate going to the Gentiles.[1]

## Paul and the Body at Rome

The body in Rome was large, and Paul knew that. He was receiving word from Rome back when he wrote his letter to Rome, six years earlier. He knew his leadership and evangelistic gifts were going to be important in building up the Roman body. He earlier wrote, "For I long to see you so

---

1. Later manuscripts add verse 29: "And when he had said these words, the Jews departed, greatly disagreeing with each other." It is found in none of the best manuscripts. Copyists sometimes added text like this to make the story more complete. In almost all cases they are easily detected.

that I may impart some spiritual gift to you, that you may be established" (Romans 1:11). He couldn't afford to be held up by resistant rabbis.

He talked about his interaction with the Roman body during this period in the book of Philippians. He said, "Most of the brethren, trusting in the Lord because of my imprisonment, have far more courage to speak the word of God without fear" (1:14). He probably was holding training meetings at his private house, and these were bearing fruit as Paul's enthusiasm for the gospel rubbed off.

On the negative side he explained, "Some, to be sure, are preaching Christ even from envy and strife" (Philippians 1:15). So they were shamefully using ministry as a means of establishing self-importance. This distortion is always made evident by the presence of competition. We've all felt it. Pride is subtle and adaptable. Here we have real believers seeking glory from their ministry.

Paul's response? They "proclaim Christ out of selfish ambition rather than from pure motives" (1:17). But, "What then? Only that in every way, whether in pretense or in truth, Christ is proclaimed; and in this I rejoice. Yes, and I will rejoice" (1:18).

So Paul considered it important to have the right motives for spiritual work, but it was even more important that the word gets out to those who need it. He knew God was really the one doing the work, so he didn't feel the need to be a perfectionist when it came to motives.

When I was a new teacher of the word at 19 years old, a brother came and rebuked me. He charged that I was heavily motivated by egotistic pride. I went into a tailspin; mainly because I knew what he was saying was true in large part.

I began to seriously consider resigning my role as a teacher. How could I justify doing God's work, when I was also enjoying people listening to me? Fortunately, I told an older believer, my mom, about my plan. She immediately said resigning was wrong.

She insisted that God teaches us how to have good motives while we are engaged in serving, not at home in the library. I realized the enemy might be using this to get me out of ministry and changed my mind. Getting the word out was more important than my state of mind.

Here in Philippians, Paul shows that his priorities were in order. Not that he approved of the poor motives, but he knew God would deal with them in time.

Paul also talks about how outreach to non-believing Romans was accelerating because of his presence. For one thing, "My imprisonment in the cause of Christ has become well known throughout the whole praetorian guard" (1:13). The praetorian guard was an elite legion of six thousand men. The most likely access for the gospel into this group was Paul himself.

Every day he would have another soldier chained to his wrist. During that day-long time together, we can safely assume that Paul was his usual self—constantly pouring out the gospel to whoever would listen. The soldiers would have also witnessed Paul's meetings with others and listened to their spiritual conversations. Considering that this happened for over two years, that means he would have shared the gospel with hundreds of soldiers. They, in turn would go back to the barracks and meet others who had also heard Paul. Jesus had become the issue of the hour in this legion.

Paul also said, "Most of the brethren, trusting in the Lord because of my imprisonment, have far more courage to speak the word of God without fear" (1:14). So, whether through meetings Paul held at his house, or perhaps the inspiration that came from his example, the Roman body was energized to a new level. We know he was preaching and teaching during this imprisonment (Acts 28:30-31). He could preach and teach in his house, just not out in public.

The gospel even penetrated the household of Caesar, according to Philippians 4, where Paul writes: "All the saints greet you, especially those of Caesar's household" (v. 22). It could refer to servants who worked for Nero's household, or, for all we know, relatives of the emperor!

## The Big Picture

The body of believers in Rome was growing rapidly, and soon became the largest in the world. Speaking of this group only three to five years later, anti-Christian Roman historian, Cornelius Tacitus, called them a "huge multitude" captured during Nero's persecution.[2]

---

2. Cornelius Tacitus, *Annals*, XV, 44.

But that's not all. It was during these two years that Paul found the time to write four more letters known as the prison epistles. They are Ephesians, Philippians, Colossians, and Philemon. Would we have these letters today if Paul hadn't been in prison? Doubtful.

A man of action like Paul, who was also at the zenith of his expertise in church planting, would have found it difficult to find time to write. But sitting in his private prison, writing was the only way he could talk to his friends in other cities. Imagine the New Testament without these books! Not something we would want to see. By traveling around and preaching, Paul could have served thousands. By writing these books, he served millions.

# 41

# AFTER ACTS

The story isn't over. The book of Acts ends with the words:

> And he stayed two full years in his own rented quarters and
> was welcoming all who came to him, preaching the kingdom
> of God and teaching concerning the Lord Jesus Christ with all
> openness, unhindered. (28:30-31)

From these verses we can quickly identify the date for the completion of
Acts. For whatever reason, the author stops telling his story abruptly in
the middle of nowhere, two years into Paul's imprisonment.

The most plausible reason why he ended like this with no real conclusion is that Luke was writing to Theophilus who was working on Paul's
defense. At this point in history, it was time to deliver the manuscript in
time for the trial.

## Facing Trial

Paul survived his trial. He expected to survive it, based on reflection on
his own mission, as he explained in Philippians:

> But I am hard-pressed from both directions, having the desire to depart and be with Christ, for that is very much better; yet to remain on in the flesh is more necessary for your sake. Convinced of this, I know that I will remain and continue with you all for your progress and joy in the faith. (Philippians 1:23-25)

However, this was not a matter of revelation, because he also allows for the possibility that he's wrong (Philippians 1:21-22).

We know Paul was acquitted because of the book of Titus and 1 Timothy. Paul told Titus, "I left you on the island of Crete so you could complete our work there and appoint elders in each town as I instructed you" (Titus 1:5). The problem is that such a trip to Crete will not fit anywhere in the book of Acts. The only place such a trip would fit is *after* the book of Acts ends. Paul must have been acquitted and then went on this mission trip to Crete.

Likewise in 2 Timothy, he asks Timothy to come and visit him in prison before he dies. And he asked, "When you come, be sure to bring the coat I left with Carpus at Troas, and the books, especially the parchments" (4:13). Yet, if you've been following the narrative in the last ten chapters of Acts, you know Paul hadn't been to Troas for five or six years at the time of the Roman imprisonment. Would Paul still be worrying about a cloak?

The evidence suggests that Paul wrote this text in 2 Timothy *after* the Roman imprisonment in Acts. He was released, he traveled again, and then was re-arrested, again in Rome. That's exactly what early Christian writers say happened.

Clement of Rome was an elder in Rome who wrote our earliest extra-biblical letter in about AD 95, now known as 1 Clement. He says of Paul, He came "to the extremity of the West."[1] That refers to Spain, the westernmost province in the empire. Paul said he wanted to go to Spain but it didn't happen until after the period covered by the book of Acts.

Likewise, the *Muratorian Canon*, another of our earliest and most reliable sources states that Paul lost his life in Rome after returning from Spain.[2]

---

1. 1 Clement 5:5-7.
2. *The Muratorian Canon*, 38

# Recapture in Rome

Roman historian, Tacitus says Emperor Nero launched a vicious persecution against Christians shortly after the great fire in Rome in AD 64. The last year of Nero's reign was AD 68, so this second Roman imprisonment must have been between those dates. Early church sources say both Paul and Peter were caught up in this persecution and put to death.

Tacitus explains in part,

> Accordingly, an arrest was first made [by Nero] of all who pleaded guilty; then, upon their information, an immense multitude was convicted.

In other words, admitted Christians were captured and tortured to make them give up more names. In this way, they eventually rounded up the "immense multitude."[3]

1 Clement 5–6 says Paul and Peter were both wasted at the same time.

It's unlikely that Christians in Nero's persecution were given trials.

Early church historian Eusebius says, Paul "suffered martyrdom in Rome under Nero" These facts are related by Origen in the third volume of his Commentary on Genesis.[4]

Although we no longer have Origen's commentary, we have no reason to doubt Eusebius on this. Eusebius has an entire chapter about Nero's persecution and that Peter and Paul were both martyred in it, contrary to skeptical scholars.[5] Why would the early church lose track of where two of their biggest heroes died?

---

3. Cornelius Tacitus, *Annals*, 15:44
4. Eusebius, *Church History*, 3:1:2–3.
5. Eusebius, *Church History*, 2:25. Clement of Rome, a very early source, agrees that Peter and Paul were martyred at the same time but doesn't mention the fire. Suetonius also says Nero punished Christians, without mentioning the fire. Gaius Suetonius, *Life of Nero*, 38:1–3. Notwithstanding these good sources and a parallel statement by Tertullian, skeptical scholars like Brent Shaw argue that the Neronian persecution never happened! His argument amounts to nothing but an argument from silence. He says, "All later sources of any consequence that connect the Christians, Nero, and the fire, including Christian writers from Tertullian to Eusebius, depend on his [Tacitus'] words." Brent Shaw, "The Myth of the Neronian Persecution" *Journal of Roman Studies*, Aug. 2015, 13. Under this method, where all subsequent sources are dismissed, it becomes inevitable that only the earliest source recounts the event. He argues in a circle, because his method assures that Tacitus would remain the only source. And he can't possibly know if Eusebius' quote of Origin depends on Tacitus, because we don't have Origin's book—only Eusebius' citation from it.
Also, if Tacitus just wanted to invent another way to attack Nero (as Shaw claims), wouldn't he pick a more sympathetic group, instead of one that even Tacitus thinks deserved to die?
This goes to show the fallacy of arguments from silence. For example, Shaw observes that the elder

# Finishing the Course

As Paul waited for the end, he wrote another letter—2 Timothy. He wanted to touch base with his premier disciple, still overseeing things in Ephesus.

The letter stresses the urgency of Timothy's struggle with falsehood in Ephesus. He also hoped to see Timothy once more. He knew he was soon to die: "For I am already being poured out as a drink offering, and the time of my departure has come" (2 Timothy 4:6).

In Old Testament law, people offered thank offerings, usually of animals. Then, sometimes they added a "drink offering," Some wine poured over the animal sacrifice. It was sort of an extra thank you.

To Paul, his ministry was like his thank offering. He talks about the Gentiles he won to faith: "that my offering of the Gentiles may become acceptable, sanctified by the Holy Spirit" (Romans 15:16). Now, he was adding a drink offering—his own life, given up in thanks to God.

He felt comforted that he had "finished the course" (2 Timothy 4:7). Paul taught that God had a specific plan available to followers who chose to be servants. He urged Timothy, "Fulfill your ministry" (4:5). Or, as the NLT gives it, "Fully carry out the ministry God has given you." That is the sense intended.

And it wasn't only apostles and upper-level leaders who had such courses laid out before them. Paul also wrote:

> For we are his workmanship, created in Christ Jesus for good works, which God prepared beforehand so that we would walk in them. (Ephesians 2:10)

In this passage, he consistently speaks of "we all" referring to all believers.[6] Notice however, following the plan is optional. Otherwise, if the plan was more like a fixed fate, Paul would have no reason to urge Timothy to fulfill his ministry. That would happen automatically.

Pliny, "nowhere in the more than 20,000 facts... so much as refer to any people called Christians or *Chrestiani*, much less does he make any connection of them with the fire." p.10 Under his logic, if this means the Neronian persecution never happened, it also should mean that Christians didn't even exist in Pliny's day.

6. See also 2 Corinthians 10:13 where Paul refers to "the sphere of service God himself has assigned to us, a sphere that also includes you." We saw earlier that the Spirit was nudging Paul one way and another in Acts 16, where he was prevented from going to Asia and Bithynia, but summoned to Macedonia. Paul and Barnabas' calling in Acts 13 fits into this picture of a specific plan as well.

So the view that many Christians have—that whatever happens, and wherever they go is the plan of God—is wrong. God will reveal his will to those who form the intent to follow, but we have to pray for such knowledge and carefully compare our plans to God's word. When our attitude and desire is to follow God's plan for our lives, he promises "I will guide you along the best pathway for your life. I will advise you and watch over you" (Psalm 32:8).

In the same book, Paul writes of another who abandoned God's plan. "Demas, having loved this present world, has deserted me and gone to Thessalonica" (2 Timothy 4:10). Here was a man who was in perhaps the most strategic place a young Christian worker could be—attending and being discipled by the Apostle Paul—the greatest church planter alive. What an opportunity!

But he "deserted." He had a plan of his own that he trusted more than the path God had laid out for him. It's a tragic tale. He remained a believer, but missed the full plan God had for him.

But even if we fail this badly, it's never too late to get back in line with God's plan. This same list mentions another deserter: "Pick up Mark and bring him with you, for he is useful to me for service" (2 Timothy 4:11). This is John Mark, the one who deserted Paul and Barnabas in Pamphilia (13:13). Paul refused to take him on the second journey because of his unreliability (15:38).

Mark messed up. But he got back on track, and here Paul endorses him warmly. So however poorly we follow at one point, it's never too late to get back on track and finish well.

Paul exulted as he faced death:

> In the future there is laid up for me the crown of righteousness, which the Lord, the righteous Judge, will award to me on that day; and not only to me, but also to all who have loved His appearing. (2 Timothy 4:8)

He knew his job was done, and he looked forward to being with Jesus, whom he had met several times. Unlike the terror and despair exhibited so often by non-believers as they approach death, Paul had the peaceful knowledge that God would take care of him.

At the end, Paul says only one person is still with him: his old friend, and our author, Luke (4:11). You can see that he had earlier finished Acts, because if he was still writing, he certainly would have reported this second imprisonment and Paul's death.

## Aftermath

The great Apostle Paul was dead, but not before he had fully preached the gospel "from Jerusalem and round about as far as Illyricum" (Romans 15:19). This expression describes an arch of two thousand miles from Jerusalem to the top of Italy and down to Athens. Then, he spent two years preaching in Rome, resulting in a big surge of growth there.

We have no good reason to doubt Clement of Rome's claim that Paul later made it to Spain, although we know nothing about what happened there. On the other hand, we do know he and Titus planted multiple local churches on the island of Crete after Acts was finished.

This was the most fruitful century for the body of Christ. The *World Christian Encyclopedia* estimates that by AD 100 there were one million Christians in the Roman Empire out of a population of 181 million. If this growth had continued proportionately for another century, every person on earth would have been a follower of Jesus.

Readers of Acts today can only envy the success evident in this period of history. We don't envy the constant persecution and suffering Paul details for himself in 2 Corinthians 11. Perhaps it's worth considering trying to turn back the clock and following more closely the pattern of ministry seen in Acts.

# Also By Dennis McCallum

*Members of One Another* - New Testament scholar Ben Witherington says of this book about authentic, New Testament-style community, "What should a real Christian community loook like? What should its ethos be, and how in particular should it function? If you are interested in these kinds of questions, then McCallum's *Members of One Another* is the book for you!"

*Organic Discipleship* - This guide to making disciples is based on the combined seventy years of ministry experience and wisdom of McCallum and his daughter Jessica Lowery.

*Walking in Victory* - This practical, accessible study of Romans 5-8 guides readers toward spiritual growth while treating the Apostle Paul's most thorough treatment of the topic.

# Other New Paradigm Books

**Dennis McCallum:**

*Christian Parenting*: A Relational Approach

*Discovering God*: Exploring the Possibilities of Faith

*Lessons from Genesis*: A Study Companion Volume 1 & 2

*Liberation*: Follow the Book of Hebrews into a Life of Radical Grace

*Members of One Another*: How to Build a Biblical Ethos into Your Church

*Organic Discipleship*: Mentoring Others into Maturity and Leadership, with Jess Lowery

*Spiritual Love*: How to Build Deep Relationships and Marriages under God, with Gary Delashmutt

*Walking in Victory*: Why God's Love Can Change You Like Legalism Never Could

**Conrad Hilario:**

*Identity*: Seeing Yourself in God's Eyes

*Searching for Wisdom*: Finding the Father in Proverbs

**James Rochford:**

*Endless Hope or Hopeless End*: The Bible and the End of Human History

*Evidence Unseen*: Exposing the Myth of Blind Faith

*Too Good to Be True?* How We Get to Heaven, What it Will Be Like, and Why We Can't Live Without it

**Gary Delashmutt:**

*Colossians*: Christ Over All; Christ in You

*Loving God's Way*: A Fresh Look at the One Another Passages

**Others:**

*Constructive Suffering Workbook*: Buidling a Biblical Perspective for Your Pain, by Amy Moreno and Lee Campbell

*Kicking the Habit*: Quitting Pornography Under Grace, by Joel Hughes